Wakefield Press

Forever Horatio

Edmund Pegge has worked as an actor in England and Australia for five decades, travelling around the world to perform on stage, in film and television. He has worked with many famous actors and directors, and enjoyed numerous encounters and adventures. Also a cricket aficionado, he divides his time between England and his second home, Australia.

For Tord
A Fellow Traveller from an
Antique Land !
Loved your story, so many
Parallels

F'orever HORATIO

An Actor's Life

With love, cheers and best wishes

(Tales from a Strolling Player)

Edmund Pegge

EDMUND PEGGE

Foreword by Dame Judi Dench

Wakefield
Press

Wakefield Press
16 Rose Street
Mile End
South Australia 5031
www.wakefieldpress.com.au

First published 2017

The author would like to acknowledge the following sources:
The front cover photo, reproduced by kind permission of David Wilson. In the photo
section, the image from *Shakespeare's Greatest Hits*. Reproduced by kind permission
of Alex Makeyev. In the photo section, three images from *Tenko*. Reproduced by kind
permission of Immediate Media. On page 14, 'Schoolboy' from *The Mersey Sound* by
Brian Patten. Published by Penguin Modern Classics, 2007. Copyright © Brian Patten.
Reproduced by permission of the author c/o Rogers, Coleridge & White Ltd, 20 Powis
Mews, London W11 1JN. On page 292, the last verse of 'Mrs Worthington'. Reproduced
by kind permission of the Noël Coward Estate.

Every effort has been made to trace copyright holders and to obtain their permission
for the use of copyright material. The author apologises for any errors or omissions
in the above list and would be grateful if notified of any corrections that should be
incorporated in future reprints or editions of this book.

Cover designed by Stacey Zass
Typeset by Michael Deves, Wakefield Press

National Library of Australia Cataloguing-in-Publication entry

Creator: Pegge, Edmund, 1939– , author.
Title: Forever Horatio: the life of an actor / Edmund Pegge.
ISBN: 978 1 74305 498 7 (paperback).
Notes: Includes index.
Subjects: Pegge, Edmund.
            Actors – Australia – Biography.
            Actors – England – Biography.
            Television actors and actresses – Australia – Biography.

CORIOLE

McLAREN VALE

Contents

Foreword

I have known Ed Pegge for more years than either of us care to think about. We first met when we were both in John Neville's company at the Nottingham Playhouse. I remember him mainly for being the most wonderful company member, always supportive and encouraging.

His life and career have taken many turns. He knew at a very early age that he wanted to be an actor, and was encouraged by a teacher who recognised early talent. Moving to Australia in his teens, he found other teachers to encourage him. He went to drama school in Sydney and from there he joined a touring company, from which he gained enormous experience.

More than most actors, he knows the importance of being in the right place at the right time, and that getting the right part is often a matter of luck. He has had his ups and downs but always manages to reinvent himself, even if it has not always been doing his first love – acting. He has worked with the best, and has some fascinating tales to tell.

Ed's self-effacing title for his book, *Forever Horatio*, implies that he has always been a supporting actor. That may be so, but he has managed to leave his mark, both in the UK and Australia. Anyway, where would the rest of us be without him?

Dame Judi Dench

Preface and Acknowledgements

The spur for writing these memoirs came from finding all the letters I ever wrote to my mother, from 1960 to the 1990s. As I had always wanted to be an actor, I was curious to find out why. Where might this compulsion lie, which has led to some interesting speculations and even a possible royal connection? This is an account of my life as an actor over the last 50 years. It is very personal and self revealing but there was a strange feeling of distance when writing, as though it was about someone else.

Not having achieved celebrity status, I knew it would be difficult getting published. I was encouraged after reading Michael Simkins's biography *Fatty Batter* which is a hilarious account of an actor's cricket life. Also *Letters from an Actor* by the American William Redfield, an account of his time in the cast of the famous Richard Burton's *Hamlet* on Broadway. Non-famous actors need an angle. I have no angle except being representative of an actor who aspired to and probably achieved his potential, but like 95% of the profession remained a working actor. The Horatio in the title, a part I played twice, refers to Hamlet's friend in the great play. I was destined to be a supporting actor.

I have been hugely encouraged over this four-year period by friends who have read parts of the text. My thanks to: Anthony Bowman, Jeanie Drinan, Alfred Bell, Jan Craig, Susie Maizels, all cornered with early readings in Sydney. My friends in the UK: Candice de Polnay, Bay Haseler, Michael Hope Lewis and Barbara Erskine, Christine Godwin, Angela Straker and latterly Roy Kendall for their honest and flattering appraisals. My special thanks to Rita Wuethrick for her patient computer tutoring.

To my friends in Adelaide: Wayne Anthoney, Lance Campbell, Wayne Groom, John Scales, Bronwen Thomas, Dr Alan Cotton and Richard Potter; to Jan Turnbull in Melbourne for reviving her memories of life in Malaya; and to Lyn Wright in Canada who has been championing these efforts. Special thanks to Kevan Carroll, who has been an assiduous proof reader along the way, to Bernard Whimpress and David Bishop for their advice, and to Ross and Alex Clayton for their keen-eyed corrections and suggestions. Finally to Michael Bollen, Margot Lloyd and Michael Deves at Wakefield Press for believing that what I have written is worthy of a punt.

Part 1

1939 to 1965

I

The Early Days

Yellow eyes pierce mine as I sit on a wooden bench in a garden under the Southern Cross. Cleo, our black cat, is calling me back to those early days under the Northern stars. Tinker, my childhood tabby, loved hunting me from the long grass. He thought he was a tiger. He would leap out from cover, grab my ankles and scamper away: those early days of innocence, soon to be darkened by death from the skies.

I was born in 1939, a war baby brought up through those years of rationing when the catch cries were: *waste not want not, heat up the leftovers, turn off the lights, make do and mend, help others and do as you're told.* These precepts still temper my actions. My early days were spent exploring the woods, hunting with bows and arrows, scrumping (pinching fruit from orchards), mucking around in boats and doing naughty things with penny bangers on Guy Fawkes night. We were Arthur Ransome boys, living the Swallows and Amazons life. Adventures in a countryside that held no threats, though imagined danger always lurked through fear of the unknown: haunted houses, Roman ruins, dark woods, eccentric village characters.

The Tapestry Hall in Old Windsor witnessed my birth, in a nursing home opposite, no longer there. It was a short walk to the Long Walk and Windsor Castle. My father had arrived from India in 1931 and built a house (still there) on the Pelling Hill Estate, near what used to be the Catholic school Beaumont College and not far from Runnymede where the Magna Carta was signed.

I believe '*place*' has a strong influence on one's upbringing. I'm sure the historical surroundings in which I grew up fired my imagination. I wanted to be an actor from the age of 10.

Even though my earliest days were lived amid all the constrictions of wartime, they were halcyon days for me. The dominant memory of my first five years was the sound of the warning and all-clear sirens. That terrible moaning crescendo, similar to the bush-fire warning in Australia, still sends shivers up my spine. The burring sound of a doodlebug and its great shadow passing over our house was a frightening experience. If the engine noise ceased it would drop and explode. Indeed, one did and fell a kilometre away on The Bells of Ouseley pub, killing three people. Earlier a bomb had dropped in the field opposite, leaving a huge crater. The blast bent our lead-light windows.

During incidents like that and when waking up from a terrifying nightmare, my mother would always be there, sitting on my bed in my tiny 'box-room', stroking my forehead while murmuring rhythmic nursery rhymes. She always read stories to me at bedtime. My favourites were about Rupert Bear.

One of my most vivid memories occurred under an upturned sofa in the drawing room when I was about four years old. It was early evening and the sirens had sounded. My father brought me down from upstairs and laid me on a mattress on the floor with the back of the sofa covering my head. It must have been the first short straw I drew. If a bomb had dropped on the house, my sister had the best chance of survival under the baby grand piano; my survival would have been doubtful.

One night I was in the land of nod when I felt a sharp pain on my bottom. Letting out an almighty scream, I rolled out of bed to find a wasp had stung me. Dad sat me on his lap beside the green lamp and explained that Hitler had sent over that wasp and that I was not to cry.

I know I dreamt a lot and had scary nightmares. A typical one was being chased by a bull right up our driveway and trying to push the front door only to find it opened outwards instead of inwards. I woke up as the bull was upon me. I can still feel its breath on my face.

There were two other experiences after the war which left an indelible mark on my memory and a physical scar to this day. We lived opposite an orchard with a bolted wooden farm gate guarding that bull in my nightmare. It was out of bounds to boys which meant it was a challenge. I used to stand in the inlet of our driveway with a pile of stones and throw them into the trees to try and knock off the fruit. I was a long and accurate thrower. Later my friend and I would sneak over the gate and pick up what had fallen. One late afternoon I was enjoying my natural gift for throwing to such an extent that I failed to stop as the 441 double-decker bus passed by.

I cannot to this day understand what possessed me to throw a stone just as the bus was in front. It shattered the driver's side window. I heard the bus's brakes screeching as I ran into our big garden to find somewhere to hide. Somehow I ended up in the outside loo. My father pushed open the door; he was standing there with the bus driver deciding my fate. My father assured the bus driver that it would do no good involving the police and sending me to prison and that he would deal with his son in the only appropriate way by giving him 'a damned good thrashing'. This seemed to mollify the bus driver who went on his way with the assurance from my father that he would pay for all damages. I was then led into Father's study and given six of the best with his very whippy cane from India.

It is a very Dickensian phrase, 'six of the best'. To call the infliction of a painful act on a person 'the best' shows what a long way we have come from those sadistic days. It was not the only time I was beaten; for trashing the rose bed it was deserved, but being late for a dental appointment, which is perfectly understandable, was undeserved, and I have been late ever since.

During this episode my mother was in her bedroom lying down. She lay down a lot throughout her life, having regular attacks of the vapours (feeling faint). My mother had many wonderful qualities but down-to-earth practicalities were not among them.

The second experience tells the story of the scar on my left arm. I was walking home from a friend's house near the river in the dark. It must have been in the late 1940s as we still had gas lamps on street corners that had to be lit. It was a windy night and the light from the lamps spread figures on the high old wall I was walking beside, making it look like someone was following me. I began to run. I was only 200 metres from home but in my terror it seemed like a mile. Thinking someone was about to grab me, I dashed into our back kitchen but couldn't shut the door – I couldn't shut the door! I jammed my left arm on the frosted glass partition, the glass smashed; I pulled my arm back and ripped a two-inch gash. Blood gushed everywhere. My mother had those vapours but fortunately my sister was at hand. She put a simple tourniquet on my arm and called the next door neighbour, a nurse who took me to hospital in her car. I had jammed the door with the doormat in my frantic action. There was no one there.

My mother was of a delicate nature, brought up in those days when young ladies did no work; they pursued hobbies. She had an exquisite hand for drawing, attended art school and developed into a minor artist. In her early years in Western Australia she was taught elocution by Lionel Logue. Many years travelling with her mother – ending up in India and getting married with servants to do everything – did not prepare her for the harder vicissitudes of life in England with a daughter and a son, even with domestic help.

In addition, because her delicate nature was unable to cope with the oppressive heat of India, her husband was forced to retire to England at the age of 49, far too early. My father's whole life up to then had been in India, having been born and raised there. He had risen near to the top in the Imperial Indian Police Force, becoming District Superintendent of Police for Bombay Presidency (an area three times the size of Britain). He had overseen visits from royalty, had reluctantly arrested Gandhi on the Salt March as he left Poona, saved the lives of villagers by shooting marauding tigers and had quelled riots between Hindus and Mohammedans. His time was in those years which led to partition and the creation of two new nations, Pakistan and Bangladesh.

Those riots were quelled not only by the power of his enormous voice but also by the respect the Indians had for him. He was fluent in three Indian languages: Hindi, Gujarati and Marathi. He used to swear at me in Hindi, calling me a *kutte ka bachaa*, which I decline to translate. If Hindi speakers read this they will raise their eyebrows. Indeed, they did when I asked three Indians chatting in St James' Park in Sydney for the correct spelling.

Despite having been born, brought up and schooled in India, my father was not entirely part of the Raj. He was seen as a white Indian like those in the West Indies. His father had been sent to India in the 1860s to be Governor of the prison in Ahmedabad. I know from hearing his stories that he never felt at home among those wet wallahs from England. He did, however, play contract bridge in the white clubs and he was a Mason in a lodge his father had founded in Ahmedabad. Hence, by being a Lewis (grandson of a lodge-founding Mason) all my private schooling was paid for by the Grand Lodge of England.

I grew up in awe and with a degree of fear of my father. Recently I have been trying to imagine myself in his shoes and I can understand why I must have added to his frustrating circumstances.

Although I inherited my mother's artistic sensibilities and sensitive nature, I did develop a commanding voice and an indignant temper. I seemed to be evenly endowed by both, but believe I had more of my mother in the early days. I was not robust, being a skinny boy with bowed legs ('rickets', I heard from a doctor walking behind me years later) but I had good ball sense and liked attention.

The predominant memory I have of my father is of him sitting in a well-worn leather armchair reading *The Times*, smoke curling up from his enamel cigarette holder, occasionally lifting his left buttock to release an almighty fart. (That, I hesitate to say, is another characteristic I inherited from him.) One day I struck a match and lit his newspaper. He rose and roared like the tigers he shot and gave me a clip round the ear (another familiar phrase from those days); I've been hard of hearing since. Even his burping was more like a tiger's roar and could be heard throughout the neighbourhood.

My father had been a man of action: a sort of Hemingway man. He was a first-rate shot, attested by the number of skins of tiger, leopard, cheetah and hyena that were brought back. His prize possession was the eight-foot long tiger skin with head. He often told me the story of how and why it was shot. This magnificent creature had killed and eaten a villager and was sleeping it off in a field just outside the village. The terrified villagers had run to my father's headquarters with this news. Once a tiger had tasted human flesh it had to be destroyed. A great retinue of excitable Indians accompanied him to the field where the tiger lay. Having given firm instructions for absolute silence on approach, he proceeded to get them to build a tree platform (a *machan* in Hindi) overlooking the doomed sleeping cat. The villagers were instructed to be armed with utensils and tins, anything that would make a noise. At my father's command an almighty noise was made. The great cat rose in the air with a mighty roar; father's shot from the platform pierced its jugular vein and it fell lifeless to the ground. A great procession followed my father's garlanded return. Pegge sahib was a hero. You can understand how this kind of story would fire the imagination of the young Pegge. There were many stories like it.

Among the many items brought back from India with such stories attached were hunting bows and arrows and a long spear. My friends and I put these weapons to dangerous use in those endless games of 'dare' and mock battles. How my eyes survived the fierce air gun pellet fights is a miracle.

My father had been a fine sportsman, skilled in polo, hockey, archery and cricket. But I knew him only as a tired, lonely man with no purpose to his life. It seemed an effort for him to play cricket with me, but he was encouraging and, thank goodness, I had some natural ability.

His old days of action were set in motion once again when I ran home from the boatyard on the river Thames to tell him how I had been sexually interfered with by a bearded ex-sailor. He had taken me to his flat nearby, having gradually befriended me during my many days fishing and boating on the river. I told my father exactly what he had done to me. The next day I was boating with a friend in the middle of the river. I saw my father striding with ferocious purpose towards the said gentleman who was working on a boat near the water. He grabbed him, a knee jerked up, and with a final punch to the jaw, he knocked him into the river. Pegge sahib was a hero again.

I have been left with a vivid memory of this incident but no scarring. Having told my father, his actions must have alleviated my guilty feelings by thumping the shit out of the perpetrator. Certainly since that incident I have had a deep aversion to the physical idea of homosexuality, but not to those who are gay. After all there are many in the theatre and I have always enjoyed their company.

Not that I condone what my father did to the man, looking back from these more enlightened days. After all, homosexuality and paedophilia have been a part of the human condition throughout the ages. If you went to boarding school at an early age as I did, there were plenty of exploratory fumblings as we tried to work out what to do with this thing that rose when touched.

There was no sex education and many parents from those days were too embarrassed to talk about it. I found out from older boys, the two sisters who lived next door and the local village girls. '*I'll show you mine if you show me yours*' was the mantra of the day. However, one of the sisters from next door did end up becoming a nun.

I remember my first kiss. Her name was Hilary Harboard. She had straight blonde hair, a button nose and had that cool Nordic look. We would meet on the 441 bus (the one I threw a stone at) which took us to our respective schools. She got off in Windsor and I went on towards Slough. We were sitting at the back of the bus and just before she got up she leaned forward and kissed me on the lips. It wasn't a peck. The rest of my journey was spent in a state of reverie with my schoolbag firmly on my lap. I clutched it tightly across my thighs for fear of showing the aroused chipolata.

Visits to the theatre had the deepest imprint on me. My mother took me regularly to the Theatre Royal, Windsor, which was a repertory company run by John Counsell. You could see the same actors in different plays every two weeks. In the company were two actors who became familiar names later, Patrick Cargill and Geraldine McEwan (from *Father, Dear Father* and *Miss Marple* respectively). But the highlight for me in those early years was the annual Christmas pantomime; being able to join in, to hiss and boo and yell 'behind you' were the best part.

In those days séances were also very fashionable. My parents called it *Planchette*. On a glossy table, letters of the alphabet were placed in a circle and a fine glass tumbler placed in the middle. All players would put a finger lightly on the glass and the appointed medium would call for the spirit to answer our calls. After a while the glass would start to move to the letters and spell out an answer. I can honestly say no one consciously pushed the glass. It could be thoughts creating electrical impulses. We once had near proof that it worked when it gave us the name of the horse that won the 1946 Epsom Derby. Its name was *Airborne* but Dad put only a few shillings on it.

During the long winter months I played more indoors – toys like a Hornby train set, Meccano, Dinky toys, card games and endless sessions on the Monopoly board. Victorian parlour games such as hide-and-seek and musical chairs were still played at parties. We had no television until I was 11 years old. I remember playing with my underground train set while watching Queen Elizabeth's Coronation in 1953. Many, many hours were spent reading and putting on little performances.

2

'Creeping like snail unwillingly to school ...'

The seed for my acting career may have been sown at Upton School, Windsor where I first appeared on stage playing Marigold in Toad of Toad Hall. It began to grow shoots at my prep school, Long Close School.

From the age of eight I travelled on the 441 bus to Slough (still operating) every day and walked a kilometre to Long Close School. Later in that first year, prompted no doubt by the stone throwing incident, it was decided I should be a weekly boarder. I remember being very upset and feeling unwanted. I was very much a mummy's boy. That was soon overcome by the likes of our classic matron Miss Blackburn who was the most lovable person if also a perfect model for Miss Piggy.

I soon felt I had another home, which would arm me well in my peripatetic later life. The school building had been an old home with a large garden. The masters were too old to serve in the war. They were all decent father figures and very good teachers. Music and drama were strong in the curriculum and I became besotted with our music teacher, Miss Susan Williams. Miss Williams recognised I had a promising singing voice, and cast me as a leading singer in the chorus of *Trial by Jury*, followed by Mabel in *The Pirates of Penzance*. To play Gilbert and Sullivan at such a young age laid the foundation for speed in performance and sharp articulation. I also played Hermia in an open air performance of *A Midsummer Night's Dream*. I particularly remember saying: 'Help me Lysander ... to pluck this crawling serpent from my breast.'

Young people today would find it weird that a boy aged 12 should be saying lines of this kind. Young boys played girls in Elizabethan times. This tradition continued right up to Elizabeth II's reign, certainly in private boys' schools (called public schools in the UK). Experiencing playing Shakespeare at that age was life-framing, and pointed me in the direction I was destined to travel.

But it was while I was playing Mabel in *The Pirates of Penzance* at my prep school that I knew I wanted to go on the stage. I had hit a top C and there was a very brief hush in the audience. That moment has always stayed with me. If a volunteer was required to speak text aloud my hand shot up.

I adjusted easily to boarding school as I always spent the weekend at home. Even though Father was mostly inactive and Mother was mostly lying down, I did have my long-suffering sister to annoy, and there was also The Gang.

I can remember every one of their names and most of them lived near the river where most of our time was spent. The Wind in the Willows was a very real story for me. We fished, swam and mucked around in boats. I was a cox for the skiff crews of the Wraysbury Skiff and Punting Club and won my first two sporting trophies for junior punting and sculling. I was thrown into the river fully clothed by a member for being a pest.

We cycled up and down the footpaths but never crossed the river. The territory in which we roamed was one or two kilometres each way from the Old Windsor lock to Runnymede and inland to the Roman ruin on top of Pelling Hill. Every weekend and throughout the holidays we were out and about in the fresh air having adventures. We were never bored; our lives were full of exploration, observation and curiosity about strange local characters. There was the Running Man and the Green Man. The Running Man would run every night at the same time past our house from the village to The Bells of Ouseley pub and run home again a little less steadily. We could never find out who he was or why he ran. We were too afraid to ask.

The Green Man lived under a boat on the riverbank. He looked like one of Robin Hood's merry men dressed in green bits and pieces. After he died they found stacks of money among his belongings. Rumour had it that he was a surgeon and was responsible for the death of one of his patients.

Across the river from his upturned boat lived Mr Holloway, the gentleman thief. Perhaps he used our Green Man to hide some loot. My uncle used to drink with Mr Holloway in The Bells of Ouseley. Nobody had any inkling as to his nefarious occupation until we heard that he had committed suicide in the Wheatsheaf Hotel in Virginia Water. He could no longer escape the tightening net.

To cross the Thames there was the jolly Mr Butcher, our ferryman. He did take you to the other side but it was only to Wraysbury, which was not permanent. You called for him by ringing the large green bell. The sound of bells was very common in those days and has always meant a reassuring connection with the past for me.

We used to muck around in an old ruined building down the road from where we lived. A bell to call in the workers from the fields was often heard. Where we lived the past was always present. The last stanza of 'Ode to a Nightingale' by John Keats says it all for me:

> Forlorn! the very word is like a bell
> To toll me back from thee to my sole self!

I see and hear that bell in Old Windsor resonating across the glades and meadows that were my wild home. And towards the end of the dying sound that sped across those fields, a grand mansion lay, which none of us ever visited. It was out of our territory, which meant it held more curiosity. But we did know that an old lady lived there on her own and that her name was Lady Follett.

One morning as I was going to school on that 441 bus, I saw a pall of smoke curling up above the ridge of the hill. Later we heard that Lady Follett had died in a fire that had destroyed the mansion. She was my Lady Haversham when I read Great Expectations and somehow I associate that scene with the opening lines of an old folk song:

> Early one morning just as the sun was rising,
> I heard a maiden crying in the valley below.

I spent a lot of time listening to the wireless, as it was called then: Itma starring Tommy Handley, Much Binding in the Marsh and Dick Barton Special Agent with the memorable signature tune called 'The Devil's Gallop' by Charles Williams, were the favourites. We regularly held musical evenings on a Sunday. It centred around our baby grand piano on which my mother and sister played. I sang songs like 'In a Monastery Garden' but I had more fun being bumped for six by my Aunt Nora's wide derrière singing 'Hands knees and boomps-a-daisy'.

Stories were told of the past, and favourite poems performed. We had a wind-up gramophone player. We listened to vinyl records of Caruso, Gilbert &

Sullivan, Chopin and, my mother's favourite, the Strauss waltzes. We grew up listening to words and music, and we lived the Christmas-card Christmases with holly, snowballs, tobogganing, carols, Santa Claus, crackers and crackling fires – all very like Dylan Thomas's recollections in *A Child's Christmas in Wales*.

It really is amazing how change has galloped faster since I grew up. My upbringing was connected to the Victorian era. Brown paper parcels were tied with string and sealed with hot sealing wax and pressed with Father's signet ring. I was beaten and told that boys were to be 'seen and not heard'. I looked forward to going on a shopping trip; being taken to the theatre or cinema was a treat, as was the annual Christmas visit to the pantomime at the Theatre Royal, Windsor.

I cried watching *Bambi* and thrilled to the action film *Where No Vultures Fly*. Cinemas in those days held a lingering sensual memory: the smell of cigarettes and celluloid, probably the reason I became a smoker. But the sweet smells of summer and autumn, the smell of newly mown grass and bonfires of smoking leaves, have always been my cherished memories.

Steam trains were still on the tracks run by different companies like LMS and LNER. We went to the same place at the same time every year for our summer holidays – Bognor Regis, made famous by King George V who was quoted as saying on his deathbed 'bugger Bognor'. He was right. The amazing fact is both my parents were born during the reign of Queen Victoria. My father was born in 1883 and my mother in 1899.

Before leaving those long days at my prep school, certain memories cling to my senses. I gag whenever I see or think of porridge and semolina or tapioca puddings, like eating tadpoles with those slithery eyes; porridge always lumpy and never enough brown sugar. Then I remember being locked away in an attic bedroom for a week, with matron giving me injections of penicillin and streptomycin for an agonising ear ache, and me longing to be out mucking about.

Finally, although I won the throwing-the-cricket-ball competition handsomely (which was most unfortunate for that 441 bus), I came second to O'Connell in the contest for best all-round athlete, who was called rather grandly the 'Victor Ludorum', the prize for which was a whacking great silver cup. It would have been mine had I beaten him in the last race but he held off my valiant effort, damn him. I can see his arrogant disregard for me, expressed perfectly in a poem by Mick Gower called 'Alsoran'. It is about a boy being beaten in a race by a blonde Adonis.

I wonder where those boys are now and what they are doing: Onions, Langley, Sly, Sturrock, O'Connell. And those masters: Mr Alexander, Mr Judd, Mr Vincent, Mr Phizzy. All gone and fading into sepia images.

Brian Patten's poem 'Schoolboy' says it all:

> *The ghosts of Tim and Maureen and Pat*
> *and Nancy and so many others,*
> *all holding sexless hands, all*
> *doomed to living, and*
> *one pale boy*
> *in a steamy room*
> *looking outside across the roofs and chimneys*
> *where it seems, the clouds are crying,*
> *the daylight's gone blind*
> *and his teachers, all dead.*

3

Father's Death and Family History

For an actor, these early memories are the bricks and mortar from which a performance is built. This well of memories is what Stanislavsky (the great Russian master of dramatic art) asked his actors to call upon in their process for making scenes real and truthful.

One of the most potent memories I have used in role preparation is that of the day I was told my father had died. That devastating sense of loss stuns and drains the body. I was 12 years old and beginning to lose my fear and look up to him.

His gruff exterior belied a buried caring. He was an old man at 70 and had strangely been converted from loosely C of E to Christian Science – the teachings of Mary Baker Eddy that refused traditional medical treatment. I remember feeling odd when attending Sunday School in their church next to Windsor station. His regular doctor kept visiting for his company and whisky. Lack of proper diagnosis, Christian Science and all those years in India affected his liver. Cyril Cuthbert Colbeck Pegge was a man to be reckoned with in those early days in India and in a sense he died in exile. Pale and yellow, he loitered towards his end.

Undoubtedly my mother's influence was more direct and longer lasting. I remember being caressed to sleep with nursery rhymes, learning to speak her ditties and sayings like 'Betty Botter', and listening to her performing the monologues learnt for Lionel Logue's classes. She often related stories of her past and repeatedly talked of how she was taught elocution by the gentleman who helped the King overcome his stammer. I never thought much about it until the film *The King's Speech* was released.

All these stimuli surely contributed to planting the seed for an actor's life. Her motherly devotion gave me the emotional security to risk impecuniousness and cope with rejection. She was always there. Indeed it felt like she was there forever as she only just missed out on getting a letter from the Queen.

My mother's family emigrated from England to Australia in 1841. Mother always said we 'came out', not 'emigrated', even in 1954. They travelled on the *Parkfield*, landing in Western Australia. My great-grandfather Edmund Birch ran a pharmacy where the ANZ bank stands now on Barrack Street. He held office in the Legislative Assembly in the 1860s and was prominent in Trinity Church affairs but died early in a fire.

My grandmother Eunice was by all accounts a very beautiful woman but flighty and flirtatious. She sent my mother to Lionel Logue's Perth classes about 1914. I suspect she met him socially. In 1917 my grandfather offered my grandmother the choice of a trip or a car, and so she took her sister and my mother to England. Although not many people had cars, Eunice had, I suspect, a greater yearning for travel and a change of scenery. She ended up spending a number of years in London and having a very close relationship with the Dean of Perth from Western Australia. How this happened in those days beggars belief. She must have met this episcopal bounder before leaving.

During the time they lived in Chiswick, Mother attended the local art school and produced some exquisite water colours of bonneted ladies. The three of them travelled around the British Isles, seemingly unaware of the First World War. Mother often talked of visiting Castle Douglas near Dumfermline for the grouse shooting, the hosts being Scottish landed gentry. Eighty years later I visited a very run-down Castle Douglas, now suitably an artists' colony, and took photos of the exact views Mother had painted. I had to get on the roof for the outward view to the sea above the trees that had grown.

There is a gap in my grandmother's storyline. She returned to Perth but found her husband had disappeared. The rumour goes that he moved to America and died a wealthy man but nothing filtered through to his Perth family. Grandmother died of cancer at the age of 46 in 1925 and is buried with her mother in the Karrakatta cemetery in Perth, which I managed to find with the help of my cousin. I cast my mother's ashes on the grave that held the remains of two generations of mothers.

One interesting note is that my mother adored her mother and reminisced about her often, but hardly ever mentioned my father. She had very few memories of her married life. After her mother died her brother Edmund, who was working for Raleigh Bros in Calcutta, sent for his sister Evelyn. She must have enjoyed a carefree social life there before travelling and meeting my father. She seemed proud to tell us many years later that she nearly married a gentleman with the exotic name of Salvador D'Arbelles. Edmund D'Arbelles would have been an infinitely more appropriate theatrical name than Pegge, but then, I suppose, I would not have existed.

Despite what has been related about my father, when he died it left me with a hollow feeling as though a prop had been removed. Twelve years old is just the time a boy needs a father. At least I had my mother and sister who gave me love and security. There were many boys who lost their fathers in the war. I had been lucky. I was also lucky with our next door neighbours.

The Hortons became my surrogate family: Adrian the avuncular father figure, Margaret the practical no-nonsense mum, Gay who became the nun, Jane, my friend to this day, David their young brother and Bonnie their English sheep dog. Adrian was a Pickwickian figure: a rounded, bewhiskered gentleman 'full of wise saws and modern instances', a bon vivant, a great judge of character and mad about cricket. I joined his Gentlemen of Old Windsor team in 1949 at the age of 10 and played regularly up to a few years ago when it finally folded. He was an assuring presence in my life after my father died.

My best friend in those early days was John Briginshaw whose father bought and restored the ruined mansion with the ghostly bell down the road. The family moved to Tasmania before we left and we lost touch. Fifty years later I met up with him. We recognised each other. We could just glimpse behind the blemishes of ageing to the children we once were.

4

The Growing-Up Years

It was time now to move on to my senior school. St Paul's School was in a dark, gothic-style building in Hammersmith, not be confused with the school attached to St Paul's Cathedral for training choristers. Getting to school was an arduous business. I had to walk to get a lift from Mr Weller in his Austin Seven car, crammed in with two adults. At Egham Station the train took me to Richmond where I boarded the District Line (part of the underground system) to Hammersmith with another walk that finally got me to school. It took me an hour and a half each way. This was in 1952 when London was smog-bound in the winter. When the smog was bad we would put our hankies over our noses and mouths; breathing would leave a yellow stain. Smog was extremely dangerous; it killed 12,000 people in 1952.

As we had a two-hour break for sport and lunch, I hardly ever left school before 4.30 pm, by which time in the winter it was dark and cold. On the return journey, without the benefit of a lift, I had to catch that 441 bus from Egham station; I never got home before 6.00 pm. With my vivid imagination it was a scary journey, what with swirling mists, gas lamp shadows and dark figures with trilby hats and upturned collars. However, during the year-and-a-half making those journeys, I never experienced any real danger.

On that District Line train I had my second close encounter with the fair sex. Robert Evans and I vied for the attention of the ice-cool ballet student Valerie Hill. She was our Estelle from *Great Expectations*.

St Paul's was a classics school of high standing. I would never get in now with my academic record. Latin was actually spoken among some of the masters. At least I can still remember the Latin grace.

I was given a bursary from Masonic Grand Lodge as mentioned earlier. Our Latin master, being a mason, was asked to keep an eye on me. He was an old-fashioned, caring, marvellous teacher with a commanding voice. His name was D.A.R. Young and he was known as 'Dary'. He had a direct influence on confirming my desire to be a performer. He often put aside the text of the Gallic Wars and read Dickens' *Pickwick Papers* and *Nicholas Nickleby* to the class. His renditions were memorable due to his robust acting of all the parts.

Another master was memorable for an entirely different reason. I was in the lowest form in the school, which was run by a well-known rowing man, Freddie Page, who had been coach of the Oxford University boat race crew. He was a fierce disciplinarian. Anyone out of line would receive his 'six of the best' which meant the errant boy, and I was one, would have to kneel on the seat of the chair and reach down to grab the base of the back legs so as to present a very tight arse. It bloody hurt. Nowadays he would be charged with a criminal act. Mind you these thrashings never did me any harm!

Mr Harbord (no relation to Hilary, my first kiss) was a much kinder gentleman who taught English and produced the school plays. I was only at the school for a year and a half but made my mark. Firstly by playing Casilda in *The Gondoliers* (it was said of my performance that 'Pegge was strikingly dignified and imperious and sang the difficult music with purity of tone'); and then, after my role as Lady Teazle in *The School for Scandal*, I received my very first fan letter ('I wonder, don't tell anyone but I think you're one of the best ones'). This came from Elizabeth, daughter of Mr Harbord whom I should have kissed but didn't. Also, I became a leading treble.

I had a wonderfully unexpected reunion with an old boy in 2009 when I made a rare attendance at a Masonic meeting of the Old Pauline Lodge. This white-haired gentleman was prompting the new Worshipful Master. He was my betrothed Luis in *The Gondoliers*. Julian Rees and I went in to dine singing our duet.

Our music master Ivor Davis was a most enthusiastic teacher and thought I had the voice of an angel. There were three of us who were the leading trebles. The prize each year for a treble was to be chosen to sing the solo in St Paul's Cathedral on Apposition Day (Founder's Day). Ivor gave it to me in 1953. I can remember vividly that out-of-world feeling hearing my voice at the end, echoing around the whispering gallery, up into the roof of the dome. I like to think my voice is still up there somewhere.

Ivor was limp-wristed and flapped around a lot. He was, it has to be said, very gay, even though that word was not in use then in that sense.

One might think that St Paul's, being predominantly a day school, would be less likely to have a paedophile master. There was no stigma attached to Ivor Davis, but there were rumours about the Christian Union Movement and a certain boxing master. We were a top boxing school. I was coached by Bo Langham – not accused of paedophilia – who amazingly had taught my uncle in 1915, the reason I went to St Paul's. He was over 70 years old when he took me for boxing. The only time I represented the school I found myself in the ring with a boy from Kings College School, Wimbledon. We went three rounds without either of us throwing a punch. I still have Bo Langham's three-page analysis of the fight that never was.

Even though I attended St Paul's for only a year-and-a-half I maintained contact with several boys and masters. These bonds were reinforced after I returned when I joined the Old Pauline Cricket Club. There is no doubt that I gained a huge advantage going to a private school. This was immediately evident in the first week of my return in 1965.

5

Journey Down Under and First Impressions

In 1954 Mother was 'sent for' by her brother (a last cry from the Victorian age) to live in Adelaide, South Australia. He thought it would be a better life for my sister and me on Father's fixed pension. It turned out to be all right for me but not so much for my sister Eunice at the age of 21.

Our departure on the *Orontes* at the end of January 1954 was a chaotic affair. Without my sister we might not have made it. We left our next door neighbours to sell the house and furniture. We were not ten-pound Poms in steerage. We had a comfortable trip lasting almost eight weeks.

I have one vivid memory during the voyage; Jill Dempster. I espied her in a deck chair. She was 19 and very beautiful. I was 14 and very weedy but she didn't seem to mind me talking to her. I can't imagine why she allowed me to hang around – perhaps I did errands for her. Anyway she ended up in a very useful position for me in Adelaide after a successful modelling career and becoming Jill Minnear. She headed the South Australian Film Corporation soon after it was founded.

An earthquake greeted us off the coast of South Australia on 3 March 1954. What struck me more was the dry, burning heat and relentless sun, beating down on corrugated iron roofs of bungalows all looking the same. It was a desolate feeling.

Another very distinct memory from those first few weeks was losing fear of the dark. I felt no danger in the Australian night; buildings held no presence of the past, shadows no longer frightened me. That feeling of not quite being at home though, has always remained. I blame the mosquitoes, the cockroaches and the flies. Insects really get to me. Maybe it is something to do with that wasp Hitler sent over when I was younger.

Also in those days there was no air conditioning. The languorous ceiling fan only moved the hot air around, but there were the 'sleep-outs'. They were to prove very handy later, even though the iconic fly wire door did creak too much in those late-night situations. Australia in the 1950s is perfectly described in a poem by John Clarke, 'A Child's Christmas in Warrnambool', which is his take on Dylan Thomas's *A Child's Christmas in Wales*: 'the distant constant slowly listless bang of the fly wire door'.

Despite these discomforts I settled in fairly quickly. After all, it wasn't a foreign country. There were many familiar things and at last a constant supply of Vegemite. Our relatives in Perth used to include a jar in the food parcels they sent to us during the war years.

6

Final Schooldays

My bursary from the Masonic Grand Lodge of England was extended to St Peter's College, one of the top schools of Adelaide. My Uncle Edmund first took me through the portals of the college which carried the school motto 'Pro Deo et Patria'; a very English sentiment. My eyes opened wide as we drove towards the beginning of my next three years. St Paul's had very little space; this was more like Eton College or Tonbridge. The playing fields of St Peter's College played the same role as the famous fields of Eton. Indeed, as I was soon to discover, the school was run on strict English public school lines. I felt at home very quickly.

However, I soon found myself out of my depths academically. The headmaster assumed that coming from a famous classics school (the 16th century scholar Erasmus was an old boy of St Paul's) I must be pretty bright. I hadn't told them I was in the bottom form. I was soon found out and dropped two streams. Somehow I don't remember being affected by this drop in status. I think I knew even then that I had other qualities.

There is a profound difference between the way education in schools is conducted today and to the way we were taught. We were allowed to tip-toe through the tulips of learning, being taught by teachers who were not necessarily taught to teach. They had the knowledge of their specialised subjects and a desire to impart it. What's more they were characters who were given apt names: Thick Bills, Trunk Vollugi, Lags Symons, Enos Miller and Bullant Palmer. Martin Ketley taught me Latin and produced the school plays and Dr Peter Wiener was our charismatic French teacher. A Doctor of Philosophy at the age of 24, he had been an intelligence adviser to Field Marshall Montgomery. In his rooms there was a photo of them at the steps of Montgomery's HQ at St Paul's, my old school. Very few boys missed one of his classes.

My interest in world affairs stems from his current affairs classes. He talked the talk of a man who had lived to the full and was keen to pass on his knowledge and experience. He inspired us to question and be curious. In one memorable class Dr Wiener said a special guest was coming to talk to us.

We were in the upstairs classroom of the original building to which led a wooden spiral staircase. We heard this clumping noise ascending the stairs, at last he appeared. As soon as the gentleman entered we all recognised him immediately. It was Douglas Bader, the famous hero from the Battle of Britain. We listened spellbound as he related his experiences.

I happened to meet Douglas Bader with Sir Lennox Hewitt on a flight from London to Sydney. I saw them up there in first class and boldly walked through. Introducing myself I said I was at St Peter's College when he had come to give a talk and saying how much he had inspired us all. I don't know how it happened but I spent the rest of the journey with them. Sir Lennox Hewitt was charming and interested in hearing about my acting career. I came away from that flight with a slightly tarnished view of Bader, however. While sitting around at Bahrain airport, his comments about the Arabs were virulently racist, displaying the attitude of a white supremacist.

Many years later I heard some adverse comments about him, when visiting a Spitfire museum, from fellow pilots who had known Bader. Their comments were not flattering. They forcibly made the point that there were others, equally as good, with disabilities, who had not sought fame and cashed in on their exploits. It was interesting to see Kenneth More play him in the film *Reach for the Sky*. I felt he was too lightweight and jolly compared with the man I met.

Our music master, John Winstanley, conducting rehearsals for the annual Christmas Carol concert, was famous for endlessly saying: 'Boys, tip of the tongue and sing through your head.'

The literally minded boys thought that silly but I realised it was good advice and have promoted that idea in speech training. He was a great enthusiast for boys to appreciate classical music. His musical appreciation class was extra-curricular but well attended. My love of the great composers was cemented in those sessions.

Again it was the Latin master, Martin Ketley, who helped confirm my acting aspirations. In my first year he cast me to play Lavinia in *Androcles and the Lion* by George Bernard Shaw. It was to be the last time I would play a female. In my second year Mr Ketley cast me in my first male role. I played the husband in *The Man Who Married a Dumb Wife* and in my final year Lord Arthur in *Lord Arthur Savile's Crime*, a play adapted into a short story by Oscar Wilde.

It was a wonderfully premature experience to be in such a sophisticated play, trying to execute lines and movement in that style. The confidence I gained doing all these school plays gave me the strength not to be put off pursuing this vocational compulsion.

Many of the boys from my years became eminent in their careers, but their fields seem to be traditionally confined to the law and medicine. When I had to meet the headmaster before leaving he gave me quite an astonished response. C.E.S. Gordon was a rather distant figure – a very tall gentleman with large feet and half-moon spectacles. His feet were on the desk as I walked in to his austere study.

'*Well Pegge, what do you want to do in life, boy?*'

'*Sir,*' I replied, '*I want to be an actor.*'

There was a long pause as he slowly put his feet under the desk, peered over his spectacles, leaned forward and, fixing me with an astonished stare, said: 'Good God boy, we haven't had one of those before. You'd better go to Elder Smith and find out what you really want to do.'

Elder Smith & Co. was a large merchant company that automatically took boys from St Peter's College who were undecided on a profession. Even in 1956 there were remnants of mores and attitudes that could be ascribed to the Victorian era.

7

Work and Theatre in Adelaide

After leaving school at the end of 1956 I did join Elder Smith & Co., but I also enrolled part-time taking English and Psychology in an Arts Degree course at Adelaide University, despite being told I was not university material! I launched myself into Adelaide's lively and prolific amateur theatre scene over the next three years.

I soon found working in an office tedious beyond belief. One image has always stuck with me. Mr Hack in the Lands Department sat in the same wood and glass compartment for many years, with 'spectacles on nose and pouch on side' as Shakespeare would have it, waiting to receive his gold watch and retire after forty years of service. I needed to escape from this kind of expectation.

Appointed to the Cement Section I found myself in a two-manned department behind a very grey looking Clem Kingston. Next door in earshot was Mr Horrocks, a very serious wobbly chinned man. There was something very Dickensian about him. My main job was to write out orders for cement in quadruplicate to be sent all over South Australia. Under this ordering pad I would secrete the script of whatever play I was rehearsing. As well as learning lines and writing out orders, I used to toast my sandwiches on an upturned electric fire. Sometimes Mr Kingston and Mr Horrocks would find their noses twitching with the smell of burning toast. I was often caught not doing any work. The final straw came when my inattention to detail had disastrous consequences.

There was an order for thirty bags of cement to be sent to Kangaroo Island off the southern coast of South Australia. I wrote out the order for thirty tons. It was duly delivered to the harbour at Kingscote where I am told evidence of the order is still visible. I was duly removed (a boy from St Peter's

College would never be sacked) and sent to the airways section of the Travel Department. This was much more fun as it was by the entrance to the building with lots of comings and goings. This section was better for my purposes. It suited my outgoing personality and I found myself instinctively becoming a people-watcher. Noting the way people walk and talk is the actor's storeroom for future performances.

My first play outside school was the lead role at the age of 16 in The Man from the Ministry by Madeline Bingham, for a newly formed church group. I was very encouraged by the critics, one of whom called me 'an actor of real ability and considerable promise'. Another described me as 'a budding Dirk Bogarde'. I've been 'budding' ever since.

I began to attend lectures at university and eagerly joined the dramatic society and other amateur groups. These were the days when it cost very little to attend university and amateur companies were of a very high standard.

My first university performance was playing Lord Withers in *Two Gentlemen of Soho* by A.P. Herbert, one of the last performances in The Hut, for the Adelaide University Dramatic Society (AUDS). It was a very stylised English play and the well-known writer/critic Max Harris gave me an encouraging mention:

> In Mr Edmund Pegge AUDS have a player with both the voice and the gift for this sort of thing ... so expertly did he roundly full blood it in the fashion.

I was then in the opening production of the Union Hall in 1958, playing the Captain in *Androcles and the Lion*. But my university performing days centred around the Adelaide University Footlights Club, which had been established before the war. Both Melbourne and Sydney universities had similar traditions out of which a number of luminaries began their performing careers, including Germaine Greer, Clive James and Barry Humphries. Of course, they were modelled on the renowned Cambridge Footlights Club.

I performed in two productions and directed the 1960 revue *Strictly Between Us* at the end of my first year at drama school. I remember finding it difficult to deal with so many differing details in a production while keeping the broad picture in mind. It turned out to be my only attempt at directing. Ever since, I have always had the utmost respect for directors. Directing requires an imaginative and incisive mind.

The Footlights Club produced an eventful *Hamlet* in 1959. Most members of the cast were struck down by flu. The director, Brian Bergin, insisted I remain playing Horatio. One critic said that I gave the most polished performance and 'was completely at home in the part, and did not share the common uneasiness'. He should have said 'common cold'. Looking back now it was significant that the man who played Hamlet became a professor of dentistry while I became a professional actor. It set a template for the way my career unfolded.

Playing Kinesias in *Lysistrata* by Aristophanes for Adelaide University Theatre Guild was a memorable experience. It was the one and only time I had to go on stage with an erection. We were a group of soldiers denied sex by the women of Sparta who were on strike. Entering with scrolls erect under our tunics brought the house down. The audience were literally falling out of their seats and it was so easy to prolong the laughter by acting suggestively. Laughter and spellbound silence feed the actor's ego in live theatre performances. Commanding attention can be a factor in making you want to be an actor.

We had a wonderfully eccentric English lecturer called Bryn Davies who was also a charismatic performer. He would stride onto the platform, his cloak flowing, and immediately take out a cigarette. His protruding, piercing eyes would fix you, then move to someone else. He would tap his cigarette onto his silver cigarette case, then make a point in his address. He would continue this routine throughout the lecture: taking the cigarette out, making another point, getting the matches out to light up – and then making yet another point. I can't remember him ever lighting a cigarette. It was mesmerising for me. He was, in fact, doing prop acting, which we call 'business'.

There is one sport which was virtually compulsory in those days for a male stage actor. I took up fencing (foil and sabre) with the newly formed University Fencing Club. It was predominantly run by Hungarians who had escaped the 1956 uprising. Modern physical education teachers would be alarmed at the way we practiced. There was a permanent pall of smoke around the piste and a pungent smell from heavy sulphurous Camel cigarettes. No one ever seemed to warm up, from which I have a niggling reminder in the groin. My only competitive experience was the 1957 inter-varsity held in Sydney. My first two bouts with foil were against Gary Watford and David McKenzie. I remember their names because they represented Australia in the 1956 Melbourne Olympics.

Fencing is the most appropriate sport for actors and is taught at most drama schools. It is an essential skill for performing in any period play or film where duelling is required. It also underpins the thrust and parry in performance. I continued fencing for the next 20 years and used this skill to do occasional stage-fight arrangements.

There were visiting performances that made an impact on me, including the Old Vic's tour of *Twelfth Night*, *La Dame aux Camélias* and *Duel of Angels* starring Vivien Leigh in 1958. This was particularly memorable because I organised a party for the cast.

John Scales, my good friend from school, had wonderfully hospitable parents who agreed to provide the venue. The invitation was passed on to the cast through the English actor David Dodimead, whom I had got to know. To my surprise he said that Vivien Leigh would be delighted to come. At that time her partner was John Merivale who was in the company. He couldn't accompany her to the party, but did come later.

Somehow I found myself in Vivien Leigh's dressing room soon after the final curtain to take her to the party in my Austin 10 Coupé. As I walked in, she had the fridge door open displaying evidence of her liking for gin. I was 19 years old at the time and must have had a lot of front to cope with this beautiful major star. Damn it, I was driving Scarlett O'Hara in my car to my party. However, Scarlett O'Hara had to pick up some dry cleaning for Rhett, I mean John, before we could leave.

I see the picture of Vivien Leigh holding court from a chair in middle of the lawn with all my friends sitting at her feet. It was a regal scene. My friend, the renowned Gilbert and Sullivan actor Dennis Olsen, who came with the actress Julie Hamilton, remembers the occasion vividly. She was gracious and beautiful; we were all under her spell. Julie particularly remembered her talking about Patrick White whom she had met, and asking us questions about what we were doing and thinking. She also remembered how Vivien came up to me during the evening, put her hand on my chest and said 'Ah, mine host'. Her eyes were twinkling. Finally, Julie remembered how much she loved animals. It was proven when George, the water spaniel dog of the house, greeted her on arrival and attached himself all evening, lying at her feet while she was holding court – ultimate charisma. I have often found when meeting highly talented people that most are humble and interested in what you have to say.

I do, however, need to set the record straight. Although I appeared to be the host, I made absolutely no contribution to the actual work that was required to organise the event. I must have been swept up in an euphoria of self importance.

One of the most memorable performances I attended during this period was by Emlyn Williams, the well-known actor/playwright. He was touring the world with his two one-man shows on the works of Charles Dickens and Dylan Thomas. He had the most magnificent voice, its richness conveying the text with clarity and colour. His voice peopled the stage from a lectern.

I will never forget the end of his Dylan Thomas performance. It was the poem 'And death shall have no dominion' and these words were the final line. He moved out of the spotlight circle which remained on the lectern. As he was about to leave the stage he spoke the line again, as the spotlight closed in, leaving a spot on the lectern. He walked out of the of the Bonython Hall side door and we heard the line again. It was spoken with a sustained pause after the '*no*' and an upward inflection on the final word '*dominion*' ringing into the night. The light on the lectern flickered and went out. There was silence for what seemed like minutes. There was a kind of muted applause, because everyone was spellbound, maybe contemplating the thought that death might not be so final.

In hindsight I believe that moment confirmed my determination to be a professional actor and in particular to do these kinds of platform performances, which indeed I did many years later.

Adelaide had a lively amateur theatre scene in the 1950s and 1960s. Television came in 1956 and took a couple of decades to dominate people's leisure time. There were many theatre groups. From 1957 to 1960 I appeared in at least a dozen plays as well as revues, playing a variety of big and small parts. I also had some very good directors/teachers.

Musgrave Horner had a lasting influence. He was an expert speech and drama teacher. Through his classes, summer drama schools and text books I learnt the techniques for clear and expressive speech. Many years later I codified these basic techniques when writing my own speech manual. Musgrave was senior lecturer at Adelaide Teachers College. What I learnt from Musgrave and his assistant Enid Lewis linked up to that which I learnt from my mother, taught by Lionel Logue, though my end had nothing to do with elocution.

Others I learnt from were Colin Ballantyne, who introduced me to the teachings of Stanislavsky; John Edmund in his academy; and Alexander Hay. He had studied at the Royal Academy of Dramatic Art (RADA), founded the Byre Theatre in Scotland, had toured in Donald Wolfit's Shakespeare Company and spent three years at The Old Vic under Sir Tyrone Guthrie. I was lucky to witness his power and technique firsthand as the First Gentleman in his production of *King Lear*. During these years I began my career in radio drama by passing my audition with the somewhat eccentric Stafford Dyson. My first paid job was in sound effects (clicking coconut shells to sound like horses hooves), followed by small parts.

In 1959 I auditioned for the National Institute of Dramatic Art (NIDA) based at the University of New South Wales. The opening narration of Under Milk Wood by Dylan Thomas was my first choice, followed by a dramatisation of a poem by Robert Browning. I believe this unusual choice helped as I was accepted and offered a scholarship. However, my journey was arrested by being called up to do national service in the army. Compared with young men in the UK who were required to do 18 months, the Australian call up was for three months and more like a rigorous holiday.

In the long run it turned out to be valuable experience. Discipline, fitness, learning to be a team and mix with people from differing backgrounds were essential building blocks for my future career. Also I became proficient at army drill, useful to have for any production about the armed forces.

Somehow I found myself in the artillery platoon, which meant no route marching. An embarrassing incident happened on manoeuvres. A mock battle was coming to an end. It was sunset and thinking it was 'all quiet on the Western Front', I took the portable loo away from the camp, placing it on a slight rise. My seated figure appeared on the horizon in splendid clarity. In no time I was surrounded by the enemy, shot many times and escorted back to base as a prisoner. The battle was lost.

An abiding part of the army seems to be the Regimental Sergeant Major (RSM). We had a typical one. He had a bristling moustache from under which poured a voice like thunder, filling the air with orders decorated with a colourful enrichment of the English language. He was like RSMs in most comedy war series.

At the end of 1959 I auditioned again for NIDA and was fortunate to win the Clyde Waterman scholarship. Without a scholarship I would not have been able to do the two-year course, without which my journey might have been longer and harder. Sometime in February 1960 I left home at the age of 21.

Everyone remembers my birthday – 1 April, All Fools' Day, when the fool at court could play a joke on the King. I always found myself playing the fool and wanting to be noticed. Many say it is an appropriate date for me and perhaps it has had some bearing on the outcome of my career.

During the few weeks before leaving for Sydney I had an experience which led to interesting repercussions. I met up with a nurse I was seeing. She came from a country town and so was living in nurses quarters. I was living with my mother. We wandered through the parklands looking for a secluded spot. Darkness had settled, so had we when a beam of light startled us. He said he was a policeman and would have to charge us but eventually let us go. We reckoned later he was probably nothing of the sort.

Just before my departure I was visiting my speech teacher in the same country town where my nurse friend was visiting her parents. They lived at the other end of town and I had borrowed an old car to visit. We found another secluded spot to park off the main street in between where we lived. Some time after midnight the car would not start so we had to walk. Arriving at the main street having not said very much, I offered to accompany her home but she refused. We looked into each other's eyes and saying nothing turned and never looked back. It was a long walk in the early hours of the morning. I felt a great emptiness as I trudged back to where I was staying. On reaching my basement bedroom I immediately set to writing a poem. I didn't think about what to write, the words flowed out of my pen and I never changed a word.

The poem was called 'Hollow Shoes' and it has acquired some history. It has been published twice in small publications but more importantly the poem was admired and re-written by a renowned English poet.

And so 'the time had come the walrus said' to embark on the big journey to an unknown future; to leave the comforts of home and find out the extent of this compulsion. It felt like liberation from 'certain certainties', as T.S. Eliot put it, escaping the prescribed expectations. Many of my very talented friends never broke away from Adelaide and consequently, I believe, never really maximised their potential, or at least tested themselves against the best. I now live back in Adelaide with the knowledge that I did at least achieve that.

8

Drama School

The National Institute of Dramatic Art was founded in 1959 and when I arrived in 1960 it was nothing like a student would find today. The whole campus was virtually a building site. Our training quarters were similar to Nissen huts; they were the early days of the University of NSW.

The teaching method and curriculum were based on those established by the British drama schools like RADA. It was classical acting for the theatre.

Our timetable was intense. We were always in a production or doing play readings in among classes on movement, speech and the history of theatre. Movement classes were taken by the formidable Maggie Barr who had worked with the famous modern movement teacher Martha Graham. Her classes were very aerobic, stimulated by the music from *Carmina Burana* by Carl Orff. Whenever I hear it my body instinctively wants to curl up and fling itself upwards with the arm reaching high. Maggie's idea was that this kind of music would help to instil in us the idea of looking for *dynamics* in performance: to go from soft to loud, from high activity to stillness. With her large, dark eyes and black hair, Maggie had a dynamic presence. She always seemed to be bare-footed, always in tights and a loose top and always filling the room with her incisive voice. A memorable moment was when she arrived one morning and, probably sensing lethargy in the air, said, 'Now girls, have you had a good bowel movement this morning?' Us boys tried not to laugh as the girls hid their embarrassment.

We had a different movement teacher for period dancing. Val Tweedie had a distinctive habit. She smoked mentholated cigarettes from a jam jar. What's more she often had a cigarette in her fingers while, for example, demonstrating an Elizabethan gavotte.

All the students loved Joan Whalley, our speech teacher. She was very attractive and knew her stuff. She had a very persuasive way, certainly for the fellas, in teaching us how performers must breathe. She would come up close behind us, put her arms around our midriffs and rest her hands on our diaphragms. *'Lift your rib cage and use your lungs like bellows'* was a typical instruction. I knew perfectly well how to do it, having had all that training in Adelaide from Musgrave Horner, but I made out I didn't. I enjoyed her lingering behind me!

Everyone, particularly the girls, loved Tom Brown. He had soft features but a resolute manner. We all had respect for him, not least because of his wide experience in the professional theatre. After I had left, I found his name on the credits for the world premier performance in New York of my favourite musical *Candide* by Leonard Bernstein. He was the stage manager.

I learnt a very important lesson from Tom. We were early in rehearsals for *The Beggar's Opera* by John Gay, a production in our second year. I was The Player who opens and closes the show. My alarm clock had not worked, and I phoned to say I was going to be an hour late. I arrived to find he had kept the whole cast sitting in the auditorium of the Little Theatre in silence. When I walked in all eyes turned towards me and Tom said that lateness was not tolerated in the professional theatre. I can hear his cold voice saying: 'Now Mr Pegge has arrived we shall commence rehearsals'. Since then I have been late for only one performance and one rehearsal during a career covering 50 years, but they were exceptional circumstances.

The eventual long-serving and immovable John Clark was our history of theatre teacher and drama director. He came from an academic background and was well-versed in world theatre and its evolution. He inspired us to read widely. John gave me the chance to play a leading role, casting me in the name part of the medieval play *Everyman*. I have always been grateful to him for that early experience in shouldering the pivotal part of a play.

Clement McCallin was our second-year acting coach. He had come from the traditional English classical theatre: ex-RADA and the Royal Shakespeare Company (RSC). He had style, stage presence and a commanding voice. Unfortunately for him he was required to teach lessons from Stanislavsky's *An Actor Prepares,* regarded as the modern actor's bible. The rumour went around that what he needed to teach the next day, he would have read for the first time the night before.

I seem to remember getting through first year without too much angst. The greatest difficulty was trying to survive on £6 per week. These were the days before decimalisation; equivalent today would be about $120. Many of us found accommodation in Kings Cross. The Cross, as it was known, is much sleazier now than it was then. It was more bohemian and arty among the drag queens and prostitutes. *Les Girls* was the most popular night club and created a legacy that led to the film and musical *Priscilla Queen of the Desert*. It was a vibrant community with lots of interesting characters, perfect for a preen of actors eager for experience.

Because of my earlier training in Adelaide, I probably gave the impression to the tutors that I was ahead of the rest. Consequently my superior manner in the second year was brought down a peg or two (pun intended). I was given small parts in the two major productions of *Peer Gynt* and *The Beggar's Opera*. The lead role of Peer was given to Doug Hall, another actor who ended up becoming a dentist.

I had gone to see Tom Brown for advice and he told me that he thought my acting was shallow. That devastated my ego and I had to dig deep to keep going. That sting stayed inside me throughout my career. Of course you could say this was good training for the rejection to come in the professional world.

My letters from the time sound like pleas from the Gulag:

All my underpants have developed holes and I have only one really warm, good fitting pair of socks.

My poor mother was bombarded with endless requests for money and mending. Here are a few other quotes from my letters:

... it's getting colder and colder. At least the cold drives the cockroaches away, but the mice still play. They wake me up at night ...

... callers that never leave, work that's hanging over, utter fatigue ...

... don't know how I'm going to live next term ...

... God, money is a damn nuisance.

I was living in an attic room in the Victoria Street actors' warren.

John Tasker restored my confidence by casting me in the James Stewart part of Tony Kirby in the Kaufman/Hart American comedy You *Can't Take It with You.* John was a lively, inspiring director whom I had met before and was most encouraging. He also cast me as the Poet in a world-premiere staged reading of Patrick White's first play *Ham Funeral.* It was the beginning of most of White's plays being produced. He was a rather austere man to meet and apparently didn't like criticism. We were invited to his flat after the reading. Most of us were sitting on the floor at his feet looking up at this rather dried-up-looking old man who spoke slowly, seemingly weighing his words.

Being part of the university our curriculum was able to include attending lectures in English and Philology. Dr Leonie Kramer's lectures on *1984* and *Brave New World* were seminal. George Orwell and Aldous Huxley were prophets. Her lectures ignited an interest in the big questions of politics and philosophy. The lecturer on Philology (the development and history of language) also ignited my lifelong interest in the evolution of speech and language.

Most students had to find part-time jobs in order to survive. I was lucky to get one in the University Bookshop where I could buy books cheaper and get paid just over £4 for ten hours work. The average worker's wage in those days was about £18 per 40-hour week.

Life in Sydney outside NIDA was limited. There was little time for leisure and even less money to pay for any. Still, we were able to see lots of films and plays: *Wild Strawberries, Black Orpheus* and Brendan Behan's stage play *The Hostage* being most memorable. We were typical students, most of us poor but finding ways of getting the necessaries to have a party. We found a cheap source of wine at a garage on the wharf in Woolloomooloo – Fiorelli Red for one shilling and threepence.

I was lucky to befriend a fellow student called Sandra McKenzie. On occasional Sundays she would invite me home to her parents' Wahroonga home on the North Shore. It was the Head Master's residence of Knox Grammar School, a soothing world away. Her wonderful mother cooked the Sunday roast and insisted on doing my washing.

Ours was a two-year course. These days it is three years and fiercely competitive. There is in the region of one chance in thirty of being accepted. After leaving you are in a profession in which nearly nine out of ten actors are out of work at any one time. I do not encourage young aspirants unless they have a real compulsion.

Today the focus of the course is different, with less emphasis on acting in the classical theatre tradition. The English acting tradition, followed in our time, built a character from outside to inside, the American tradition from inside to out. Theatre performances require the actor to project; movie acting requires inner thoughts to convey what the character feels and thinks. Theatre was the dominant form of entertainment in those days. Television had only just arrived and Hollywood was a dream too far. Many top Australian actors went to NIDA, led by Cate Blanchet and Mel Gibson.

Sadly, practitioners and teachers have gradually slid down the American path and embraced more inward preparation suitable for screen acting. That is where the main body of work is to be found. As a result, I have noticed a decline in clarity of speech in plays on stage and certainly on the screen.

The age of mumbling is upon us.

9

The Travelling Player

Theatre and radio drama were our main sources of income after graduation. My principal employment over the next three years came from becoming a Young Elizabethan Player.

John V. Trevor was the creator of this exciting modern version of the travelling player. His idea was to devise potted versions of the Shakespeare plays being studied for exams and take the performances to schools.

The Young Elizabethan Players (YEP) began touring about 1958. Before teaching at NIDA Clement McCallin was one of the first leaders. He was renowned for being able to extemporise in iambic pentameters due to his vast experience playing Shakespeare. I did my audition soon after completing the NIDA course in 1961 and began my professional acting career in February 1962. It proved to be the best experience any actor could have as a first engagement.

John adapted the plays to the approximate running time of just over an hour and in such a way that seven actors, five men and two women, could cover all the parts with simple changes of clothing and props. The stage could be anywhere as we had various sizes of rostra with a sloping winged curtain as a backdrop behind which would be a rail with costumes over a rack. The plays were stripped down to their skeletal storyline but always included the famous speeches. There were usually three companies touring each year, covering four states. We travelled from school to school and town to town in an eight-seater minibus towing a caravan with all the equipment.

My first tour was the most memorable. Our company leader was Doreen Warburton who had been in Joan Littlewood's Theatre Workshop Company in London's East End. Two of the other actors subsequently made names for themselves: Peter Couchman became a well-known radio and television presenter in Melbourne and Mark McManus will be remembered for being

Taggart in the Scottish detective series. Another member, a sweet girl called Janice Dinen, was seriously short-sighted which led to a tragic accident in London. She fell off the standing platform of a double-decker bus.

There was one other very essential member of these merry bands of players; each company had a manager who looked after the administration. He had myriad tasks: accommodation, paymaster, driver, stage-managing lights and music, liaison duties with the schools and mediator. Our company manager was Tony Gould who was ideal to fill all those roles. It is very important in a small group on a long tour that everyone gets on. Tony was an excellent mediator. He eventually became a high-flyer in arts administration.

We rehearsed two plays, *Twelfth Night* and *The Story of Prince Hal*, on the stage of the Elizabethan Theatre in Redfern. Prince Hal was a cobbled story taken from *Henry IV Part 1 and Part 2* and *Henry V* following Prince Hal's early escapades, with Falstaff and his gang, to becoming king. I was cast as Prince Hal and Aguecheek in *Twelfth Night*. They were prime parts to kick off one's career.

It was exciting rehearsing on the stage where I had watched the incomparable Rudolph Nureyev with Margot Fonteyn on their tour of Australia. John Trevor directed us with focus on the text and the mechanics of telling the story. But my fond memory is seeing him sitting on the stage behind a desk upon which lay his book for notes and a large glass of milk laced with brandy. Rehearsals were long and intense over a period of two to three weeks. We began at 9.30 am with warm-up movement and speech exercises, then rehearsals from 10.00 am to 6.00 pm with less than an hour for lunch.

During this rehearsal period I searched desperately for accommodation that I could call a base and where I could leave a few belongings. I eventually found a tiny back room in one of the terrace houses in Forbes Street, Darlinghurst. It looked over an alleyway of despair – drunken brawls and prostitutes. To have a warm shower you had to light a tiny fire with paper and bits of wood.

This tour would be taking us the length and breadth of Queensland and then to South Australia. I was glad to be on my way to Brisbane and about to earn a regular salary of £29 per week, equivalent to about $600 today. Our opening in Brisbane was a baptism of fire. Jaffa sweets were occasionally thrown from the gallery with voluble sniggering. We had been prepared for these possibilities. The leader would stop the performance, say a few stern words and then pick up where we had left off with greater intensity.

After the two matinee performances in Toowoomba, the Arts Council put on a dinner for us and the visiting UK actor Michael Denison and his wife Dulcie Gray. He was playing Professor Higgins in *My Fair Lady*. This was to be the first of many welcoming functions which we called 'bun fights' where we met the locals and had to make polite replies to such questions as 'So, what do you do for a living?'.

Another new and premature experience was being treated as celebrities by the students. Young girls in particular were desperate for our autographs in case we became famous. We even received fan mail.

It was a comfortable beginning to what lay ahead. Our journey out of Toowoomba took us on to the endless flatlands of the west through Roma to Charleville. We spent long hours travelling into the sun on dusty dirt roads, the monotonous landscape chasing the ever-receding mirage. And then there was the heat. It was my first experience of the real outback; such a far cry from the green fields of England.

After heading north through Blackall to Barcaldine, we turned east to play in Emerald then north again for Charters Towers. We took it in turns to drive these vast distances. To give an idea how vast, driving from Emerald to Charters Towers took eight hours. After 108 km to Clermont we then drove 373 km on a dirt road without seeing anybody. That was driving a minibus with eight people, towing a heavy caravan on dusty, pot-holed roads.

Charters Towers was memorable for two reasons: we played in a grand old theatre where Dame Nellie Melba had performed, and I nearly broke my ankle. It was the first time I became aware of Doctor Theatre. When on stage in front of an audience you are unaware of the pain; adrenaline does the job of a painkiller. I have never missed a performance.

We travelled up to Cairns via the semi-tropical Atherton Tablelands. It was such a contrast to the dry flat plains of the interior. Lush green forests covered undulating mountains, their peaks caressed by mist. A rich crimson sunset fired the myriad colours of the plants, soothing our weary senses.

A panoramic view of the cane fields leading to Cairns and the sea greeted us as we emerged from the ranges. The most dramatic sights in this part of the world are when they burn off the sugar fields. Vast fields of leaping, licking flames, producing a heavy sweet smell, reminded me of classically painted scenes of hell.

I remember sitting with Mark McManus on Ellis Beach near Cairns entertaining two girls from a local drama group. The beach was backed by a mountain range that dropped gently down where palm trees embroidered a pristine stretch of gold sand that looked across to distant islands. There was nobody around. Mark began singing 'Moon River' and his voice seemed to hang in the air, stopping time. It is the only song of which I remember all the words.

Mark had a perfectly placed tenor voice. He would entertain in many pubs on our tour singing Scottish folk songs. His singing of Feste's song 'When that I was and a little tiny boy', towards the end of our performances of Twelfth Night will always stay with me. He had a strong chiselled face with a pug nose – I suspect from his time as an Olympic boxer. He was a powerful actor and in those days his potential could only be realised in the UK or the USA. He quickly became a leading player in the theatre and on television in London.

He certainly had little trouble charming the local residents on tour, as troubadours have done since days of yore. However, on a later tour of Queensland I scored the rogue prize in that department.

I have toured plays in the UK, USA, across Australia and NZ. Queensland tours are always the toughest due to the vast distances, but this particular tour was even tougher than most. I estimate we performed for roughly 14,000 school children and travelled about 6,500 km over a period of three months. It was the best baptism into real theatre that any actor could wish for. By the end, our bodies ached and our minds were only just hanging on to the lines. 'How much longer?' was the common cry.

In fact, we had to have regular word rehearsals. One of these took place when we broke down. We were in between two towns in the outback with two tyre blow-outs. Our company manager had got a lift from a rare passerby. We made a camp fire.

We were all sitting in a circle speaking lines in a non-expressive way, called a 'line check'. It must have sounded like chanting because slowly we became aware of being watched. We could just tell that a group of Aboriginal people were submerged in the surrounding bush. The air was electric with the presence of an unseen audience. Before we finished they had disappeared. There was a strange silence between us. Maybe we had stepped on that ancient, traditional oral path of theirs.

After touring Queensland we were soon off to South Australia with a newly rehearsed production of *Macbeth*. Adelaide is about 2000 km from Brisbane.

We travelled up to Streaky Bay, over to Whyalla and Port Augusta, and then as far north as Woomera, a town noted for being the headquarters for the atom bomb experiment and subsequent rocket launching trials. Our travels back south took us through most major towns all the way to Mount Gambier in the south-east.

In Balaklava, Mark McManus and I were billeted together with the local baker and his family. We were shown our room with apologies: they only had one spare bedroom. There was one double bed with a long hump down the middle; a bolster the baker's wife had placed there to divide the bed. After she had left we went into a gay routine as to who should have which side. We fell about. And so, my friends, I slept with Taggart.

Touring Shakespeare in the outback of Australia had strong romantic appeal, even though the reality was bloody hard work. It also appealed to a famous actor who happened to be in Sydney, Albert Finney. Karel Reisz, the film director from Britain, and Miriam Brickman (casting) were looking to film the story of Ned Kelly, with Finney in the title role. Somehow Albert Finney heard about the YEPs and had talks with John Trevor, but sadly nothing came of that or the film.

As I began rehearsals for the next tour in January 1963 to play Alonso and Trinculo in *The Tempest*, Theseus and Oberon in *A Midsummer Night's Dream*, I was thinking about the big move overseas. I had written to Michael Langham, director of the Stratford Memorial Theatre in Ontario, Canada. He replied saying he could give no guarantee of work.

For my second tour, we hit the road towards the end of February and came to rest, exhausted, at the end of August. New South Wales being more densely populated, we did many more performances than on the previous tour in Queensland. In one week in Newcastle we did 12 performances to tricky audiences. They were predominantly urban students in state schools. At one point during a performance of *The Tempest* at Newcastle Boys High School I had to snap out of character during a Trinculo speech to tell boys in the front row to shut up, before snapping back into character. During the performance of *A Midsummer Night's Dream* these students employed 'the hissing game'. Every now and then you could just hear a hissing noise when there was remonstrating acting. Most of them came up to us after the show to apologise.

This tour was facilitated by another wonderful company manager. Geoff Rothwell was efficient, understanding, diplomatic and unflappable – except for his hands, which flapped a lot around his dark-complexioned face and big nose. However, I was not so happy on this tour. It was hot and tiring, there were many more performances, and egos were clashing.

In Narrabri we performed in their very run-down town hall. There were primitive facilities. We all shared a dressing room with many small creatures; there were no loos and only one wash basin with a dribbling tap. We left sweaty and angry. As we pulled away from the premises a mutual curse was cast: 'Hope the bloody place burns down!' was the cry. Well, it did. We read the headlines in the local morning paper in the next town. In retrospect, I was surprised we were never questioned. We could have left a burning cigarette.

We spent a very relaxing weekend in Moree, a very outback town. It was my first experience of 'the camp fire': the iconic scene in many Australian paintings. Through stories told by the local teachers, I was made aware of the plight of the Aboriginal people. They had been given houses to live in, alien to their nomadic existence. Features like floor boards were ripped up for firewood. The image stuck in my memory. Another image I remember: luxuriating in a hot artesian spa, which was a blissful place to get relief from the endless mosquitoes and flies.

In a six-week period we travelled over 1000 km to Broken Hill in the west then a considerably longer zigzag return journey. Our first port of call was Wellington, where we met the polo fraternity at a huge barbecue. I say huge because a whole tree was burning. After the initial, very Aussie standing back and having a look at us, the polo folk became most hospitable and gave us free passes to their carnival in Narromine the following weekend. The area was famous for polo.

I was billeted with a charming couple who became friends for a while. Tony and Brooke Maurice invited me to stay with them after the tour. The carnival was great fun. On the Monday morning we mounted our mechanised horse with sore heads and began driving west into the sun on mostly dirt roads for 600 km.

After leaving the town of Deniliquin we had an experience not uncommon in the bush: taking the wrong turn and getting bogged in thick mud for two hours. We dug the truck out twice, took the caravan off a couple of times and tried in vain to push it up to the truck, which we had managed to get out. Eventually we had to unload the equipment to get both truck and caravan on to firm ground. Then came the back-breaking job of carrying the equipment about 100 m through the mud.

You needed a strong constitution to keep going. Here is another quote from one of my letters to give you a coal-face idea of what it was like:

> Played Albury last Wed. to huge audiences then had a very cold, tiring trip to Tumut where I became quite ill. Fortunately we were billeted in homes. Only just managed to do the shows. Actually another member of the company came down with the same thing, a kind of gastric flu. I was sick on the Wednesday night and had very little sleep. Saw the doctor who said it was due to fatigue and cold, so true, I could hardly keep my eyes open and could not stop shaking even though I was by a fire. Took the tablets doctor had prescribed, went to bed with two hot water bottles and a pile of blankets at 8.00 pm and didn't get up until 10.00 am. I was cured.

You can understand why actors feel like exploding when they hear remarks like 'so what do you do for a living?' and 'it must be jolly good fun being an actor'.

One extraordinary event on this tour was the ultimate in the adage 'the show must go on'. We were set up to play *The Tempest* in Goulburn. For some reason John Maxim who was playing Prospero was travelling from his home outside Sydney. The rest of us had travelled down the night before and stayed over. It was getting very close to curtain-up for the late morning performance but John had not arrived. Just before our company manager was about to announce that the show could not go on, John appeared, breathless and ashen faced. He got ready, nothing was said and we did the show. During those great lines of finality towards the end of the play ('Our revels now are ended ...')

floods of tears streamed down his cheeks. Cautiously we approached him after, to be told that his mother had risen early, crossed the road to get a newspaper and been knocked over by a car and died on the way to hospital. We were speechless. He did not miss a performance.

Indeed over a period of about eight years with three companies touring each year in similar circumstances to those I have described, very few performances had to be cancelled.

I was not meant to be on the 1964 tour of Queensland but was asked to take over the parts of Horatio in *Hamlet* and Orlando and Corin in *As You Like It* from an actor who had to leave. Our intrepid director John V. Trevor flew up with me through a violent storm, eventually landing in the mid-west town of Blackall to slip me into the productions. In the next town, Longreach, the actor playing Hamlet fell ill. Logically, John Trevor should have given me Hamlet and he should have played Horatio – it would have been more believable – but John took over, script in hand. It would have taken a huge stretch of the imagination for the audience of outback school kids to believe that John was a virile young prince. He was in his 60s, very gangly and bespectacled with a deep baritone voice. I remained Horatio.

During this performing period, however, I learnt something not taught at drama school: the value in creating stage business with a prop. As Corin, I had a toy lamb on wheels, led by a piece of string with nodding head. I made *baaa* noises while feeding it with a bottle. It is such an ego boost hearing laughter that you've *milked!*

This half-tour took me to towns and schools visited two years ago and I was greeted like an old friend. In Charters Towers we played to a huge audience in an open air theatre at Thornburgh Church of England Grammar School; how very English. Playing Shakespeare in the open air is also very English, but playing *Hamlet* without microphone enhancement directly into sunlight was seriously difficult, particularly in the ghost scenes. We did play in many bizarre stage areas. The most bizarre was a chicken run, which is very Australian.

This tour was much the same as before but for one experience. It concerns and probably supports the old view that actors are 'rogues and vagabonds'. It happened in Townsville and I tell this with some shame and no bragging rights.

I was billeted with the young local surgeon and his wife, both from Sydney. She had been a model and had been used to sophisticated company. I met her husband the night we arrived and discovered he had been in the fencing team for Sydney University when I came up for the inter-varsity fencing championship in 1958. He happened to be on night duty for the next three nights I was there. After the school performance in the afternoon his wife took me on a trip in her station wagon. She wanted to show me the unique dance of the brolgas, gracious long-legged swamp birds that perform an extensive mating ritual. Maybe the subject matter got the better of us – we quickly found ourselves in the back part of the vehicle.

That night I lay in bed feeling very awkward about what had happened when I heard a tap tap tap on the wooden partition between our rooms. Queensland houses are mostly built of wood. She slipped into my room and told me how unhappy and bored she had been, despite having three gorgeous daughters (who used to climb all over me at eight o'clock in the morning). I really wasn't the prime mover in this tryst.

The surgeon suspected foul play, and the upshot was that I needed to leave town a little earlier after he challenged me to a duel. I would have been in disgrace two centuries ago for not honouring the challenge.

I believe this kind of touring to be unique and incredibly gruelling. All the touring I did in later years was with greater ease, less pain and in more exotic places. But the lessons I learnt and experiences I had gave me a solid frame of reference for the future. As far as I know there is no record, account or estimation of the profound effect John V. Trevor's merry band of Young Elizabethan Players had on those thousands of school children over eight years. John Bell continues his legacy but I have yet to hear any acknowledgement.

Soon enough I was back in the metropolitan bush waiting for the phone to ring.

10

Work in Sydney Town, the Metropolitan Bush

I was back in Sydney by the end of August 1962, exhausted and happy to be out of work. However, by the middle of October I was doing my first commercial. It was to be the first of many and thank goodness for this bread-and-butter work. There was considerable snobbery about doing commercials among the pure theatre actors. There was a sense of tarnishing the finely tuned actor's craft and casting a blot on your credits. The commercial was for Schweppes and I was very happy to be paid £9. This kind of job would be worth about $6000 in Australia today.

My first television drama was *Prelude to Harvest*, about the first settlement in 1788. I was cast as Lieutenant Dawes by Colin Dean for the ABC. I was very nervous at first and must have been overplaying because at the end of a scene during rehearsals Colin came up behind me and said quietly, 'I know you have been to drama school to learn how to act, now you need to learn how not to act'.

It was a good time to come into the acting profession in those early days of television. New drama productions and plenty of commercials were needed on top of the regular radio and theatre work. My first year as a professional actor was extremely successful. It came to an end in a flurry of work in television and radio.

My second television drama for the ABC came soon after. Alan Burke cast me as Paul, the juvenile lead in *My Three Angels*, playing opposite Anna Volska, who became John Bell's wife. It was a strong cast that included the renowned Gordon Chater, Owen Weingot, Dickie Davies and Murray Rose, the champion Olympic swimmer, making his debut as an actor.

Then to my astonishment Alan gave me the part of Ferdinand in *The Tempest*, with Max Oldaker playing Prospero and Reg Livermore playing

Ariel. This would turn out to be the first Shakespeare play to be recorded as a television drama in Australia. Most of the leading young actors had been auditioned, but my advantage was having recently worked for Alan. As I soon found out in the profession generally, directors like to acquire a stable of actors they go to first when casting.

I was extremely nervous playing such an important role on television with so little experience. It seems that I was most concerned about making the romantic scenes come alive with the kind of acting-truth needed for the screen when in such a theatrical play. I certainly looked the part. It would be interesting to judge the acting from today's standards. I suspect too theatrical.

Although Colin Dean had told me not to seem to act on the screen, television productions in those early days were nearer to performing a play on stage. We rehearsed the play in a rehearsal room marked out by tape with token props and furniture. The camera crew came in to mark where and what they would shoot, then we all moved to the main studio where we performed on the built set. When it was recorded they tried to take most of it in one take. It was a little similar to the way sitcoms were shot in front of a live audience not that long ago. Tensions were high with everyone afraid of making a mistake.

During this period towards the end of 1962 I successfully auditioned for ABC radio drama. I did many radio plays over the years I was in Australia and had some success in London as well. My radio career in Sydney culminated in two leading roles: Guy Hamilton in *The Year of Living Dangerously* (played by Mel Gibson in the movie) and Scott in *Fire on the Snow*, a play specially written for radio by Douglas Stewart. Both these productions were directed by Frank Zepple. Radio didn't pay well but it was regular work and for a select few it was their main source of income. I even picked up the odd radio play when on tour.

The agent's perennial response to queries, especially when all your friends seem to be working, is that there's nothing for you at the moment; it's very quiet but it should pick up later. The life of an actor hangs on that phone ringing, as long as it is not a hoax. A friend of mine played a very nasty trick on me. I picked up the phone one morning in 1964 and this American voice said he was calling from Hollywood to ask if I would be interested in doing a screen test for a movie to be shot in Australia.

I was completely convinced. In the end this 'friend for a brief while' felt he had to come clean. It was Michael Thomas, a scriptwriter, after he had helped me in my first one-man project. It was a cruel jest; actors' egos are very brittle. He himself did get to Hollywood. I last saw him in London after he had made *Scandal* which was a major film credit. Having not heard of him since, Mike Molloy, a well-known cameraman and a mutual friend, emailed Michael to say we had caught up. In his reply he mentioned me with a snide remark about my gullibility. Those who never really make it often like to put down others. Michael Thomas never really made it.

At last I had found pleasant accommodation by way of an L-shaped room in leafy Potts Point. Rent was £3/10/– per week ($160 equivalent today) but 'entertaining young ladies in the room was not allowed'. It feels now that we were part of ancient history. The rule was soon overcome. This was the place where I began my love of Mahler; it was where I heard that Kennedy was shot, and where I entered into the first of my engagements to be married.

In 1963 I began doing plays at the Independent Theatre. The company was run by the benign autocrat Doris Fitton, who had a keen eye for promising young actors. I performed in three productions and many play readings in between touring and television work. A significant unpaid performance was a play reading of *Zoo Story* by Edward Albee with Mark McManus.

Mark played the manic part of Peter; I played Jerry the victim. Looking over the kind of parts I played, this role at that early time in my career in a sense became a template. Over the years I have played a number of cowardly, dishonourable characters. Perhaps my behaviour in Townsville had something to do with it. In my estimation it seems I was unable to confront an unpleasant situation. Consequently the charming, fun exterior has been a cover up for a basic weakness. Maybe this is picked up in auditions. Of course underneath I was full of deep insecurity and doubt in my ability. Many an actor has suffered this.

Despite the purists I enjoyed doing commercials. They didn't tax the acting psyche, did require a dexterous skill and paid well (eventually). The next commercial was for Chesterfield cigarettes with the lovely 1963 Miss Australia, Tanya Verstak. We had to drive a red Austin Healey Sprite sports car on a country road, be stopped by a flock of sheep, light up a Chesterfield, take in the country air and drive off into the sunset. Not an unpleasant way of earning £80, though an unthinkable way of taking in the 'country air'. In those days just about everyone smoked. Actors used to have specialised training in how to handle cigarettes and pipes on the screen.

The beginning of 1964 was a very busy period. I was rehearsing *The Tempest* at the ABC and *Sweet Bird of Youth* at the Independent which was followed by a part in Robin Lovejoy's production of *JB* by Archibald MacLeish. After auditioning for Tom Brown's high-profile production of *Henry V* starring John Bell, I heard I had the part of the Duke of Gloucester. It was to be performed in a huge tent for the third Adelaide Festival of Arts in February/March 1964. I experienced deep disappointment when looking for my part in the text. The Duke of Gloucester only had one significant, suspending line: 'I hope they do not come upon us now'. I was drowned out by aircraft noise in most performances, as the tent was under the flight path.

During this time, John Gielgud was touring with his one-man Shakespeare recital. A group of us drummed up the courage to go backstage. He seemed to have been extremely moved when he was delivering the 'Fear no more the heat of the sun' speech from *Cymbeline*, which seemed to cast a spell over the audience. He explained to us that he was thinking of President Kennedy who had just been assassinated. That moment in time for our generation when everyone remembered where they were and what they were doing when the news broke.

The great actor was very gracious and most impressed with what we told him of our performing Shakespeare in the outback. There was something in his presence that elicited that holding-of-breath, awestruck feeling. It is a quality that real stars have – charisma. I certainly experienced that years later when meeting and working with star actors. They standout as if the air is pushed back around them, and when they speak you feel compelled to listen. And it is not just actors who have that presence; I remember being momentarily awestruck passing Imran Khan, the cricketer, on a street in Chelsea.

In those days you could often find visiting performers at Vadim's restaurant in Challis Avenue. This bijou restaurant was run by Vadim who was, I believe, an émigré from Russia. I remember meeting Micheál MacLiammóir there, when he was touring with his one-man show *The Importance of Being Oscar*. It was frequented by members of the Sydney Push when they weren't at their pub. Among the cast list for the Push were the likes of Clive James, Germaine Greer, Robert Hughes, Martin Sharp, Richard Neville and Barry Humphries; a leading group of fiercely intelligent students who ended up being *éminences grises*. Much has been written about them and the Push in those days. They were heady days; just being on the periphery of their company was exciting. They were at the forefront of the rebellion against the stultifying, anti-intellectual status quo of Prime Minister Robert Menzies's era, which was steeped in suburban 'you've never had it so good' smugness.

Three of these leading lights never came back to live in Australia. I happened to meet up with Germaine on a plane when she was returning to see her ill father. She spent most of the conversation railing against Australia and, in particular, complaining that no university had invited her to lecture or hold any office. This anti-intellectual, tall-poppy syndrome has not entirely disappeared.

It took many years before Barry Humphries was accepted in his own country. I saw his first show *A Nice Night's Entertainment* in the Macquarie Radio Theatre. It was a biting send-up of suburban Australia but audiences found it difficult to laugh at themselves in those days. Barry was certainly able to laugh at himself when I told him how grubby he was. He had a room in Chico Lowe's boarding house in Elizabeth Bay where I had a cleaning job after leaving NIDA.

Plotting the downfall of the Ming Dynasty (Ming was the nickname for Robert Menzies) continued late into the evening at Vadim's with alcohol secreted in coffee cups. We were still in semi-prohibition. Kings Cross was throbbing with alternative life styles and lively debate. Rosalyn Norton was the resident witch, just along from the Macleay Bookshop. The Chandler/Bogle murder case was gripping the collective imagination, and an amusing alternative greeting to visiting artists was staged by University of NSW students. The Beatles were staying in the Sheraton hotel, the great pianist Arthur Rubinstein was staying in the Chevron hotel opposite. About 300 gathered outside jeering at the Beatles and chanting '*we want Arthur*'. I am sure that would not have offended John Lennon. Don't worry I am not going to say I met Lennon – but I did meet Rubinstein many years later.

The Troubadour was a folk-singing coffee lounge in Rushcutters Bay near Kings Cross. You entered through curtains into a scene from the Left Bank in Paris. Through the haze of smoke, passing posters on hessian-draped walls, you lay on cushions and languidly listened to highly acclaimed folk-singers and guitarists. Tina Date, Gary Shearston, Alex Hood and Marilyn Henderson with Sebastian Jorgensen (classical guitar) and Tony Morrison (flamenco) were the talk of the town.

It was a copy of The Troubadour in London's Earls Court. That is still open; the one in Sydney has long gone. Michael Thomas, of the hoax phone call, was able to persuade the manager, Jim Carter, to let me try out a one-man reading of *Under Milk Wood* which he helped devise. Nerves were soon dispelled, perched on a stool I let Dylan's sensuous, rat-a-tat words caress the ears of the eager listeners. It was so well received I got paid and was invited to add a reading of Dylan Thomas's short story *Live Like Little Dogs*.

Soon afterwards I joined the cast in a platform performance of *By Royal Command*. John Bell had adapted this version of *The Hollow Crown*, about life surrounding the kings and queens of England, first performed at The Old Vic in London. I took over from Arthur Dignam.

This was the time I became aware of possibly being known as 'the take-over kid', 'the second-choice actor' and the 'sorry-you're-too-young' or 'too-old' actor. Robin Lovejoy who had directed Mark McManus and I in *The Zoo Story* said he couldn't cast me in the same part in a full production as I was too young. Ken Hannam had asked me to step in for three performances of a play he had directed and wished he had cast me in the first place. In addition, in September of 1964 I had just returned from taking over parts in the YEP tour of Queensland. Many more instances would occur throughout my career. On the other hand I was often also in the right place at the right time – the chance meeting and a timely phone call are all part of every actor's life.

After returning from the Queensland tour I decided it was time to take the big step. In September I booked a berth on the SS *Flavia*, an Italian liner leaving for Tilbury Docks, London on 6 January 1965. The fare cost £143: about $1,500 equivalent.

I was worried that I may not have sufficient savings if no work came my way before leaving. That was soon dispelled by being cast in the part of Valère in Moliére's *The Miser* at the Independent Theatre for which I would be paid £4/7/- per performance. It was directed by Alexander Archdale, an English actor of the old school. He also played the lead and proved a martinet in his other role as director. He was a very wobbly actor with shaking body parts but a commanding voice. I got on well with him but he was horrid to those less well trained.

There were many like Alexander scattered throughout the old British Empire. Perhaps they felt they hadn't quite made it at home or just got stuck from a visit. I came across him again many years later in London when I was attending the annual Stage Cricket Club match against the Cross Arrows on the Nursery Ground at Lords. There was Alexander Archdale talking earnestly to old stage members. He had been a member before the war. He greeted me profusely but soon asked me for a loan. He was down and out. The colonies in those days were fertile pastures for black sheep from high blown English families.

A timely piece of casting happened in November. It came from Ken Hannam. It was a very small part in a televised production of a Restoration comedy called *The Recruiting Officer* by Farquhar, which had a significant history in early Australia. It was the first official play ever performed in the penal colony around 1800. Thomas Keneally wrote an account of that history in *The Playmaker* and Timberlake Wertenbaker wrote a play based on his book, called *Our County's Good*, in which her cast is made up of convicts and the leading lady is about to be hanged.

Leading the cast was arguably one of the finest Australian actors since Peter Finch: John Meillon. He was also the leader of the Pack, a hard drinking bunch of highly regarded Aussie actors. His HQ was the Royal Oak Hotel in Cremorne where he was regularly attended by the likes of Bill Hunter, Max Cullen, Bob McDarra, Johnny Ewart and Walter Sullivan. One needed a strong constitution to keep up with them. I was a piss-weak pisspot but they were fun days.

Ken Hannam was soon to join the many Australians, particularly in the entertainment industry, who would spend many years overseas. I would be part of his actors stable but also would become a lifelong friend There was a general feeling in those days that if you wanted to grow and test yourself against the best, you had to go to Europe. For an actor then the Mecca was London; these days it is Hollywood. As for me, I was going home.

A casual meeting with the well-known director Robin Lovejoy proved salutary. His advice was, 'Don't think yourself a failure if you don't make it and don't be afraid to come back'. That Polonius-type precept was trenchantly worded in an article I happened to read recently, quoted by the British poet Andrew Motion about Henry Lawson and his unhappy two years in London before the First World War:

> If you didn't go, it was because you suspected you were no good; if you did go you were a traitor; if you went and came back you were a failure.

In those days you couldn't win.

In one last throw of the dice before embarking, I somehow got hastily engaged. Before I left Sydney to spend Christmas with the family, I was invited to a barbecue in Point Piper, one of the most exclusive suburbs. I met a Sydney actress and invited her back to my L-shaped room and introduced her to Mahler's grand classical music. Prompted by the soaring sounds of Mahler's second symphony I proposed. In true Aussie style (most unlike me) I slipped a beer ring on her finger. We agreed, however, to put the engagement on ice until she came to London.

Well, all sorts of things could happen on a long sea journey.

II

Return Journey

Crossing the world by ship was coming to an end. Convicts sent in sail ships took 8 months to reach Botany Bay, steamships took 6 to 8 weeks, and aeroplanes now take 19 hours. Still, I was glad to have experienced this slow mode of travel. It did become somewhat monotonous but there were plenty of distractions.

A small group of us from Adelaide, which included lifelong friends Mick and Rosie Johnston, met up with a lively group from Sydney, some of whom I knew. We decided we were the jet set, making lots of noise, dominating games and sporting activities and generally behaving badly. Playing *tombola* (bingo), deck quoits, deck tennis and being outrageous at fancy dress balls all sound twee. These activities were part of a bygone age belonging to my mother, who did several steamship voyages. Here is a description from a letter I wrote to her from my journey.

> Today we crossed the Equator and the appropriate ceremonies were conducted by King Neptune and his court. I was officiating as a lawyer whose job was to admonish the victims for not having crossed the Equator before and pass sentence. They were all duly messed up with eggs, spaghetti, bits of meat and forced to kiss a rotten fish in front of the throne. The stewards really began the free-for-all by emptying buckets of water over everyone; even the Captain got a drenching. Then down came the rain, a fitting entrance to the Northern Hemisphere. We all fell into the pool followed by a mountainous German lady who jumped in with all her clothes on and just about emptied it. Tonight we have the Grand Equatorial Ball and the choosing of Miss Flavia.

Mind you these kinds of hijinks are in televised contests these days.

There were a few young married couples and 'dozens of scrumptious single girls sunbathing in brief bikinis' but one girl stood out:

> I've latched myself on to a very swinging, good fun girl from Sydney. She is an extremely amusing, worldly-wise journalist from the *Sunday Mirror* with a glorious name – Blanche d'Alpuget. She tells me the 'd' indicates an aristocratic background. I'm very impressed. What's more she thinks she went to school with Lyn Rainbow [my fiancée].

Blanche had blonde hair, generous lips and a comely shape; I probably thought at the time that I had won a prize.

An embarrassing moment happened on top deck late on a hot night under the twinkling stars of the Indian Ocean. We were leaning back against some rails, relaxing with a cigarette and discussing the meaning of life. As I turned my back to the heavens to make a point, I threw my cigarette butt towards the side of the ship. I was in the middle of persuading Blanche to my point of view when I felt a tap on my shoulder. I looked up into a gnarled oak-tree of a face belonging to a member of the crew, who proceeded to admonish me about my cigarette butt. It hadn't reached the sea; it was smouldering in a lifeboat. '*Prego non fumare in lifeboat, non fumare in lifeboat!*' he kept repeating as he went away, quite unconcerned about anything else. We fell about laughing.

On Saturday 23 January 1965 we berthed in the port of Aden for nine hours, which gave us time to explore. An incident happened when Blanche and I were walking through Aden Old Town. I believe this incident was the seed for her writing a certain passage in her novel *Winter in Jerusalem*. We had taken a risky trip by taxi that dropped us near the crater town called Old Aden, deemed strictly out of bounds by the British Authorities. We had a guide but he walked very quickly in front of us and we lost him. Here is my description in a letter:

> We found ourselves amongst the squalor and poverty in the streets and back alleys, passing deformed beggars, men lying on stretcher beds by the roadside fasting, heavily veiled women, goats by the dozen, cattle, flies and groups of boys with piercing eyes of hate. As we emerged into a wide open area of rubble where it seemed Aden's washing was hanging out to dry, something hit my back. That group of boys was throwing stones at us. We started running and luckily found our taxi driver. We flashed passed rows of smart flats running for miles down the main highway where the British live.

Here is the quote from her book *Winter in Jerusalem*, from Danielle's point of view as she wanders along the paths and winding alleys of old Jerusalem:

She shivered all over at the idea that underneath lay collected a lake of the human blood shed century after century in these lanes: a sharp blow to the paving could make it gush again.

We chose to alight at Port Suez and were taken by coach to Cairo from where we beheld the Sphinx, stood in awe of the pyramids and were hoisted up on belching camels. On our way to visit the gold mask of Tutankhamun all our senses were attacked, with pungent smells and chaotic sights and sounds on the streets of Cairo: vehicles being driven with horns blaring scattering goats and children, and people hanging on the outside of every crammed bus. We had crashed briefly into the Third World.

Genoa was our final call before our journey's end at Tilbury on 6 February. Being winter in Europe, Blanche had decided to wear her cream and russet fur coat. With her blonde hair and ruby lips I had the devil of a job keeping at bay the rampant goggle-eyed Italian men determined to pinch her comely behind. Again in her book *Winter in Jerusalem* I came across this passage being experienced by her character Danielle while shopping in Jerusalem:

> ... if she wandered along Saha-el-Din Street looking for a watch shop, helpful young or not so young men would trail behind until one or other worked up enough courage to grab at her bum.

At Tilbury docks I descended the gang plank behind Blanche. We stopped, our eyes met, we smiled and walked away. My friend from St Paul's school was there to pick me up, and so began my life as an actor in England.

Part 2

1965 to 1973

12

Connections in the 'Scepter'd Isle'

Romantic notions of England have been handed down through the centuries via Shakespeare, Blake and Brooke. Stepping on to the concrete quayside at Tilbury docks on a cold, wet day in February does not encourage those patriotic feelings that arise when singing *Jerusalem*. Waiting to greet me was my friend Gary O'Brien and his charming wife Lesley. We all crammed into Gary's Triumph Herald and as we cruised through the streets of London, I felt at home. I had known Gary since my schooldays at St Paul's and was delighted to meet his wife who is still a very good friend of mine. They were taking me to stay with 'Hamlet' in Wimbledon.

Alan Hannam had played Hamlet in the student production at Adelaide University in 1958, in which I played Horatio. He had topped dentistry and married the second-placed student Pauline Hannon (they one vow-elled each other) and was in the UK to top up his credentials. I did not outstay my welcome as my connections with St Paul's school provided work within two weeks of arrival.

I was taken by Gary to our old school on the first Tuesday afternoon as choir practice was just finishing. I was talking to Mr Harbord, Mr Cummings and Mr Cook (the Sur Master, or deputy headmaster) by the main entrance. It was a long, cold stone walkway down to the Great Hall which was, incidentally, used by Field Marshall Montgomery, an old boy, as his HQ during the latter part of the war. I heard rapid footsteps approaching and saw Ivor Davis, our twinkling music master, eager to join us. He stopped in front of the group, looked up at me and said, after a very brief pause: 'Edmund Pegge, you still have the most gorgeous blue eyes.'

I froze and could have melted into the stone floor. The other masters laughed it off as though it was typical of him, which of course it was.

Mr Harbord, who had produced the school plays I was in, happened to have two brothers who ran the well-established Gordon Harbord Theatrical Agency. An appointment was made for me within a few days. I made my way to St Martin's Lane near Trafalgar Square with photos and CV for the appointment. With a degree of trepidation I knocked gently on the oak-door entrance to a slim three-storeyed building. I was about to knock again when the door creaked open. It was as if a ghost had opened it. My eyes dropped and there was a hunched back. A head tilted, peering up at me and introducing herself as Gordon Harbord's wife, and told me to go up.

I climbed the oak-panelled stairs, heavy with the past; the walls were covered in theatre posters and photos of stars in West End productions. I was greeted by a bespectacled, wispy-haired gentleman who introduced me to his brother Bill, and David their Scottish accountant. Gordon Harbord was a slightly effete, old-fashioned theatrical gentleman. His brother was quite the opposite: a stocky, beer-drinking chap who, like me, loved his cricket and golf. I was happy he was to look after me. I knew we would get on well.

Spotlight is the UK's actors' directory run then by the kindly Cary Ellison. Bill had phoned him that afternoon to be told that David Perry at Ipswich Repertory Theatre was looking for an actor to play Paris in *Romeo and Juliet*. Being recommended by the Harbord Agency, I was offered the role without an audition. This all happened in the first week of my return. By the following Monday I was on my way to my first job in England on £9/10/- per week during the two weeks' rehearsal and £17 per week playing. I was thrilled and excited. I had a good part in a prestigious repertory company within two weeks of arriving, all through the connection with my old school.

Talent alone does not guarantee success: connections, chance meetings, being in the right place at the right time, if the face fits, and luck, all contribute to how well your career develops. I had joined the biggest lottery game in the world. My first step was into the English repertory (rep) system.

Most major towns throughout England and Scotland have a theatre and many had a permanent company. An actor could gain fairly regular employment having acquired a reputation on this circuit. The danger, soon to be discovered, was coming across those actors who had never moved on from the repertory circuit. They became known as 'rep actors' as they had acquired a hammy or mannered style of acting. This was due to the system of fortnightly and, in the earlier days, weekly turnover of plays. In fortnightly rep once the season opened you would be performing the show at night and rehearsing the next play during the day. It was almost an enforced routine throughout the system. In between you had to find time to learn your lines, grab a meal and do your washing. Rehearsals began at 10.00 am and frequently ended at 5.00 pm. You would then need a rest and a light meal before going on stage for the evening show at 7.30 pm. Most shows came down by 10.30 pm. You would be on a high from performing and need to wind down with a drink or three and a proper meal. Then it was home to theatre digs to learn lines for the next show. One hardly ever watched television and there was even less time or energy for any hanky-panky! It was near to a monkish existence. I found myself working 16-hour days.

This system did not allow an actor to get deeply involved with the role. One actor asked a director what his motivation should be in a scene. He replied 'the cheque at the end of the week'. What is more, the plays were not all potboilers (e.g. Agatha Christie whodunnits and light comedies). They had to be spread through a season to keep the punters happy so that earnest directors could indulge in plays by Brecht, Shakespeare, Osborne, Pinter and the like. It was understandable that this treadmill could cause some actors to slip into bad habits. I managed to get out of the system at regular intervals to do television.

So there I was in Ipswich, an ancient town in Suffolk on the East Anglian coast. It was famous for wool and Cardinal Wolsey. Years later the Arts Theatre was renamed the Wolsey Theatre. Incidentally, I discovered a very apt phrase experienced by actors which is derived from wool processing. Men called tenters would stretch the wool on hooks to dry. 'On tenterhooks' is a perfect description every actor experiences, particularly on opening nights. The phrase as we know it today means 'in a state of agitated suspense'.

I found myself in rehearsals for *Romeo and Juliet* on the Tuesday of the week after arriving. That was amazing enough, but by the following Monday the company was hit by a crisis. Kenneth Poitevin was playing Sandy Tyrell in the first week of their current production of Noël Coward's *Hay Fever*. We had similar backgrounds and were similar types. He had been taken to New Zealand in his early teens and had recently returned. His father had become seriously ill in NZ, so Kenneth was immediately released by the company. I was asked to take over at 11.30 pm Monday and, peculiar to Ipswich, would have to play a matinee the next day.

I was up most of the night learning lines with fellow actors helping out. I had one run-through in the morning, went on at 2.30 pm carrying the book, and by Wednesday night I performed without the script. I can tell you those tenterhooks were jumping around. Talk about being thrown in at the deep end of English theatre.

Romeo and Juliet went well except for the last night. There was an apocryphal story told of John Gielgud in his earlier days playing Escalus, being played by Roger Bizley in our production. When Gielgud came to the final lines of the play it was claimed he inverted the last syllables of their names. So one heard this glorious voice uttering the famous lines:

For never was a story of more woe than this of Romiet and his Julio oh oh

We had told Roger he would make that faux pas by the last night. Playing Paris, at the end of the play I was lying dead in front of him. We came to the last night. He had succeeded in not giving in. He said the lines correctly but then went into a long series of oh oh oh ohs, which caused the sword lying along my body to shake violently as I tried to contain my giggles. I was a corpse corpsing (theatrical slang for laughing uncontrollably). Others on stage also couldn't contain themselves and the audience noticed. A cardinal sin had been committed.

Guy Slater playing Romeo was furious. After the final curtain he grabbed Roger by his Elizabethan collar and began to manhandle him towards the Opposite Prompt (OP) exit which led to a lane outside the theatre. Apparently blows were thrown in between a stream of invective; poor Roger eventually appeared in our dressing room looking dishevelled. It was as well they didn't have their Elizabethan rapiers with them. Guy was a serious actor and rightly felt that Roger had destroyed the tragic impact of the play, because the audience noticed and began to titter.

Corpsing is not exclusive to theatre but it occurs quite often, mostly without the audience noticing. It is actually a painful experience.

In a later season playing Wickham to Philip Dunbar's Darcy in *Pride and*

Prejudice, to cope with our suppressed convulsions, we had to gradually recede to the mantelpiece upstage. With our faces turned away from the audience, it was necessary to shout our lines out in between long pauses. Philip, who has remained a friend since, did something with his lugubrious long face that would set me off.

A little old lady attending a performance of *Macbeth* at Ipswich Rep also had everyone in stitches. She was sitting in the front row at a Tuesday matinee performance knitting. When the actor playing Macbeth came to the lines 'tomorrow and tomorrow and tomorrow' she was heard to say to her friend, 'Ooh, that'll be Friday'.

My first two weeks in English theatre were, to say the least, eventful. The next play was *The Hollow*, an Agatha Christie whodunnit. These plays were less demanding but tedious to act in. The characters are one dimensional and you can't do much more than learn the lines and avoid bumping into the furniture.

Ipswich Rep had a reputation for being adventurous, stemming, I suspect, from Sir Peter Hall's tenure. I was nervously excited to find I had been cast in one of the leading parts in the following production. Horner in *The Country Wife* by William Wycherley was a dashing, unscrupulous rake, and the play was a Restoration romp.

Restoration plays require highly stylised acting. Philip Voss, a well-established, classically trained actor, was cast as Pinchwife. Again I was thrown in at the deep end as he became impatient with my inexperience in this style. My confidence was encouraged by our director David Perry who laughed heartily at my playing, but it wasn't until the second week that I felt confident in the part. Despite my own reservations the local critics were generous. The Ipswich *Evening Star* said that I played the part 'with verve and excellent timing'. I did well enough to be invited back for another season of plays the following year.

The modern rep actor had a somewhat suburban mentality: finding financial security going from one repertory company to another for a season. It was different from touring towns in the same play or plays from a base. A touring company was on the move, playing in a variety of venues and towns. On tour we enjoyed friendly accommodation under the caring eyes of theatrical landladies. There was this wonderful network of homes throughout the country that particularly catered for actors in short spells. It was a peripatetic existence, requiring generous, understanding friends who provided a base-home for belongings. My hosts for storage and the occasional overnight were old friends of the family living in what was called the 'gin and tonic belt', Sunningdale near Ascot.

A Vespa scooter was my first means of transport. Negotiating around Hyde Park Corner was like being on the dodgem cars at a fair. We all flew around trailing a scarf without head gear. I even rode to Ipswich in the rain.

The Government did provide a safety net from poverty. The National Insurance stamp system meant you could sign on when out of work and get unemployment benefit. Chadwick Street unemployment office in Victoria became a friendly meeting place for out-of-work luvvies (a slang term for over-theatrical actors). There was no shame in signing on as everyone paid 15 per cent of their salary when in work. It went into a separate fund that held money to cover benefit, National Health and pensions. When you signed on you got your National Insurance stamp franked which eventually would affect your pension. I once saw a Rolls Royce parked right outside.

Back in London at the end of my first season in Ipswich, I found very comfortable accommodation through Philip Voss. It was in Honiton Mansions on Kings Road, Chelsea, over the still-standing Jaeger shop. The flat belonged to the well-known theatre director Colin Graham. Colin was noted for his opera productions of Janáček and Benjamin Britten. He was into leather gear and motorcycles. A charming man whom I hardly ever saw.

Soon after moving in my first television role came along. *Death Happens to Other People* was to be the first of many parts I would play set in the two world wars. I was paid £30 for the week's work. It was videotaped in the Cardiff studios of the BBC. The director was Hugh David, with whom I would work again in Australia. A very boyish-looking Simon Ward was the lead actor.

A commercial followed, for Carlton cigarettes, produced by J. Walter Thompson Advertising Agency, one of the biggest in London. Shot on location over a period of three nights around famous sights of London, it was on an epic scale. The theme centred on something exciting happening in the background every time I lit up a cigarette: fireworks exploding behind

Westminster Abbey, fountains springing to life in Trafalgar Square, flowers being revealed in Covent Garden. In the early hours of the morning we filmed at Les Ambassadors, a gambling club for the rich and famous by Hyde Park, and, finally, they had me waiting on the Embankment for the sun to hit the new glass Vickers building which, of course, it failed to do. They even hired a helicopter to take shots of me driving. This bigger-than-Ben-Hur commercial cost £10,000 out of which I was paid £120 (my weekly salary in theatre was £15).

I mention all this to show how much waste there was in advertising, and probably still is. The commercial never went to air. It was an exciting job for me to do so soon after arriving. It certainly did the ego no harm as crowds gathered wherever we were filming. I also made a long-lasting connection with Liz Perry, Derek Causton's PA. He was the Account Executive, a kindly Irishman who liked a drink. Liz and her husband Philip Johnston entertained me in Singapore and Hong Kong years later, and her sister provided a home away from home outside Newcastle when I was playing in seasons at the Flora Robson Theatre in Jesmond Dene.

More than any other artistic profession, acting requires good connections for survival and to ease the uncertainties of a here-and-there existence. Some actors in prestigious companies like the Royal Shakespeare Company and the National Theatre or in long-running West End shows can find a degree of stability. Soap operas provide that in television.

I found myself doing another television play in June of 1965: a small part as a television director in *Common Ground* for the BBC starring George Baker, Judy Parfitt and Barbara Lott. George Baker became well known for the *Wexford Files*. It was reputed that he also dubbed some of George Lazenby's lines in the Bond film *On Her Majesty's Secret Service*.

The next connection would prove extremely fruitful. I went with my old friend from Adelaide and NIDA, Briony Hodge, to see *The Right Honourable Gentleman* in the West End starring Anthony Quayle. We went backstage to meet him. He was a gracious gentleman and keen to help. He suggested I write to John Neville at Nottingham Playhouse. My letter was timely as he was casting for the annual schools tour: shades of the Young Elizabethan Players with not so far to travel. I auditioned for the part of the Knight in

Mirandolina by Goldoni at the *Spotlight* offices in Leicester Square. It only required reading lines from the play in front of John Neville and Richard Eyre. John set me at ease by taking off the Australian accent. (A humorous book on the Australian accent entitled *Let Stalk Strine*, was very popular at the time.) I heard very soon that I had got the part. Little did I know then that Richard Eyre would become one of Britain's leading directors and be knighted. This production was to be one of his earliest as a professional. It would also lead me into further work over the next few years, though I never worked for Richard again. Sometimes the road from early connections can become a cul-de-sac for future opportunities.

Nottingham Playhouse run by John Neville was like a mini-national theatre. This was no ordinary rep. Firstly, the repertoire included Noël Coward's *Private Lives*, Shakespeare's *Richard II*, Bertolt Brecht's *Schweik in the Second World War* and Arthur Miller's *Death of a Salesman*. Secondly, there were no rep actors in the company. The likes of Judi Dench, Edward Woodward, Michael Craig, Alan Howard, Harold Innocent, John Tordoff and Ronnie Magill graced the playhouse stage. I would also meet Alfie Bell there, who would become one of my lifelong friends.

The schools tour would only last about four weeks in August/September, but I was in the frame for anything else being cast. And what a something else that would turn out to be. John announced that a three-month tour of West Africa was being planned for early 1966. The plays were *As You Like it* and *A Man for All Seasons* and he wanted to know who was available. Surprisingly not many of the main house company wanted to be away for that length of time. It would take to the end of October before the cast was announced.

On returning to my London flat I met up with my fiancée, about whom I had slightly forgotten! Lyn Rainbow had arrived from Australia and, as I was not around, had found herself a very classy flat overlooking the Embankment. Soon after her arrival we both realised that marriage was not for us. Domesticity didn't seem to be quite the thing to be doing at the centre of the Flower Power era of 'love is all you need' and 'let's turn on, tune in and drop out'. Lyn soon fell into a job understudying in the West End production of *Barefoot in the Park*. We hardly ever saw each other again.

It was standard practice that as soon as you were out of work, you sat down and wrote cards to all the casting directors. You told them what you had just done and hoped they would keep you in mind. I was soon known by over twenty casting directors. Much depended on this vital link to directors in all media and theatre. Agents would put forward suggestions from their client list for parts in television drama, movies, commercials and training films. If your face fitted with what the casting director imagined the director was looking for, then you would be asked to attend an interview. For every interview you would be one of several actors up for the same part. On average you had a one in six chance. One of my cards worked. I got a small part in an ITV play called *Cure for Tin Ear*.

Much to my delight found I would be playing my scenes with one of the great Australian actors and the ex-wife of another one. It must have been early days for Leo McKern (*Rumpole of the Bailey*) in television, but he was a highly respected theatre actor, having worked at the National and the RSC. He had come over with a regiment of Aussie actors after the war that included the likes of Bud Tingwell, Vincent Ball, Bill Kerr and John Tate. Playing the female lead in this modest drama was the ex-wife of Peter Finch, Yolande Turner.

I have one vivid memory of this production. I had been Leo's chauffeur in the Rolls Royce used in the show. Leo and I were in the back seat of the 'Roller' being driven back to London exchanging dirty limericks. It became more of a competition, which he finally conceded with my 'There was a young man called Perkin ...'.

I spent some time back in my home village of Old Windsor, staying with the Horton family (our next-door neighbours), painting their house and catching up with some of the local village characters. One of them, Lesley Griffiths, was particularly eccentric. A Bible-reading man, he was seen every night waddling down to the Fox and Castle pub, feet splayed like a penguin's, in 18-inch bell-bottomed trousers smoking a pipe. You would swear it was Jacques Tati.

Observing human movement and gesture are very important for an actor's kitbag. Remembering a stored gesture can lead to nailing a character. This approach seemed to be the way Laurence Olivier worked. I saw him for the first time on stage in *Love for Love* by William Congreve at the National Theatre in which the Australian actress Madge Ryan was playing. I also caught up with Geraldine McEwan who was in the company. She remembered me from her early days at school with my sister in Windsor.

Despite being more in work than out, I had to borrow money from an aunt to keep going before receiving the fee from the television play. Actors regularly wait weeks to get paid. At last the news about West Africa came through early in November. The company was going. I would be playing Roper in *A Man for All Seasons* and Oliver in *As You Like It* – good parts. Rehearsals would begin on 5 December with continuous work for four months and a fantastic opportunity to see something of Africa.

I cannot believe what I wrote in a letter after my euphoric news. I began moaning that I would have to give up my flat, store belongings, live out of a suitcase and lose ground in television because I would not be around. Actors in work always seem to worry what they're missing out on. Looking forward to the end of a long run of a play is a common feeling. Then after two weeks there are further moanings about not being in work. Accordingly, it was not surprising that I wrote what would turn out to be a prophetic remark: 'Of course anything could happen between now and Christmas, like a revolution in Ghana'. Almost: it occurred in Nigeria.

The whole scenario began with Ghana breaking off diplomatic relations on 12 December. Through pressure from the press and the government the British Arts Council was forced to withdraw our tour. We were used as a political pawn. John Neville and Judi Dench had led the company to Ghana, Sierra Leone and Nigeria before and played in Nkrumah's palace. Now a coup d'état had taken place there, Nkrumah had been deposed and we were all devastated. This happened after we had been rehearsing for three weeks. The tour was surely off.

However, the Arts Council managed to reroute us through Southeast Asia with a possible short tour in Europe to follow. As someone else once said: all's well that ends well.

One incident during rehearsals for A *Man for All Seasons* harked back to my to my first television role. I had stopped rehearsals and launched into a great chat about what Roper was doing on stage in this scene. From the gloom in the stalls came Michael Rudman's voice. 'Stop thinking, Ed. Just act.' Slightly different from the time in Sydney when I was told to stop acting. But that was film as opposed to stage acting.

John Neville was known for his practical jokes and naughty bits of business. When playing Richard II he had done something to make Maggie Jordan corpse to such a degree that she left a puddle on the stage. Judi Dench, renowned for being a giggler and easy to corpse, happened to be in the wings watching. She wasn't in the show. She decided vengeance on John was required. She got her own back for his previous japes and to support Maggie by coming on as an extra knight in armour at the end of the play. He was caught off guard to the extent of muttering an extra line: 'Who is this very small knight? Have him removed.'

There was this wonderful camaraderie and fun, and some serious drinking done, led by the likes of James Villiers and Ronnie Fraser. We all played hard and worked hard. Of all the companies I have been in, Nottingham was the most memorable. Many well-known people passed through, probably because of the high standards and rich talent of actors. One day I even found myself having lunch with Lord Snowden.

All things considered I could not have expected to do much better than I did in my first year on this main thespian highway. London is still regarded as the Mecca for theatre actors.

13

'Tea with the Sultan back to the Dole Queue'

The company would not be reacquainted with Nkrumah, but would be having tea with the Sultan of Perak. We were on our way to Southeast Asia.

Included in the company were some well-known actors like James Cairncross, Geoffrey Hutchings, William Russell and Edgar Wreford. There was also Geoff Kenion who became a lifelong friend and instrumental in providing further work. John Neville believed that everyone had equal value in a company, even though there were stars like Judi Dench and Edward Woodward playing in the main house. Ours was very much a company of actors.

We left a cold and snowing Newcastle on Saturday 12 February at midnight after the final performance in the UK of *A Man for All Seasons*. It was freezing as we travelled overnight by train to Euston Station and on to Heathrow. After touching down at Zürich, Beirut, Karachi and Delhi, we finally arrived on the tarmac at Bangkok airport, having done the 'milk run', as it was known. I shall never forget the blast of hot air when the doors were opened.

We stayed overnight and spent the day visiting the Floating Market on the Klong tributaries. Long, lean taxi-boats driven by extended churning propellers to avoid the weeds screamed up and down the river. It was as busy as any high street with hundreds of small craft selling produce, and families living in houses on stilts in the water among the smells of incense, oil and decay. Our tour would be starting in Penang but instead of flying straight there we had to fly to Singapore and stay overnight. Our flight had been delayed, then cancelled, then re-directed via Kuala Lumpur, put on, put off. We were exhausted when we finally got there, but at least we had five days to recover by swimming pools.

It was not surprising that Penang felt easy-going and familiar to me. It was founded in 1786 by the father of William Light, who laid out the city of Adelaide. Penang had only recently become part of the Federation of Malay States in 1957, the year Malaysia was granted independence. Malaysia was the last major piece removed from the colonial pink jigsaw. Consequently, much of Penang felt like home. The capital was called Georgetown, with place names like Downing Street, Buckingham Street, Pitt Street, Fettes Park, Macalister Road and Love Lane. There couldn't be a more English sounding name for a town than Butterworth, which was on the mainland. One got the impression that Malaysia was happy to have been part of the British Empire. Apart from troubles in the 1950s leading to the Indonesia–Malaysia Confrontation, which was happening while we were there, it seemed to be a most successful hand-over.

Penang was idyllic for our first stop, and audiences were very responsive. They were predominantly expats from Britain and Australia, though there were also many Malays and Indians who had been schooled in Shakespeare and English History. With plenty of swimming, golf, sunbathing and interesting history to explore, it couldn't have been a happier beginning.

Our next stop was Ipoh, an important administrative centre known for its tin mining, lying 200 km north-west of Kuala Lumpur. In those days it was also well known for its playboy sultan, the Sultan of Perak, who invited the company to tea in the banqueting room of his vast, white palace 50 km outside Ipoh. We were told of his bizarre lifestyle: he created his own music, painted mostly female nudes, played with a huge model railway that went through several rooms, had his three Muslim wives but played up with others and sneaked into nightclubs. At afternoon tea I sat next to one of the princesses who was exquisite, but her shyness and faltering English made her difficult to talk to. Richard Eyre, however, was getting on very well with the older princess. He told us that she virtually proposed to him, pleading with him to stay or take her with him. Despite their wealth, I suspect it was an empty life for them.

During our eight days in Kuala Lumpur we had free time to explore and meet people. Our opening night audience included the President of Malaysia, Tunku Abdul Rahman and the British High Commissioner, with the standard reception ('bun fight') after the show. Most dignitaries seemed keen to greet us wherever we went. It had been a part of the theatrical touring culture for many years when opera, ballet and plays toured the world. Sadly the accountants find it too expensive these days. In this sense the world is less global except for pop concerts. We were well received and during the 'bun fight' we did a lot of arranging for visits, parties and golf. We were taken to visit a rubber plantation, the Batu Caves and a pewter factory.

One contact turned out to be very lucrative. An account executive from Lintas Advertising asked a group of us to do six commercials. I can't remember what for but I do remember the fee: £116/13/4 for five hours work, more than three weeks' theatre earnings.

I had a memorable game of golf at the Royal Selangor Golf Club. At one of the short holes there was a swamp in front of the green. I duly hit my ball into it. I moved off, assuming I had lost the first ball. Not a bit of it: as I approached the swamp a blackened figure hailed me. 'Sahib, I have your ball!' A dripping black foot appeared with a ball – possibly mine, probably not – clutched in his toes. Of course, payment was required and I was obliged to play that ball.

He was one of the many indigenous Malays called Bumiputeras, literally translated as 'sons of the soil'; and this man *was* taking it literally. He spent every day fishing out balls from the muddy swamp with his feet. These people invariably did menial work and were seen as the low caste in Malaya, like the untouchables in India. They were positively discriminated for by the government and their lot has improved.

My good friend from Adelaide, Frances Horner, had married Dharmalingham, an Indian Malay, and was living in KL. Frances was the daughter of Musgrave Horner, my speech and drama mentor in those early days. With them I had my first experience of eating in a marketplace of open restaurants where you experience the essence of the East through all its bustle and smells. Most evenings after the show we went to the Royal Selangor Club, one of many such private clubs that are still to be found throughout the major cities of Southeast Asia. The sun had not quite set on the Empire.

Kuching, our next stop, was nearer to the edge of the Indonesia–Malaysia Confrontation, though the conflict concluded in August 1966. We were there in February, March and April when there was still enemy activity, which made it unsafe for us to visit a longhouse (literally a long house built for communal living by the Dayaks). It was very disappointing as we could have experienced how the indigenous Dayaks of North Borneo lived.

We witnessed a lot of army activity due to the 50,000 troops stationed nearby. Patrols were still repelling Indonesian infiltrators and there was some fighting on the Kuching/Seria road where we would soon be travelling. The company was invited to the residence of the erstwhile White Rajah (King), occupied by the Governor of Sarawak. The State of Sarawak had been ruled by the Brooke family since 1841 when the Sultan of Brunei granted it to James Brooke for suppressing the troublesome Sea Dayaks. It was handed down from father to son until Charles Vyner Brooke ceded the state to Britain and it became a crown colony after the Second World War. It was an extraordinary anomaly that this huge area of North Borneo was owned and ruled by an English family for over 100 years and then for more than 10 years run by the Colonial Office in London. It wasn't until 1957 that it finally belonged to its own people, becoming part of Malaysia.

To get to the Governor's mansion we had to cross a strong-flowing river by long, covered canoes. It was scary. The local indigenous headhunters, called Ibans, paddled us from the front of their canoes, and we were cheered to safety by a group of British soldiers waiting to go upriver on patrol. All these experiences have crowded out any recall of the reason for our being there. I have no memory of where we performed; all performances must have gone smoothly; after all, danger and disasters are more memorable.

Our next port of call was the Shell Company town of Seria, where we hardly felt we were in a foreign country. We stayed at the European club: played golf, tennis, swam and they even held a dinner dance for us on the last night. We visited an oil field and – a poor substitute – watched a film about the Dayaks and their longhouses.

Further along the coast was Jesselton, now named Kota Kinabalu. It is the capital of the State of Sabah at the north-eastern point of Borneo. These journeys were taken by bus and truck and there was an air of danger as we bumped along these roads that had seen some action in the past. Again, we had a wonderfully relaxing time with our hotel right on the beach. I have a warm, lingering memory of snorkelling in the South China Sea in crystal-clear water admiring the myriad colours of sea creatures.

Our Southeast Asian adventure was coming to a close. At all opening nights we would meet the local dignitaries. Manila was no different, but we were slightly surprised to be formally presented to the president and his wife after the show. We were lined up in a row and Mrs Marcos came along giving each one of us a present. I received a pair of pearl cuff links.

During our stay a few of us younger actors were entertained by a group of very beautiful Filipino girls from wealthy families. We were taken to their homes, which were secluded behind high walls with barbed wire. Armed soldiers guarded the entrance. Talk about being chaperoned. We soon became aware of the huge gap between rich and poor when visiting sights in the city.

I teamed up with Geoff Hutchings for the return journey. Geoff was often seen on UK television programmes and was one of those character actors people feel they know. Sadly he passed away in 2012. We spent a night and morning in Hong Kong getting clothes made. Then it was back to Singapore and on to Ceylon.

I had arranged to stay over on the way back with a friend from my growing-up years in Old Windsor. He had become Managing Director of Horlicks in Colombo. Hugh Roddy and his future wife Sarah were living the colonial life. His driver picked us up at the airport. We drove sedately along potted-palm-lined roads, native eyes cautiously following our progress. His wooden house surrounded with verandas was modest, but there were three servants. The old *apu* (head servant) was a typical ancient retainer. Those kinds of servants were still around many years later. Hugh's driver took us sightseeing to Kandy. We visited the Temple of the Tooth, had our ears assaulted by the Kandyan drummers and watched a medicine man graphically miming how an upset stomach can be cured by sipping his potion. It was a very funny piece of street theatre.

We were booked to fly to Bombay on Air Ceylon's one and only plane but it had broken down somewhere in south India. We waited at the airport in that heat without air conditioning. Some hours later the plane arrived. Six hours later they announced its imminent departure. We were walking across the tarmac when excited Air Ceylon employers ran up to our group. Nodding their heads from side to side in their inimitable way, they told us the flight was cancelled. Eventually we left Colombo at 7.30 am on a BOAC VC 10 direct to

London. Well, not quite. We dropped down in Bombay and Cairo and arrived at Heathrow at 9.30 pm. What's more, that was regarded as a quick trip. As I look back at that brief but somehow long time in Ceylon, I feel as if I had been in one of those black and white Humphrey Bogart movies.

14

Back to Reality

Driving through drizzle up the M4 from Heathrow under grey skies to no fixed abode was a timely reminder of reality. I have been lucky to have good friends. Mick and Rosie Johnston from Adelaide, who were very accommodating on the good ship *Flavia*, found floor space in their flat. Work was lined up in three weeks time to do a tour of *A Man for All Seasons* for the schools around Nottingham, this time playing the Duke of Norfolk. This tour took me through to the end of May, which meant I had been in constant work for six months. But it was a far cry from Manila to Mansfield.

A few years later I saw a production of *A Man for All Seasons* at the Savoy Theatre with Charlton Heston playing Sir Thomas Moore. One of the key elements to my mind for having star quality is charisma or magnetic presence. Charlton Heston had absolutely no presence on stage. His performance was dull, due mainly to his droning voice. He had no lightness or sense of humour. He was terrible. I had an urge to yell out 'Moses!'. The production had a very short season. I am sure it is something to do with initially being trained for stage acting. Heston could project a few feet into a camera but not beyond the footlights.

I managed some visits to the theatre, including to a modern-dress production of Hamlet directed by Peter Hall. David Warner played Hamlet as a radical student with a long scarf and saying the lines in an ordinary way. It was the first time I had seen a Shakespeare play in a contemporary setting. It was also the beginning of a trend whereby lines are spoken with little regard for the poetry. So you tended to hear something akin to: 'Tobeornottobe – that'sthequestion'.

As the eminent speech teacher Patsy Rodenberg points out: the text in Shakespeare and the classic repertoire is written as 'heightened speech with the boring bits cut out'. You cannot make out it is everyday speech just because it sounds unnatural, or that young people can't understand the language. They understood the film of *Romeo + Juliet* with Leonardo DiCaprio.

One of the most memorable traditional productions of a Shakespeare play I saw was *Othello* at The Old Vic in 1965 with Laurence Olivier in the main role. His performance was a mighty tour de force However, at the end of one of the performances, it is reported that he had an out-of-body experience. According to Frank Finlay, who was playing Iago, he took flight in this performance, came off stage in a high-octaned state slamming his dressing-room door. Frank went to his door and asked what was wrong when he had given the most brilliant performance. Olivier yelled: 'Yes I know I have! but I want to know WHY!' My speculation is that he had totally suspended his conscious mind and was acting from his sub-conscious. He was not aware of acting. He was flying on gossamer wings.

For me Laurence Olivier was the greatest actor of our time if not of all times. He was mesmerising to watch. His versatility was phenomenal. In repertoire during a later season he played Mr Puff, a fop, in a matinee performance of Sheridan's *The Critic*, a Restoration comedy. In the evening, the title role in Sophocles's *Oedipus Rex*. Then he would play Archie Rice in John Osborne's *The Entertainer*, with all that loose unctuousness. In addition, he was a powerful movie actor and a matinee idol.

Before going to stay with family friends in Sunningdale I sold the Vespa scooter and bought a 1960 Austin Seven which was actually one of the first minis. As a point of comparison, I bought it for £150, paid £17 per annum road tax and paid about five shillings and five pence (5/5d) per gallon of petrol, actually similar to today's prices in relative terms. A car was needed for swanning around the pubs and houses of friends in Wentworth, Ascot, Virginia Waters and Windsor. I was fortunate to be part of a racy group from the shires of Surrey, through my early connections in Old Windsor. Their company eased the down times and even led to casual work, which sustained me over a period of 25 years.

An urgent call had me racing up to London to meet an American record producer at the Dorchester Hotel. He was planning to record an audio version of *A Midsummer Night's Dream* with John Gielgud playing Oberon. I auditioned for the part of Lysander. I felt a brief moment of importance as I strolled past the chauffeurs standing by their Rolls Royces and casually swung through the revolving doors of the Dorchester as though it were habitual. I didn't get the job. Occasional posing is necessary to keep up the spirits. Many years later I was back at the Dorchester, on the forecourt doing garden maintenance work. Posers are always found out.

Needing to find new digs, I got a room in a flat with four girls in Cornwall Gardens off Gloucester Road. This was a sure-fire way of puncturing the mystery and romance that a fellow might have for the female sex. A deviant might have enjoyed it, but the bathroom was never not festooned with drying knickers. I shared a room with one of the girls and had to promise not to peep during undressing times. Of course I did the right thing, being an honourable gentleman. It seems extraordinary that she agreed but she was the only one who was engaged. That must have made the difference.

I was out of work as an actor for three months from June to September 1966. For almost the first time I felt the actor's ennui when the phone doesn't ring and the money is running out. However, it was in the height of summer. I joined the Stage Cricket Club and the Stage Golfing Society. I also played for the Old Pauline Cricket Club and The Gentlemen of Old Windsor Cricket Club, called The Gents.

The Gents was founded in 1948 by our next-door neighbour Adrian Horton in Old Windsor. I first played for him at the age of 10 and have only recently closed my innings after 60 years. Those three months on the dole were spent playing cricket and golf, staying healthy in convivial company. I didn't need to look for alternative work. Those were the easy days.

The drought was broken with two commercials. I'm fairly sure one was directed by Richard Lester. Commercials paid a low shooting fee but, whenever shown, paid residuals which could turn out to be substantial. Many subsequently famous film directors like Lester and Ridley Scott cut their teeth on shooting commercials. But, as a general rule, if you happened to be in one of theirs you would be unlikely to work for them in a movie. Actors doing commercials were looked down upon. I think it suggested to the high flyers that you were just a jobbing actor. This became less so after we all saw Laurence Olivier doing a commercial for Kodak.

There are very few auditions after which you hope the job is not offered. I went to the Ambassadors Theatre to audition for the part of the detective in *The Mousetrap*. It was the part originally played by Richard Attenborough and would give me one year of solid work at £40 per week but it would do my career no favours. In addition, it would likely deaden my acting psyche with tedious repetition playing a potboiler eight times a week. I decided it wasn't right for me, but it was ideal for a new friend David Pinner, who was primarily a playwright. He got the part, and it provided financial security while he wrote his plays.

Having no home base can be a debilitating problem for a roving actor. I had to spend a depressing period on my own in an Earls Court bedsit. Fortunately, that situation didn't last too long as Geoff and Sarah Kenion invited me to stay in their flat in Maida Vale. This took me through to when I was booked for a return season at Ipswich which commenced immediately after the next job. The next job came out of a dinner party in late September.

I was sitting next to a girl from Sydney who was secretary to Michael Hayes, a drama director working at the BBC. He was casting for a BBC studio production set in 1066 called *Conquest*. It was a stylised re-enactment of the Battle of Hastings with Alan Dobie playing William the Conqueror and Barry Ingham playing King Harold. Janet Suzman was also in the cast. Michael Hayes couldn't find a proper part for me but asked if I wouldn't mind being a glorified extra. He assured me I would be paid as an actor. Extras were supernumeraries who filled out the moving background in the crowd scenes. They were regarded as the bottom rung of the drama ladder but essential. They had their own union and many made a living by it. It was regarded as a no-no for trained actors.

Rodger Mutton and I ran about with flags on top of poles representing the battle and playing various non-speaking roles. We had great fun over six weeks rehearsing in the barn of a church hall with plenty of laughs and a running bridge table. It was a good break because most directors build up a list of actors they like working with. Hayes must have been pleased with my attitude. The following year he cast me in the guest lead role in an episode of *When the Boat Comes In* playing opposite James Bolam. The episode was called 'Whatever Makes You Think the War is Over'. The part was Mr Buell, an inherited factory owner whom Bolam's character was trying to close down. Another story in the rich English vein of class conflict.

The year rounded off very neatly for me. Towards the end of October I began rehearsals for *Pride and Prejudice* at Ipswich playing Wickham (in which Darcy and I corpsed). This was to be followed by J.B. Priestley's play *When We Were Married*. Then I was invited to stay on to be in the world premiere of a play. It was an adaptation of Charles Dickens' last novel *The Mystery of Edwin Drood* by Michael and Mollie Hardwick. I was cast in the role of Drood/Datchery, a part I would play again. These two plays were directed by Derrick Goodwin. I became one of his stable of actors.

The year 1966 ended very well and I was already being considered for John Neville's new company from Nottingham Playhouse to go into the Flora Robson Theatre in Jesmond Dene, Newcastle upon Tyne.

15

'Ye Wor a Canny Fella, Will'

Two separate seasons were spent among the 'why I man' Geordies of Newcastle upon Tyne, Northumberland. Very soon after the last performance of *Pride and Prejudice* in Ipswich I was chugging my way up the A1 in my Austin Seven to rehearse *Measure for Measure* in Nottingham. The production would then be taken to Newcastle. It was to be staged in modern dress and John Neville was keen for me to play the part of Barnardine (a dissolute prisoner) as an Australian convict. He said he got the idea from the line 'I've been drinking hard all night long'. He would often come in during rehearsals just to hear that line.

A notable comedian was playing the part of Pompey the clown. Bill Maynard was probably best known latterly for playing Greengrass in the television series *Heartbeat*. Letting loose a stand-up comedian on a Shakespeare play can be tricky for other actors. I found it difficult to know when to enter as Bill was extemporising with cleaning equipment among the audience. Being a modern production we heard lines like: 'Pray madame would'st thou pass me up the Duraglit?' One other member of the cast was the voice of K-9 in *Dr Who*, John Leeson. He caused panic in one performance when one of his contact lens popped out. He was heard to mutter 'lend me your eyes upon the floor'. There was a crowded stage with actors moving gingerly doing a lot of looking-down acting.

This production had been staged at the Nottingham Playhouse with Alan Howard playing Angelo and Judi Dench as Isabella. Judi's performance was mesmerising. Her innate goodness and warmth infused her performance to make it memorable.

She Stoops to Conquer was the next production. Being in a premiere company I had to play smaller parts. I played Marlowe's father. The actor cast as Marlowe was Jerome Willis who was older than I but well established. It was not the first time I had played an older part to an older actor. I had played the older brother to William Russell's Orlando in the Southeast Asian tour of *As You Like It*. Russell was an established player like Jerome.

Before the end of the run of *She Stoops to Conquer* Jerome and Alex Glasgow had devised a platform performance celebrating Shakespeare's birthday. It was a very Tyneside celebration. The folk singer Alex Glasgow, who became famous for writing and singing the theme music for *When the Boat Comes In*, was a native Geordie and a left-wing crusader. The title of his final song is the heading for this chapter. He was one of the most prominent folk singers of that era but ended his days quietly in Perth, Western Australia.

There was a moment from the platform performance that lingers. At the end of the very moving speech by Mistress Quickly lamenting the death of Falstaff there is a long silence until Nym, whom I was playing, suddenly says: '*Shall we shog? The King will be gone from Southampton'.* It is one of those moments you can only experience in the theatre. And what a word for Shakespeare to use to break the spell – shog. Translated into modern parlance it means 'piss off'.

I spent six months overall living in Newcastle and still found it difficult to understand the Geordie accent. It is a thick brogue of its own which had to be toned down by the actors playing in the comedy series *Auf Wiedersehen, Pet* in which Geordie builders go to work in Germany. Here is a written example. It is the first verse of the song Alex Glasgow wrote for the Shakespeare celebration:

> *Ye wor a canny fella Will, Canny Will*
> *Wiv a mighty powerful quill, Canny Will.*
> *Aall them pomes and sangs and plays*
> *It's nee wunder we aal praise Canny Will*

This dialect had a sister dialect in Hamburg, a similar northern port in Germany, and I heard that people from these areas could understand each other. I certainly couldn't understand the local mechanic when taking the car in for a service. It calls to mind how left out I felt when I tried to join in a football game on the vast foggy fields of The Inch in Perth, Scotland, during a Christmas holiday. The boys spoke Gaelic and never passed the ball to me. I was 10 years old at the time and must have looked a forlorn figure in the mist, shivering in shorts.

Despite the initial feeling that one was in a foreign land, Geordie folk on the whole are very warm and friendly – unless one came across someone full of the potent Newcastle brown ale. I found myself at a left-wing party, and being contrary, spouted some right-wing views. I was soon in a punch-up with a pugnacious Geordie Marxist. Many actors tend to be inclined to the left wing of politics and this company was particularly so. Whenever I hear Eric Burdon and The Animals, particularly singing *The House of the Rising Sun*, it brings back those days in Newcastle upon Tyne.

I mixed with people at both ends of the social and political spectrum. Angela, the sister of the girl I met filming that first commercial in London, was married to Charles Straker. The Straker family had been mine owners and were part of the landed gentry of Northumberland. I spent many weekends with them. He was a good example of an Old Harrovian: a very hearty golfing, shooting, fishing chap, into all sorts of ways to make money. He and Angela were great fun and very generous. They took me to all their lunch parties and picnic race meetings. Two of the girls from the flat I shared had married into this group. I have always been amused by these upper-class characters and have played a few. I have been waiting for them to disappear with the British Empire but there are still remnants in the shires of old England.

At the other end of the social spectrum, Mrs Lashley was my first Geordie landlady in theatre digs. She was married to a truck driver and often had her father to high tea. This was held every evening at 5.30 pm. It was usually a full roast dinner, typically roast beef with Yorkshire pudding and spotted dick. After the performance we would come home to sandwiches and cocoa. When I first arrived and was shown to my room, Mrs Lashley was proud to announce that the singer Tom Jones had slept in my bed.

Her father was an interesting man. He was a Durham pit-miner and a great storyteller. His patrician face was chiselled by hard physical labour, and his broad brogue voice took me down the mines describing what it was like. He was a proud man. I could understand why those mining communities, led by Arthur Scargill in the early 80s, fought so hard to defy Margaret Thatcher. Mining communities were deeply entrenched, bonded by that hard and dangerous life. This meeting with the old pit miner would prove invaluable when later preparing for a part as a miner.

There are many theatrical landlady stories. One such was told by the ebullient Harold Innocent. Harold was a portly gay gentleman with a face resembling a wobbly moon. A member of the Nottingham Playhouse Company, he was great fun, possessed a wicked wit and had recently been on television. He was touring with a show in Bradford and had arrived at the front door of his digs waiting for his hostess to open the door. When it opened the landlady looked hard at Harold and after a slight pause said very emphatically 'Queer!' Harold went red and said 'I beg your pardon, Madame.' She said, 'Queer I should know you.' The word *queer* had a different meaning up North.

On my way back to London I called in to Stratford-upon-Avon to catch up with John and Anna Bell from Sydney, doing their season with the Royal Shakespeare Company before returning. There was a long tradition that classically trained actors should begin their careers 'spear carrying' in one of the major companies. It was seen as an apprenticeship, playing minor parts at first. Many of the great actors spent seasons with either the RSC or the National Theatre. In hindsight I should have gone down that road more travelled. But I was playing significant roles in respected repertory companies. I didn't fancy spending a number of years rushing about the stage saying the odd line. However, I did miss the opportunity to be in the company of the great actors in those days.

I spent the summer of 1967 in London before returning to Newcastle for a longer season in October. I managed to pick up some 'bits and pieces' work again via a dinner party contact, plus two days on a Carry On film. My fee for being the bowler in the opening sequence in *Follow That Camel* was 24 guineas (£25/4/–), a quaint figure left over from the 19th century. In six days I earned more than four weeks' pay in the theatre but I was still crying poor.

The *Carry On* film would create some fan mail, despite my brief appearance. I recently bumped into a massive crowd of *Carry On* fans at a convention attended by Jim Dale at the National Theatre. I told one of them that I had been in Follow That Camel and was besieged for my autograph.

I recall during the filming of *Follow That Camel* being very put off by Phil

Silver's behaviour. The American comedy actor was playing the lead and rather typified the loudmouthed American, throwing around his star status, unlike the quiet and modest Peter Gilmore. Peter had starred in musicals in the West End and in the television series *The Onedin Line*. Modesty is not a quality I associate with American actors.

I was still of 'no fixed abode', so it was good to find myself up north again in October to do four productions at the Flora Robson Theatre in Newcastle upon Tyne. The first would be *Much Ado about Nothing* in which I would be playing an old man again. I had a lot of fun playing Verges and it was for Derrick Goodwin, a gentle actors' director with whom I had worked at Ipswich.

This was a very up-to-date modern production with a coke machine in the set, an actor entering on a Vespa scooter and everyone in flower power, hippie clothes, all accompanied with Beatles-style music. What's more, the tabs (front curtain) were left open during the interval, and I had to sit on the front edge of the stage with the other low-life characters eating an imaginary meal.

Mother Courage and Her Children by Bertolt Brecht was traditionally staged. I remember Germaine Greer playing the Mother in a student production at Sydney University in the early 1960s. Germaine could have had a career as an actress; in a sense she did. I was cast to play the Swedish Commander and other 'bits and pieces' throughout the play which I had the temerity to refuse. My one and only appearance was in Scene 2. I was home by 8.45 pm every night of the run. It was accepted custom that if you did not appear after the interval you did not have to wait for the curtain call.

During the run of *Mother Courage* we began rehearsals for two plays at the same time. Two more different plays you could not wish to find: *The Homecoming* by Harold Pinter and an adaptation of the Charles Dickens' novel *A Christmas Carol*. *The Homecoming* was about a seriously dysfunctional family. I played Joey the dim-witted boxer. The wobbly moon-faced Harold Innocent played Max the father whose barbs were razor sharp and typical of Pinter. There was one speech by Max directed at Joey that stuck in my mind:

> ... that's your only trouble as a boxer. You don't know how to defend yourself, and you don't know how to attack. Once you've mastered those arts you can go straight to the top.

Once *The Homecoming* was running we began rehearsing another play, the delightful story of *Pinocchio* by Brian Way. This accompanied *A Christmas Carol* during the day for children. I was asked to play the Clown with no lines to learn.

In *A Christmas Carol* Peter Pratt, the well-known Gilbert and Sullivan performer, played Scrooge and I played the ghost of Jacob Marley and Christmas Past. During one performance, while playing Christmas Past magically conjuring examples for Scrooge to be a better person, a long string of prop sausages dropped down from the flies above, swinging right in front of my face. There was an astonished silence. The swinging string of prop sausages was like a metronome. As our heads swivelled back and forth watching it, Peter said to me 'Spirit, you do indeed perform miracles'. The audience caught on and we all laughed together. It was a shared corpse and therefore okay.

I was apprehensive about playing a non-speaking clown. Once we started playing to an audience though, Clown came alive. I was often among the children in the auditorium and experienced the magical power of mime, the original form of communication: a seminal experience for an actor.

That is the only time I ever performed in a Christmas show, though that whole scene was a subculture in theatrical circles. Many dancers and singers in musical theatre depended on this three-month pantomime season every year. The joke saying for these performers was 'Oh dear, November and no Dick'. Dick was short for *Dick Whittington*, the well-known pantomime.

Back in London in the new year of 1968 a connection from NIDA days found me in a ghastly flat share in West Kensington. Here is how I described it:

> I'm in a tiny room in a large, draughty, cold, dirty flat shared with two women, separated from their husbands, and their three screaming snotty-nosed children. In another room there is a croupier who creeps around late at night after returning from his job in a night club.

It sounds like a setting for an existential play. What is more, it was in this flat that a dubious gentleman approached me with the view to taking a package to Rhodesia for which I would be well paid. Who knows where that road would have ended.

During in-between periods I would be put up for a variety of long and short engagements. After returning from Newcastle I took a light step towards Shepperton Studios for a part in a film starring David Hemmings called *The Best House in London*. I was to meet the director Philip Saville and the writer Denis Norden. They looked slightly dismayed as they approached. 'Oh dear,' said Denis, 'we were looking for someone to play Swinburne [the 19th-century writer] who was short, fat and ugly.' I was six foot one, slim and not unattractive. Crossed wires often happen in this business.

The new year of 1968 arrived with the possibility of another overseas tour. It came from a general interview I had had with John Counsell at the Theatre Royal Windsor before going to Newcastle in 1967. He bowled me over with the prospect of being in a company that would tour the USA with four English plays over a period of three to six months. This whole project was firming up in March to commence in June, when I was offered a short return season at Newcastle Playhouse in *Henry IV Part I* which would finish at end of May. It was sweet scheduling.

I was given two minor roles, those of the Duke of Northumberland and Sir Richard Vernon, but also the major task of being the fight arranger for the last quarter of the play.

Choreographing battle scenes with actors of varying fighting abilities was tricky and caused serious problems during the run. I conducted research at the British Museum on 15th-century weapons. Under Shakespeare's stage directions 'alarms and excursions' I had worked out realistic sequences of fighting with long and short swords and pikes. The actors were drilled relentlessly but some were not as sharp as others. It was startlingly busy; clashing swords and actors careering back and forth across the stage, dry ice billowing everywhere and sporadic uproar among hastily spoken scenes. In the second week fatigue and over-confidence almost proved fatal. National newspapers proclaimed: 'Wounded Warriors Threaten Walk-out on Henry IV' (*Daily Express*) and 'To Strike or Not to Strike' (*Daily Mail*).

Poor David Strong, playing Sir Walter Blunt, received two head injuries, one near his eye; Neil McLaughlan failed to parry a thrust from an eight-foot pike and staggered off stage dripping with real blood. Still in his chain mail, he was treated by surprised doctors in hospital after the show. The cast threatened to go on strike unless St John Ambulance was in attendance in the wings during, what the *Daily Mail* reporter described as, 'ferocious battle scenes'. There were full houses for the rest of the run.

The Newcastle venture was a huge success. There were some memorable productions such as *Oh, What a Lovely War!* and *Close the Coal House Door*, an original work about the local pit mining communities. John Neville believed the theatre belonged to the people but he did not believe in playing down to them. Bread and circuses among the classics was his menu. It was a sad day when I heard that the Flora Robson Theatre was to be bulldozed to make way for a big road junction. One wonders now whether this concrete crawl is progress. The Flora Robson wasn't just a building; it housed dreams and memories – 'sounds, and sweet airs that give delight and hurt not'.

Now it was back to London to rehearse for the Grand Tour.

16

Westward Ho!

Not often does one job immediately follow another. Rehearsals began in Windsor the week after the last night in Newcastle. For the summer of 1968 I was living within the geographic territory of my upbringing: rehearsing in a theatre at the base of the great tower of Windsor Castle where in the garden under the battlements I had seen a performance of *The Merry Wives of Windsor* – on the meadows down the road to Datchet there had been memorable visits to Bertram Mills Circus – Down Peascod Street was my first school, Upton House – the road over the bridge near the theatre led to Eton College – a little further on was the preparatory school I had attended. To the east down the Straight Road from the Long Walk was Old Windsor, where I was born and grew up, only half a mile from Runnymede where the Magna Carta was signed on an island. Much of the landscape and a few of the buildings in Windsor town would still be recognised by Sir John Falstaff riding around on his escapades with the merry wives.

I cannot emphasise too strongly what powerful imprints the geography and landscape made on me from those growing-up years. It feels like history is in my blood and bone. That is why I want my ashes to be scattered in the field above Pelling Hill, the centre from where I roamed. What better place to pick up my journey as an actor than working in my home area.

The tour to the USA was sold on the idea that the Theatre Royal Windsor had close connections with the monarchy, and that we would be presenting four classic English comedies. However, at the beginning of rehearsals for *An Ideal Husband* on 20 May it was very much touch and go.

The American Department of Immigration had refused John Counsell's application, but John had connections in the Foreign Office. The refusal was overridden through the persuasive efforts of the UK ambassador in

Washington. We were going anyway because three separate tea cup readings confirmed that a big trip was imminent: my mother had read it in her teacup, Mary Kerridge (our leading lady) had seen a moose and an eagle (symbols of Canada and USA) in her cup, and one of the other actresses had been told by a fortune teller. We certainly see and hear what we want to see and hear, but perhaps there is a force that should not be entirely ridiculed. It meant a trip of a lifetime and constant work for six months on relatively good money. Our weekly pay at Windsor was £25, on tour it was £104. It was above the Equity minimum and meant one could actually save.

Of course there has always been this myth that if you appear in front of the public you must be wealthy. Film stars earn squillions, chorus girls just enough to live on. It is the profession of extremes. The average earnings of a working actor over years would be considerably less than a bank teller's. So many people think I am well off and in constant work because I appear on television. Nothing could be further from the truth, particularly when you add the verifiable and constant statistic that 89 per cent of actors are out of work at any one time. So I was to be on the outside of that statistic for a while, with the bonus of being in places I would not normally go to, and meeting people I would not normally meet. That's the quid pro quo of the travelling player.

From May to August I was able to re-connect with family, friends and generally mix with those types at weddings and cocktail parties that made *Four Weddings and a Funeral* so hilarious and true. My friend Monica had the traditional wedding; married in a local village church attended by the Alice Band brigade called the Sloane Rangers and their Hooray Henrys.

I used to call them the 'Yuk Yuks and the Wah Wahs' because that was the way they sounded in their speech. They were easy targets for 'sending up' and they were good for me as models for future roles. Indeed I had already played one – Sandy Tyrell in *Hay Fever* – a role which I was about to perform again. Monica became a lifelong friend and her mother was kind enough to arm me with an introduction to a very famous contact in Hollywood.

The plays to be taken to the USA were Oscar Wilde's *An Ideal Husband*, Noël Coward's *Hay Fever*, George Farquhar's *The Beaux' Stratagem* and George Bernard Shaw's *Mrs Warren's Profession*. Among those in the cast were Elizabeth Counsell, Stephen Moore and Linda Marlowe, who all made names for themselves. Mary Kerridge was a leading lady and her husband was well known for being a traditional actor/manager and very conservative. In fact it was unlike most reps I have worked in, which tended to be left-wing and provocative. The Windsor policy was focused on taking safe plays with stars on the try-out circuit for the West End. The rest of the cast were fine theatre actors, it being early days for becoming familiar through television.

An Ideal Husband was my penance play. I had the walk-on walk-off part of Mason the butler. Most of us had two good parts and one not so good, with one play out. The old adage is only partially true that 'there are no small parts, only small actors'. Career actors need a wide canvas to grow their potential.

After three weeks of rehearsal the season opened on 10 June. The following day we began rehearsals for *The Beaux' Stratagem* in which I would be playing Squire Sullen – a drunken, boorish, country gentleman. We would be playing and rehearsing the four plays before leaving for Montreal on 19 August. Life was hectic before departure: giving up digs, selling car, drinks parties in London, breaking up with current girlfriend and falling in love again. I also had to cope with an endless stream of family and friends wanting to see me after the shows, all insisting I visit them before leaving. 'Coach load for Ed' was often heard over the tannoy (intercom) after the show.

17

Touring in North America

We flew to Montreal two weeks later than originally planned, due to the cancellation of the Montreal Festival and problems with French Canadian Equity who finally backed down. We were fortunately part of a salvage package. The city had hosted Expo '68 and with the Anglo/French mixture it was buzzing. We played in the Theatre Maisoneuve, a big new theatre with difficult acoustics. We were well received and given a thumbs-up critique from Jacob Siskin, unlike Toronto, our next stop, where we ran into a notorious critic. The Royal Alexandra Theatre was a traditional 19th-century theatre with gilt and seats in boxes on the side. We all felt very much at home. However, we were assailed by the most vitriolic critique I have ever read. The poison came from the pen of Nathan Cohen seemingly trying to outdo the famous New York critic Clive Barnes. His opening paragraph is worth quoting:

> The smell of dry rot and mould which came from the Royal Alexandra stage last night was due only incidentally to the age of *The Beaux' Stratagem*. What really accounted for the decrepitude was its perfunctory production by Theatre Royal Windsor.

We were told Cohen always dipped his pen in bile but despite his review the locals came.

From Toronto we flew to San Francisco, the flower power city, where we played the Geary Street Theatre in the city centre where it was all happening. One night after the show Stephen Moore and I went to a bar and listened to this guy playing 'Piano Man'. Billy Joel was unknown then.

San Francisco was heaving with 'the beautiful people' and the gays were flaunting their new-found freedom. In many ways 1968 was a seminal year, with the student revolutions shifting the status quo of proscribed thinking. It could be claimed that there were some parallels with the *Les Misérables* story.

Mayor Daley sent in the troops and a student was shot on the campus of Kent University in Chicago. We were there in the aftermath of that incident.

Quite often the financial structure of touring companies is based on shifting sands. Our producer Robert T. Gaus announced a serious lack of funds. I was owed $700 back pay. There was a rumour he could go bankrupt but somehow the situation was saved. There was even talk of the company being flown back home for Christmas and returning in the new year; playing a season at the Ford Theatre in Washington DC, then going on to the Caribbean (calling in on Noël of course). It was pie-in-the-sky talk: nothing came of it. One minute it was all falling over, next they were talking turkey, extending the season.

After our week in San Francisco we flew to the actor's promised land: Los Angeles – Hollywood – Tinsel Town. And what a week we had there. Not many actors would have performed a Noël Coward play in a cavernous open-air theatre. Our producer had booked us in to the Greek Theatre where José Feliciano had held a concert the night before and where Neil Diamond had recorded the *Hot August Night* album. It seated 5000 and on our opening night about 500 people spread themselves over the first 10 rows which began beyond a vast orchestra pit. We were not miked and so found ourselves yelling the lines; Noël would have cringed. It was an extraordinary experience speaking the lines of a domestic comedy into the night sky above mostly empty seats.

Before leaving London my friend Monica Gordon took me to meet her mother who had been at school with Kirk Douglas's wife and had maintained a strong friendship. She gave me a letter of introduction and her phone number.

On 17 September Anne Douglas invited me to lunch at their home on North Canyon Drive. Anne picked me up from the bus stop in her snazzy Mustang. Their house was a real home, nothing ostentatious. In fact it would not have been out of place on the north shore of Sydney. It was a wide house with a sloping lawn at the back leading down to a swimming pool and tennis court. To the right was a very large outhouse which was Kirk's mini-theatre.

On this particular day Kirk had just received the script for his next movie and was upstairs reading it. The movie was *The Arrangement*, directed by Elia Kazan and released in 1969. He joined us for lunch in a very cosy dining room with another gentleman. I was sitting a metre away from the dimple.

He was generous in his conversation, asking all about the company and my connection with Anne. I tried to be very relaxed, making out that he was really just another actor, but I know that I felt very much in awe of being in the presence of a Hollywood star. He must have picked this up because before he left the table he said:

'I expect your company would be interested in seeing how a Hollywood star lives. Anne, you make the arrangements.'

It occurred to me later that the manner in which the invitation was uttered smacked a little of 'come to the zoo for specially chosen people'. Still, I was thrilled to be able to say to the cast, 'Kirk's invited you all for the day at his home'. I scored a big brownie point in the eyes of the company.

The following Friday nearly all of us in the touring company went to Anne and Kirk's for lunch and an afternoon of swimming and tennis. It was interesting to hear later from some of the cast that he had become a little concerned that I was getting on so well with his wife. I must have tweaked a jealous spot in Kirk Douglas. Perhaps I should not have beaten him at tennis. One could see how he got to where he was with that fierce competitive spirit.

Anne and he were very gracious and seemed genuinely to enjoy our company. Kirk went further and arranged for a group of us to visit the Paramount Studios, where *The Molly Maguires,* starring Sean Connery and Richard Harris, was being filmed. We were taken on a conducted tour through the vast set and afterwards we met the director Martin Ritt. It was agreed by all, that apart from the open air venue, our week in LA could not have been bettered.

Up to then we had flown the first part of the tour beginning in Montreal. It would become bus and truck for the middle part of our tour. Although it was more tiring, it meant we would really see the country and meet more people. We began travelling north to Portland, Oregon, via Redding and the Cascade Mountains, passing the glorious snow-capped peak of Mount Shasta, through the mighty pine and maple trees with their leaves just turning to the rich red and golden colours of the Fall. From then on, until we reached Atlanta,Georgia, I kept a daily diary.

We opened in Portland with *The Beaux' Stratagem* in a brand new auditorium. Many of these venues were multi-purposed, requiring microphone enhancement (where mikes are placed at intervals along the front of the stage). This required considerable adjustment to speech sound levels and clarity. Our performances were well received and we found Portland to be a very friendly town.

Some friends took me for a drink at The Goose Hollow where I met two queer sculptors and Maria, a sexy screwed up barmaid. They invited me back for coffee to their home where Al Cosby, the coloured partner with very fixed eyes, tried to show me his latest exhibits. Maria gave me ample protection.

We played in the Opera House in Seattle, another modern barn with microphone enhancement. Next door Hubert Humphrey, vice president and Democratic presidential candidate, was performing his one-night electioneering stand, which probably meant fewer punters for our show. But afterwards we had a grand party thrown by the British Council, dancing until 3.00 am. Our accommodation, however, was a sleazy joint called the Moore Hotel which could only be described as a brothel. Topless girls from the nightclub serving breakfast were a bit disturbing while eating one's scrambled eggs. A compensation was being driven around by Angela Slater who looked like Julie Christie. Did I pick her up from the dance or was she a topless waitress? You can see how a gullible English boy can be led astray in this Sodom and Gomorrah country. Some details didn't make the diary.

I have found generally when travelling that many towns and villages invariably have something unique to declare. Our next stop was the pretty little country town of Walla Walla which was the centre for pea growing. Then it was on to Caldwell in Idaho County, known for gems and growing potatoes.

An 8.00 am call had us on the road for the long haul through the state of Arizona with a two-hour stop in Salt Lake City and an overnight in Provo. We just had sufficient time to view the Book of Mormon and the tablets of Joseph Smith. America is full of odd-ball religions, none more so than this polygamous cult of worthy citizens. At least they survive; the Shaker cult died out because sex was banned.

The next morning we left early for Flagstaff, Arizona, so that we could take in a detour along the Grand Canyon. The great gap is awe-inspiring as you look down into this vast abyss, with its rock formations standing like trophies that seem to move with the shifting ochre shadows.

After playing to a most responsive audience, the next morning we were on our way to Tempe, Arizona, just outside Phoenix. The venue for our performances there was unique. The Gammage Auditorium was Frank Lloyd Wright's last design. I thought he must have been thinking of his wedding day; the building looked like a huge cake made of marzipan. What's more the acoustics were shocking and the sound system inadequate. From one point in middle of the auditorium the actors were inaudible.

Like all groups there come times when you need to let off steam and behave badly. A party was being held in one of the hotel rooms which broke out into the corridors. Cast members were chasing each other trying to drop ice cubes down each other's backs. This Nevsky ice cube battle was broken up by our dear leader. A perplexed John Counsell stood in the corridor aghast at our behaviour. He was like a headmaster saying we were irresponsible and we must cut out this tomfoolery. It was like a scene from *Tom Brown's Schooldays.*

Dale Parkinson was our American tour manager and very much part of the hijinks. He went out of his way to make sure that we not only enjoyed our time in his country but saw as much of it as possible. Our next day's travel would take us to Albuquerque, New Mexico, but he arranged a detour through the petrified forest in the Painted Desert. We were riding the scene from a Western movie and stunned by the primordial landscape, where mountains have been cut and eroded into strange shapes by the elements. Then to hold a piece of petrified wood that has been crystallised into stone of varying colours from millions of years ago was a profoundly connecting experience.

Turquoise was the word as we entered Albuquerque. We headed for the old part of town where the Indians carve the turquoise into jewellery and bought our Christmas presents. It seems from my diary entry that we learnt nothing from the reprimand from our dear leader. A few of us were taken by our hotel manager and friend after the show to various topless bars. We ended up back at the hotel in the manager's room:

> Had a very jolly evening, drinking tequila, listening to Indian tribal music. About 4.00 am we were saying goodnight in the corridor when John Counsell burst from his room, which happened to be next door, in a great rage. He was shaking with British indignation in his shorty pyjamas. The coach next morning was chilly and we received a monumental blow-up for giving the British a bad name.

Poor John. And it was not the last time he would be in despair over us.

Our motel in Odessa, Texas, was right by the Pacific Railroad. We were kept awake by real shunting that night. Odessa had acquired a replica of the London Globe Theatre which was beautifully constructed and acoustically perfect, but we didn't play there. I have no record, nor can I recall why. Maybe it was seen as a trophy, a museum piece not to be used. It could only happen in America, as indeed a sentence I wrote that night: 'Witnessed a car accident and went to bed'.

There were a few towns where we were left to our own devices. Denton, Texas, was one. The local university had forgotten we were coming. Their new theatre was set up for their own performance of *Romeo and Juliet*, so we had to play in their very cramped old theatre. Our motel was on the outskirts of town in a desolate area, no restaurant in sight. We were rescued by a Texan state cop bristling with firearms who guided us to a pizza joint.

I was looking forward to our next port of call. After bumping in to the huge, over 2000 seater, McFarlin Auditorium in Dallas, Stephen Moore and I went off to explore the scene of the Kennedy assassination. It was an eerie experience, walking from the Book Depository building down to the bridge via the grassy knoll.

Americans love building big. The Jones Hall cultural complex in Houston covered a whole block with seating capacity of 2900. It had a contracting ceiling to make the place cosy at just over 2000. But one feature was scary for actors. The only way to get on stage from our dressing rooms was by two lifts. One had to stay in the wings for the whole performance when you weren't on stage. Like the Greek Theatre in LA, playing *Hay Fever* was a daunting experience. Laughs took so long to reach us that it became impossible to time anything. Even half full it felt empty, as our connection with the audience was on a thread.

We went by air to Oklahoma City, then on by coach to Boulder, Colorado, a town built on a more human scale; it had character and a charming old hall more suitable for our plays. This was where I first threw a frisbee. I thought it was a recent invention as it was unknown in UK and Australia but its history went back a century. The origin was found in 1870. A baker in Connecticut, William Frisbie, came up with a marketing idea for selling his pies in re-usable light tin pans, by putting his name on the base. In the 1940s students at Yale University began throwing the pie tins, base up, to each other and throwing them back.

Fort Collins, Colorado, was the first of only two times I have ever smoked pot. We were billeted in a dormitory on campus and found ourselves among very friendly students. After the show two girls took Stephen Moore and me to the Spider's Web, a folk/hippie coffee lounge. We were then lured by a hippie couple to their lair where funny looking cigarettes were passed around. Although I smoked in those days it affected me badly. I had a monumental hangover, not good for tackling another vast auditorium the next day in Denver. At least we found a more intimate and European atmosphere in the gas-lamp part of town. The fall was beginning to make way with the first signs of winter. That night it snowed.

Kansas City was full of young American farmers wearing blue jumpers. In Liberty, Missouri, fleshy, young waitresses entertained us at the Pink Pussy nightclub. Southwest Missouri State College in Springfield was noted for not expecting us but throwing a great party after the show. A dark-haired girl from Birmingham in the UK was very excited by our visit and became enamoured with Michael Malnick. Being a gentleman he restrained his natural impulse, which came out in extreme twitching of his gammy leg. There were many incidents where young female students would be very forward when meeting us. I received many exclaimed remarks like: 'Oh my god, you look like Prince Charles' and 'I just love your English accent'.

It seems such an anachronism how intensely in awe of British monarchy so many Americans are. Could the worshipping of a seemingly higher or rarefied being be the simple answer?

We were now in the third week of October and on our way by air via St Louis and Peoria to Chicago. It was turning out to be a long, tiring, zigzagging tour but we were all looking forward to our week in this mighty city. However, it did not start well. Although there was some excitement in finding ourselves near where the rioting took place during the Democratic Convention, the Lincoln Park Hotel was not what it seemed. Not only was it seedy but we were told a nurse had been murdered in her room two weeks before. It was rumoured the Mafia owned it. After two nights we were moved to the Pick

Congress hotel, only to be told that a businessman had been murdered in his room only a few weeks before. As Mary Kerridge said at the time, which was worthy of a line from Maggie Smith in *Downton Abbey*, 'At least he died in comfort'.

After the first night we were invited to meet the cast of The Second City. They performed late shows of improvised satirical sketches in a downtown theatre. The *Laugh-In* show came out of this company. They were a very lively and amusing group and we got very involved with them. After their show we would retire to the Oxford pub, made famous during the riots for being used as a medical centre, and would be asked to leave at 4.00 am. 'Hey Jude' was the song at the time which brings back those few heady days or rather nights.

On a night we had off we were able to see their main show first, which was improvised but in a firm structure. Then in their late show which was totally improvised they invited us to join them. I was too scared but Stephen went up and gave a very good account of himself improvising the part of a butler in a sketch on Sherlock Holmes. The ideas for these late night shows came from the audience. They were a brilliant bunch of performers but then improvisation is more central to American actors' training.

On another night after the show we all went to Skelly's nightclub to take in a brilliant stand up comic. Mort Sahl was more than just a comedian. He was a radical commentator, noted for his fierce political satire. His style was to hold a newspaper and crack scathing but wise comments about current events and politics from the various articles. He eventually lost popularity, even with the liberal left, by exposing the lies. People do not care for too much truth.

This week in Chicago was perfectly rounded off for me when a local girl I had met took me to the Art Institute of Chicago. One American painting stood out for me: Edward Hopper's *Nighthawks*. There is no doubt seeing the originals makes a huge difference to your appreciation. They are alive. Leaving the gallery I wandered down to the great lake and gazed in awe at the man-made beauty of the Chicago skyline, as the sun was setting behind the skyscrapers.

Quite a few towns and cities are mentioned in American pop songs. We all remembered Glen Miller's song 'I Got a Girl in Kalamazoo' when we got to the town of the same name. We met a bevy of young ladies after the show in yet another new auditorium. However, we all behaved impeccably, so we couldn't genuinely change a particular word when singing it on the coach as we were leaving.

Sweet Briar in Virginia was an exclusive girls school of 700 students set in magnificent surroundings. It was patrolled by dozens of Pinkerton detectives. We were sure they were there not only to look after their safety but also to maintain their chastity. We spent a polite and early evening playing records.

On arriving at Richmond, Indiana airport, we were met by a bevy of Earlham College students and transported in their cars. We performed at the strangely named True Blood Field House in a gymnasium seating about 1500. Unlike Sweet Briar College in Virginia with their Pinkerton detectives, there was a surprising amount of freedom for the students, even though Earlham was a co-ed Quaker College. It was founded in 1847 and noted for being the most internationally diverse liberal arts college where everyone called each other by their first names. Most students lived on campus in Friendship Halls, so it was not surprising they were able to throw a pretty wild party after the show.

There was a mad moment of excitement when a group of about ten of us raced out into the fields to go riding. Stephen Moore and I managed to mount the only two white gelding horses (the college is noted for its unique Equestrian Program run entirely by the students). We ended up at two o'clock in the morning under bright moonlight on a hot night, riding bareback each with a girl behind us. This wild romantic experience was somewhat blighted by my falling over a sewage pipe while walking back.

We only spent one day and night on the campus of John Carroll University in Cleveland, Ohio. I was very glad to have at least some time there as I was able to catch up with my godmother. Bunch Anding had been a friend of my father's in India. Some years after her husband died she met Cleveland's William A. Feather, an elderly author and publishing millionaire whom she went to work for. Bunch was a very attractive lady, well into her later years, and spoke in that lovely lilting Hindi accent. She had been very supportive of my wanting to be an actor and was delighted to see me touring in what seemed like the Queen's theatre company. Bunch was of a snobbish nature and would exaggerate my achievements. Towards the end of her life I visited her in a nursing home where she proudly announced me as the Director General of the BBC.

Now for Louisville, Kentucky, where a company party in one of our hotel rooms began in the style of a London cocktail party but slowly degenerated into a scene more from *La Dolce Vita* with a touch of Tarantino. Very rarely does a large touring company get together on their own. This was the only time and probably just as well.

It began sedately with our leader John Counsell giving a pat-on-the-back speech, and saying there was still a good chance of extending the tour and playing in Washington. Eventually the seniors and goodies filtered away, leaving nine of us to play out the night. We had begun to play charades, the game played in *Hay Fever*. Richard and Peter (the unrelated Gales throwing the party) had made a wicked cocktail.

Somehow the game became strip charades. People were losing their clothes rapidly. Shirley Cain had been defrocked and most were in their underwear. The Tarantino trouble started when Richard removed Dale Parkinson's shirt. Our company manager was well and truly intoxicated. From the depths of what in hindsight was a feeling of shame or inferiority, he smashed a bottle and with the jagged ends threatened Richard's face. He stormed out screaming 'who do you think you are?' (a good name for an ancestry programme). According to one of the early leavers, poor Dale went to his room declaring he had cut Rick's throat, and left saying 'look after the company money, Steve and the boys are after me'. It sounds like a line from a movie and probably is.

The most memorable part of our visit to Indianapolis was going back to see the girls at Earlham College Richmond where we had ridden white horses in the moonlight. Four of us hired a car. It turned out to be a magical day as this account from my diary shows:

> It snowed most of the afternoon while we watched the 1st eleven soccer team playing. Really felt like home. Grounds were beautiful – tall yellow/brown trees all around. Forbes, a big jolly girl, cooked a stew and baked some bread and we all sat round a chest in their tiny sitting room lit by candles. Four of us went to see the film *Juliet and the Spirits* and returned to a folk singing party from which we left at 2.30 am.

That was a very typical social scene in those days and much needed downtime for travelling players.

During our visit to Atlanta we had the strange experience of wandering through the leaf-covered undulations that were the trenches from the American Civil War. Continuing in *Gone with the Wind* country we were able to visit Boone Hall outside Charleston, South Carolina. It was an eerie feeling driving down the long avenue of oak trees that is the entrance. Their moss-draped branches had joined together forming what seemed like a great shroud; apposite on learning they covered the living quarters of the black slaves.

Then I saw her standing in front of the porticoed mansion – Scarlett O'Hara declaring she would never be poor again. Except she didn't declare it there, nor was the film shot there.

There were times when we were allowed to stay over from where we had just played if our play out was first up in the next city. Michael Malnik and I stayed over in Atlanta. The coach took the cast for *Mrs Warren's Profession* to Cedar Falls, Iowa. The management agreed we could travel the next day by hire car but to arrive in plenty of time for a performance of *The Beaux' Stratagem*.

We set off at about 1.00 pm as we reckoned it would take between three and four hours to drive from Atlanta to Cedar Falls. What we hadn't taken into account was missing exits on freeways and driving rain. We were cruising for a couple of hours then the rain hit us. Wipers were going frantically but not clearing sufficiently to enable us to see two turn offs. By 5.00 pm we were still well over a hundred kilometres out and desperately looking out for a phone booth: no mobiles in those days. Anxiety was mounting to panic; poor Michael's gammy leg was becoming uncontrollable. We were still on the road at 7.00 pm but we managed to get a call through to the theatre. Our half-hour call was 7.25 pm for an 8.00 pm performance. We were in town by twenty minutes to eight but it took us another 10 minutes to find the theatre. There was great relief when we appeared, except on the part of the wardrobe master. He was most put out. He was to go on in my costume and read my part of Squire Sullen. The atmosphere after the performance was to say the least tense. John Counsell's face got redder as his anger mounted. We had committed a heinous professional crime.

The final part of this thespian trek took us through Greensboro, North Carolina, and Indiana, Pennsylvania, up to Burlington, Vermont, in the heart of the snow country. Then a few days in New Haven, Connecticut, home to

Yale University. Stephen Moore and I left New Haven earlier than some of the others and were able to spend the last six days of the tour in New York.

It was a magical time. I did everything a tourist is supposed to do. We were booked into the Wellington Hotel on the corner of 7th and 55th streets in the heart of Manhattan. Times Square was just down the road, Central Park was two blocks away, the Museum of Modern Art and the Rockefeller Centre were a stone's throw and 7th street ran parallel to Broadway only two blocks away. Felt fearful viewing the forest of skyscrapers from the top of the Empire State Building. Felt calming and more real watching the skaters on the Central Park ice rink, with the skyscrapers as a mighty backdrop.

As Christmas was approaching, the Rockefeller Centre had a huge Christmas tree sparkling with fairy lights as a backdrop to its ice rink. Then magically on the Saturday it snowed, making the roads and sidewalks treacherous. I slid past Tiffany's on my way to a theatre, one of five shows in that week. The musical *Hair* had just opened; we were rapt by its boldness. I think it was the first time I had ever seen actors naked on stage. It was wild and thrilling, breaking most of the rules of musical theatre.

At the Alvin Theatre on Broadway we sat in a box seat near the stage and witnessed a brilliant performance by a black newcomer. A young James Earl Jones was starring in *The Great White Hope*, an Arena Stage production from Washington DC.

One of the most lingering memories for me was sitting at the bar where Dylan Thomas used to drink. I sat in the very same spot where he may have had his last drink, in the White Horse Tavern.

Our final curtain closed in Bayside Long Island a few days before leaving. Our coach to Kennedy Airport left at 5.00 pm. Stephen Moore and I only just caught it having rushed from the matinee of *Hair*. The lit-up skyline of Manhattan was breathtaking as we crossed the bridge, the final backdrop to our American dream. It was as if we had ourselves been actors in a bigger play.

Our final journey was sleepless and jolly, of course. Then, from the skiing slopes of Vermont, I was soon looking out on snow again, this time from a bedroom window in Barnet. It doesn't quite have the same ring.

18

Back at Base Camp and Back in Rep

Coming home felt like total exhaustion after climbing a mountain. Statistics tell the story: we had travelled 39,000 km, played 104 performances in 45 university and civic theatres, mostly by coach and averaging 700 to 800 km between stopovers.

There are rare times when you hope the phone doesn't ring and you can drop out for a while. When visiting my agent the day after returning, his first words as I entered the room were:

'Do you want to go to Farnham Rep? Nine weeks doing three plays.'

'Give me a break,' I said.

'They want to know straight away. You start rehearsals on 3 January.'

So with only two weeks rest I picked up the rope to grapple with the new words of Goldoni's *The Artful Widow* playing Milord. The bonus with work in Farnham: I could stay with my very good friends Lesley and Gary O'Brien, the couple who picked me up at Tilbury Docks. In many ways little seems to change when you return to England. Lesley has been living in her quaint, cottage-like house for almost 50 years. The only thing she has changed is the husband: now married to Bill Whymper, a fellow actor.

Performing a play every two weeks was certainly better than the bad old days of weekly rep. In his autobiography *Arguments with England* Michael Blakemore has written an agonising account of his experiences in weekly rep during the 1950s. He felt compelled to leave Australia to pursue a life in the theatre, inspired, as I was, by Laurence Olivier and armed with connections from Robert Morley. There were similarities in our early acting experiences but Blakemore went on to become a brilliant theatre director and one of the best writers on the theatre. He took the path through the major companies. I chose the smaller companies. 'What if?' has been a timeless self-inflicted question, which can be entertaining but in the end is pointless.

The Castle Theatre in Farnham was a 16th-century converted farmhouse seating 167, a far cry from the vast auditoriums of America. It was situated in the shadow of Farnham Castle that overlooked a charming market town dating back to the Norman Conquest. Evidence was found to suggest that some form of professional theatre had been conducted in the castle since the 7th century. Mummers were summoned by the Bishop of Winchester to perform for the Royal Court.

The converted farmhouse was opened as a theatre in 1939 and with it came a ghost story. The story was that of Jolly Jack Tar. After sailing the seven seas in the navy he returned to marry his beloved to find her married to another. It is said he hanged himself in the barn building. Black cats and ghosts have often been part of the tradition in old theatres. I was also told of an eerie incident that happened in Farnham during the Battle of Britain. The wife of a pilot was walking her dog, happened to glance up a side road and saw at the top of the road her husband pausing and walking on. Apparently at that precise moment he was shot down and killed.

A network of high-class repertory companies had emerged during the 1960s. This was propelled by an explosion of exciting new playwriting, which was heralded by John Osborne's *Look Back in Anger*. These new plays (some were called 'kitchen sink' drama) would be mixed in with the classics and the pot-boiling whodunits and farces. It was something of an improvement on the shallow, class-ridden plays of the 1950s and producers giving equally shallow directions such as 'quicker darlings – eyes and teeth'.

The terms 'producer' and 'director' changed during the 1960s. A producer became known as the arranger and money man for movies and big shows. The director became entirely associated with the actors and the creative process. Haranguing, bullying producers made way for directors who cultivated performances. They exercised interpretation of the text and broke away where possible from the box set: the traditionally painted scenery on flats. Caroline Smith at the Castle Theatre was exactly that kind of director and her choice of plays typified this new breed.

While performing the Goldoni play about sophisticated Italians, we began rehearsals for *The Daughter-in-Law* by D.H. Lawrence about a pit-mining

family in the Derbyshire coal fields. This was followed by Shakespeare's
Taming of the Shrew in which I would play Lucentio. Being cast as Luther in
The Daughter-in-Law, the pit-mining husband in a working-class family, was a
breakthrough for me. On the surface this was casting against type coming as I
did from a soft, middle-class background, but Caroline felt I could be stretched
to become convincing. I spent what time I could listening to the Derbyshire
accent in the BBC oral library. I had in my mind that proud pit-mining father
of my landlady in Newcastle upon Tyne. Within the limited time – at least I
had two weeks not one – I prepared using Stanislavsky's tenets, building his
life outside the text. I received good notices for the performance but I was
enormously helped by a moving performance from Christine Welch playing
the wife.

During the two weeks performing *Taming of the Shrew*, a group of us from
the cast prepared the structure of an improvisation based on a day in the life
of Elizabethan England. We toured this through the local schools involving all
the students improvising incidents in a market place. This kind of interactive
performance was very much ahead of its time. It was still early days in the
gradual break away from text-driven plays.

I was looking forward to a break. I had been in constant work since
February 1968. But I could hardly refuse a return to Theatre Royal Windsor
while still based in Farnham. It was a pleasant journey through Windsor Great
Park having purchased a reliable chariot with my savings from the tour: a 1961
VW Beetle for £250.

It was, however, a play out of the old repertoire and often done in weekly
rep. *French Without Tears* was a classic comedy of its kind, written by Terence
Rattigan. We had great fun in rehearsals with our frightfully toffy director
Joan Riley. She had a cut-glass accent and swore like a trooper. Her directions
were sprinkled with the 'f' and 'c' words. But the way she spoke them didn't
sound rude or ugly. Appropriately in the cast was Jeremy Child (*Judge John
Deed*), an Old Etonian and a Lord, with Timothy Carlton Cumberbatch, an
Old Harrovian whose mother was a Bowes Lyon. He and Wanda Wentham are
Benedict Cumberbatch's parents.

There has been some disquiet in the profession concerning the perceived
advantage of actors coming from the elite schools. Eddie Redmayne and

Damien Lewis from Eton and Benedict from Harrow received barbed criticism from the political left in 2015. The same was being muttered in the 1960s. The point the critics miss is that whatever school they went to they would have been successful. It is called natural talent. So much of British drama is based on class conflict. You couldn't have Bob Hoskins or Dennis Waterman play King George VI with a stutter. Equally, you wouldn't expect to see any of the above actors play working-class types. Michael Caine only just got away with playing an officer in *Zulu*.

During the run of the play Timothy invited me to rent a room in his house in Barnes. It was an attached town house with a garden in a very cosy part of London. Barnes was like a country village centred on a pub and a pond. It was popular with actors, artists and musicians. Opposite Timothy's house lived Julian Bream the classical guitarist, whom we often heard practicing. Dennis Waterman, with whom we often played darts in The Sun Inn, lived around the corner. I felt very much at home. I also took delight in watching Concorde fly over every afternoon.

Towards the end of rehearsals after I had moved to Barnes, the sin of being late happened. From Barnes it was a quick run out to Windsor via the Chiswick flyover and the M4. Timothy had left earlier and was fortunate to get through an incident on the flyover. He told our director Joan Riley that it was highly likely I would be late, due to a cow tied up to a railing just before the end of the flyover. It had wandered up from the field, which is still there. I duly arrived late to be greeted by Joan's clipped telling off: 'I suppose you are going to come up with a cock-and-bull story of being delayed by a cow!'. I had arrived breathless with my tutor from NIDA Tom Brown's words echoing in my ear: 'Now that Mr Pegge has arrived we shall commence rehearsals!'

I committed another unwritten theatrical transgression during the run. There is a scene in the play known as the India rubber scene and my character interrupts. I was playing chess with the well-known character actor Bruno Barnabe when over the tannoy came 'Ed, you're off' – meaning I had missed my cue to enter. Fortunately it was a scene that could be improvised; the audience never knew. 'Being off' is regarded as a theatrical crime.

This was a period of to-ing and fro-ing between Windsor and Farnham. I had a welcome break for a few weeks and went up to London for several commercials without success. Then, just as I was about to start rehearsal for *The Frogs* at Farnham, I had to turn down a lucrative commercial. That bloody Irishman Murphy and his law hovers around most actors' lives. But I was thrilled to be invited back to be in the classic Greek play by Aristophanes. I was to play Aeschylus, a harridan landlady in drag, a donkey and a corpse.

I soon discovered there was something else in the air on my return. I became very friendly with our director. It is not always a sound career move to get involved with female casting directors, agents or theatre directors. If you fall out it could affect future work. However, Caroline and I had a mutually pleasant involvement for about a year. Her family home was nearby. Her mother and sisters lived in a gracefully declining mansion but they also had a skiing chalet in Switzerland. It was my first time skiing, which was a somewhat humiliating experience. I gingerly slid from the top too soon and was swept aside by flying children. A lingering memory from this period would be getting a whiff of a Gauloise cigarette. Everyone seemed to smoke in those days. Even the great man gave his name to a brand – *Olivier*, which of course I smoked.

Farnham is not far from Guildford and divided by the Hog's Back. Despite that rural name it still has an air of gentility. Our audiences were predominantly upper-middle-class retirees and an increasing commuter population. I made an extraordinary connection after a matinee. I was introduced to an elderly couple who had lived in India. Colonel and Mrs Adey had lived in Poona and unbelievably had lived at the back of where my cousin Phyllis Smithwick lived with her doctor husband Harold. Apparently he had saved the life of one of their children. What is more they knew my father. I find those kind of chance meetings create a reassuring sense of belonging.

With only a short break I was back at Windsor in June rehearsing the play adaptation of *Wuthering Heights* playing Hindley, Cathy's drunken brother. There was an extraordinary connection to come out of this time spent in Windsor, after a terrible accident to a first cousin. Joan Ashby (nee Pegge) was killed but her husband Stuart survived. He spent many months in Heatherwood hospital near Ascot, not far from Windsor. During one of my visits I met one of his nurses who happened to be male and West Indian. To my astonishment he introduced himself as Lennox Cumberbatch. I was sharing a house with Timothy Carlton Cumberbatch.

Lennox told me his family two generations ago were slaves on a sugar plantation, that there was a custom with some West Indian families to take on the name of their English bosses. I mentioned this to Timothy who confirmed in a matter of fact way 'oh yes the Cumberbatches owned sugar plantations in the West Indies and some did take on our name'. Lennox had certainly moved on since those days.

Patrick de Courcey O'Grady, ex-public school and from a not-dissimilar background to Timothy, became a most unlikely saviour when needing part-time work in lean times. Patrick had thrown me in the river when I was 12 years old. He was still living with his wife Mary, who had been at school with my sister, near our old home. Patrick sounded frightfully posh but had taken up mowing lawns for the wealthy. He elevated his mowing into a full landscaping business and employed some very eccentric people from time to time, as well as providing work for friends of mine.

Landscaping gardens for a friend's business was an ideal part-time occupation. It was physical work in a variety of pleasant surroundings. I could come and go or be late if an interview came up. Apart from keeping fit and earning much-needed cash, it was endlessly amusing. I worked for Patrick on and off over a period of 25 years.

His two more regular assistants were like characters out of a play. Dick Bonham Carter was an expert on roses. He came from the same Irish gentry family as the actress Helena. He lived in a caravan. His custom was to travel in it to each job and stay overnight. He would often get asked to move on by Patrick's clients, being outside their houses, or by the police. He once inquired in a workman's café if they happened to have *pâté de foie gras* in a very loud, upper-crust voice. It was cringe-making.

The other character was Lord Addington. He was a genuine hereditary lord in the House of Lords but was found by Patrick living in a dosshouse in Sunbury. He came from an old family of landed gentry in Norfolk who had fallen on hard times. He had a brother who was mad. He lived in a car and looked like a Neanderthal with matted hair and burning eyes. Addington had had some kind of career in Rhodesia but respectability had passed him by.

Anecdotes about people met along the way are, I believe, important for the actor's reference library. It is the bread and butter for playwrights.

19

Family Connections

The summer of 1970 came with a warm secure feeling: three plays, two television dramas, five commercials and a radio series. With money in the bank I was off to spend a week with my cousin Marilyn's family in Ireland. The Smithwick family were a well-known brewing family in Kilkenny. Smithwick beer had been brewed on the site of the ancient monastery of Saint Francis Abbey for 300 years. John Smithwick began the family tradition in 1710 but finally Walter Smithwick had to sell to the Guinness family in 1965.

My father's brother Arthur Pegge eventually went to Rhodesia from India and his other brother Frank went to South Africa. Arthur's daughter Phyllis married Harold Smithwick. Harold had become a doctor and had gone to live in India where he met and married Phyllis and they lived behind the Adey family in Poona whom I met in Farnham. They then went to Rhodesia. He died soon after UDI was declared and Phyllis decided to move to London because Marilyn, their only child, was desperate to train for the stage. That was all she ever wanted to do, as it was for me.

A doubtful but interesting ancestral connection, which could have some bearing on our mutual compulsion to act, was discovered a few years after this first meeting. We both came from a far-flung colonial family with no immediate connections to the theatre. Marilyn was very sociable and had met Bridget Boland, a very well known screen writer, who had discovered something interesting about a possible ancestor of ours in a book about Charles II.

Catherine Pegge was an actress during the reign of Charles II and a friend of Nell Gwyn. Catherine came from Yeldersley Hall, Ashbourne in Derbyshire, the daughter of a Baronet Sir Thomas Pegge who had to flee England during the civil war. It is recorded that Catherine's liaison with the King began in

Bruges and she was possibly his first mistress. She had two children by him: Charles FitzCharles who was acknowledged as the 1st Earl of Plymouth, and a daughter Catherine. We discovered that Charles did marry but died aged 23 without issue. Catherine married Sir Edward Greene, had one female child who became a nun. Recent doubt has arisen about Catherine being an actress though she did know Nell Gwyn. There is, however, a genetic connection with Thomas Pegge's lineage.

In 2015 I visited the family seat. I had arranged to stay at Yeldersley Old Farm thinking it would be part of the stately home complex of Yeldersley Hall. I soon found out that our real family seat is a dairy farm and has been for 400 years. I could sniff it on approach. Sir Thomas' father would have been the original Squire Pegge (in a round hole). It is conjectured that Sir Thomas elevated himself to become ADC to King Charles. My story might have made an interesting *Who Do You Think You Are?* programme.

Staying at Kilcreene Lodge among the Smithwick family was a transporting experience. The Lodge was built circa 1690 and was rich in history. It wasn't a large mansion but had an expansive withdrawing room and a separate billiard-room-cum-library, with front and back stairs leading to the servants' quarters and lots of nooks and crannies. It was set in a casually picturesque garden with a lawn sweeping down to a lake fed by the nearby river Breagagh (try pronouncing that) and the obligatory croquet lawn. For many years it was renowned for being a retreat for the rich and famous. It was regularly visited by members of the Catholic aristocracy.

The incumbent Smithwicks of Kilcreene were Marilyn's uncle Walter, his wife Molly and their family, consisting of Peter, Paul, John, Anne and Judy. It was a home from home. I get a warm feeling every time I think of my stays there particularly over Christmas. Our names were frequently prefaced with 'cousin' in phrases like 'what will you be wanting to do today, cousin Edmund?' spoken with that gently cadenced warm Irish accent. We often spent the late evenings in the back kitchen from where Miss Quinlan ran the house. 'Quinny' was their faithful live-in housekeeper who kept a keen eye on our needs and behaviour. We sometimes caroused well into the night in her kitchen. If it went on too long or too loud there would be rap tap tap from the ceiling.

I have only just discovered that many years ago certain famous guests were doing similar things. It is reported that James Cagney and Tyrone Power, Hollywood stars of their generation with strong Irish connections, were guests. Peter and Paul remember watching Cagney dance on the parquet floor of the drawing room. Walter and Molly loved entertaining and being entertained.

Cousin Marilyn shone for a while as an actress but after marrying and having a daughter named Katharine, sadly she died in her 50s. I keep in touch with Katharine and I am glad to report there was no compulsion to be an actress. She is a school teacher: far more sensible.

20

Moving On

Living in England in the 1960s and '70s, gave a feeling that one was at the artistic epicentre of the world, especially in such a liberating climate where eccentricity was cherished. Great Britain was leading the way in fashion, music, literature, theatre and acting. It could be argued that we lived in a time that witnessed the greatest ever: actor, boxer and pop group – Laurence Olivier, Muhammad Ali and The Beatles. And our health was looked after by the National Health Scheme (NHS), much envied and admired by other countries.

What is more the summer of 1969 was one of the hottest. By the middle of October there had been no rain since August. Among the various jobs I had in this period was filming on a documentary to promote Great Britain. It was called *Sporting Britain* and took me on locations around outer London and North Wales. Career-wise it was poor compensation for failing to get a part in the filming of *The Battle of Britain* plus a part in a West End play starring Rex Harrison. But it was heaps better than being out of work.

It was a pleasant and easy job with no lines to learn. Petite Eve Mack and I were filmed doing leisure activities: country walking, canal cruising, angling and pony trekking. But there was one activity that freaked me out. In North Wales I was required to do a rock climbing sequence. The experience is graphically imprinted on my memory.

Three professionals were booked but one didn't turn up. This meant I had no stunt double, so I had to climb. They gave me the gear and we walked up to the base of the rock to begin. I glanced across the valley to the shrouded peak of Mount Snowdon and saw an uncanny sight. Much higher than our location was a train pulling itself up along a ridge of the mountain. It was a surreal silhouette that made me feel puny.

After giving me basic instructions the pro climbers went up first to belay the rope that I would be attached to. The cameras rolled and I climbed to about 40 feet.

'Cut! Ed, can you do that again for us.'

I glanced down and froze with fear.

'I'm stuck. I can't move.' I called out, as I looked down to the valley below.

I had climbed up close to a sheer rock face. It was alright going up but coming down ...! The pro climbers above kept reassuring me. I knew I was safe but I was stuck on a four-inch ledge. Every time I came down I had to swing my leg into space over a protruding ledge and try to find a foothold by feel. After three turns my muscles felt like jelly. I closed my eyes and hung from the rope. I heard a faint voice.

'Can you please come down now? That's a wrap.'

My listless body came to life and I descended gingerly. The ground underneath my feet was a most reassuring feeling. I do remember it being a frightening but exhilarating experience. Since then I am a slightly different person: even more scared of heights.

On the final day of filming my agent called to say the BBC director Mark Cullingham wanted me for a part in an episode of *Take Three Girls*. But the casting circumstances had a familiar ring. I was replacing another actor. What's more I was to play Steve, a gay bronzed Aussie. Again not type casting, I'm neither gay nor muscular, but it was the first of a few Australian roles I would play on television. The series was very popular at the time. It was about the lives of three girls in a London flat, of which I had firsthand experience. The girls were played by Lisa Goddard, Angela Down and Sue Jameson.

After a constant and lucrative period of work I was quite happy for not much to happen leading up to Christmas of 1969. I was picking up some radio drama work at the BBC and just getting into the voice-over market. There were in later days actors earning sizeable, regular annual incomes from just voice-over work. I worked with three of them: Patrick Allen, Ray Brooks and Robert Powell. My bread-and-butter work came from commercials and training films.

I have always enjoyed reading poetry aloud (probably because I like the sound of my own voice). An old school friend from St Paul's invited me to put together a poetry recital for a Service of Compline in an Anglican church in Kensington. I asked Libby Counsell from Theatre Royal Windsor and the American tour to join me. We chose appropriate poetry like Eliot's 'The Journey of the Magi'. Our offering was very well received and encouraged me to pursue this skill I had for oral performance; it would have far-reaching repercussions.

My interest in poetry was hugely stimulated by a female lodger in the Barnes house. Timothy had invited a lovely American female author to share. Judith Thurman came from New York and had attended the bluestocking Vassar College. Her love and knowledge of poetry was prodigious and she gave me the skill and confidence to deconstruct the text of poems for oral presentation. She became a well-known biographer, receiving high praise for her books on Isak Dinesen/Karen Blixen and Colette.

I had time now to pick up my rapier again. I had not fenced, except in the landscaping sense, since my days in Sydney. I was lucky enough to find a fencing master who had been the Professional World Sabre Champion. George Ganchev had fenced for Bulgaria in the Olympics, had turned professional and set up his piste in Queens Club, the elite tennis club in Baron's Court. He had a perfect physique for fencing with an ego to match. He was well aware of his presence in the world and talked of his ambition to get into movies. Then one day he disappeared having talked about going to America. I never heard from him but serendipity brought us together. Many years later I was driving a car down Sunset Boulevard, as one does, spending a few days in LA. I happened to look briefly to my right and at that precise moment there was George Ganchev striding along the sidewalk; fairly long odds for an encounter such as that. We caught up and he had indeed breached the walls of fortress Hollywood. He was a sword-fight arranger on movie sets and gave private fencing tuition. He did do a screen test to play James Bond but said they had trouble with his accent. Since then I was told that he had gone back to live in Bulgaria and attempted to become President. There was no end to the delusions of George Ganchev.

As usual I had kept going with commercials and landscaping up to March 1970. The residuals from the five commercials gave me a very good year financially. I received a cheque for £500 for the Gillette razor ad, and all you saw of me was my cheek. The average weekly wage in theatre was about

£40 per week. The aim when shooting a commercial was to try and not be featured full on. Even better was to be left on the cutting room floor and the accounting department not told. That happened on a British Rail ad I did that featured Jimmy Savile – more on him later.

As it turned out, 1970 would be my last year spent mostly performing seasons of plays in the rep system. I believe that by the end of the year I had made a subconscious decision not to get stuck in the world of the 'theatre'. Working every night six days a week meant you spent most of your time with fellow thespians. You had little time or opportunity to meet people outside the theatre, and you tended to become a myopic member of the 'luvvie' society: 'Oh darling, I've just given my Polonius at Bradford'. I lacked that devotion that Judi Dench and Simon Russell Beale have, which you need to noticeably succeed. I can honestly say I had no ambition to be a star or famous, only a little bit well known.

The Marlowe Theatre Canterbury beckoned with three plays. I would be playing Sandy Tyrell in *Hay Fever* for the third time, Orsino in *Twelfth Night* for the second time and Datchery in *The Mystery of Edwin Drood* for the second time; not exactly extending myself but I would be playing opposite my cousin Marilyn Smithwick in *Hay Fever*. There was not much more I could get out of playing the three roles again. Sandy Tyrrell is a stock two-dimensional character. However, with the part of Orsino I thought of playing the opening scene as though he was about to have a sexual climax. After all, I argued, he was a hot blooded Italian. In the opening speech of the play there is the line:

> *Enough! no more:*
> *'Tis not so sweet now, as it was before.*

I spoke the lines with that spent feeling after a climax. Our director David Riley was all for the traditional languid, lyrical approach. I think it came off as there was an amused audience response.

The Marlowe Theatre then was built as a cinema in the 1930s retro style in the middle of an open area called The Friars. It was not a theatre that you would expect to hold any past. But there was the story of an old stagehand who was killed falling from a ladder. It had been handed down that strange things had happened from time to time.

I was doubling the parts of Drood and Datchery again in *The Mystery of Edwin Drood*, the play adapted from Charles Dickens' last unfinished novel, which premiered at Ipswich in 1966. After the disappearance of Edwin Drood I appear as this older character Datchery who has been surmised by many theorists as being either Drood or Neville Landless in disguise. On the night of the dress rehearsal we didn't finish until nearly 2.00 am. David Riley, our director, had been watching from the dress circle. He was tired and completely immersed in the play. He came down to the green room where we had all gathered for notes. When he saw me he froze.

'I've just seen you passing me on the stairs to the dress circle.'

'David,' I said, 'I've been here all the time – since the end.'

He went white as a sheet saying he definitely passed a figure on the stairs. That is when we learnt that the theatre was haunted. Of course, there is a more logical explanation: David's consumed state of mind projected my image. I prefer the haunted story.

While I was on that pilgrimage to Canterbury earning a very basic salary, my bank balance was getting welcome injections. I had filmed five commercials early in the year and residuals were flowing in. Soon after that season at the Marlowe I was up in Manchester playing an Aussie soldier in an episode of *Family at War* for Granada Television. Playing the lead in that series was the Scottish actor Mark McManus, my old friend from Sydney. He had moved on, and much further on with the Taggart tag. We caught up for a drink once in the bar next to the Royal Court Theatre. Sadly that was the last time I saw him.

I took John Scales, my old school friend from Adelaide (his parents' house was where I held the party for Vivien Leigh), to a production at The Old Vic. He remembers to this day a dazzling display of acting. It was, of course, Laurence Olivier giving us his Shylock in *The Merchant of Venice*. This particular production was significant. During the run at The Old Vic he was beginning to lose his nerve remembering lines. I believe it was the last stage production he would be seen in. It was known in the theatre as 'drying' and has always been every actor's nightmare. It happened to me twice.

John also came along to watch me give an equally dazzling display of being a chauffeur-cum-business associate in an episode of *Troubleshooters.*

We were shooting my role picking up Patrick Allen, playing the guest lead, in a limousine on Marylebone Road. John was most amused when on 'action', I stalled the vehicle not once but several times. He said it was like watching a learner driver in Australia do 'kangaroo hopping'.

Troubleshooters was a very popular series in the 1960s and 70s. Geoffrey Keen, Robert Hardy, Philip Latham, Barry Foster and Australia's own Ray Barrett were the leads. Patrick Allen, the renowned voice-over artist, and I were the only guests on this episode. We found ourselves sitting around waiting while the regular cast bickered with the poor script editor as to the veracity of their dialogue. We often heard the line 'He would never say that'. They knew their roles so well that they could and often did improvise scenes. Cyril Coke was the director, a charming gentleman with a paternal air like a business executive. He cast me from looking through *Spotlight*, the actors' directory. This only happened a few times in my career. Hundreds of actors have a half page with a photo in this door-stopper book. There is no way an actor cannot be in it.

As an actor you are only one phone call away from something that can turn out to be different, exciting or career changing. In the summer of 1970 I received a call that was not the latter, but it was different. My friend Geoff Kenion, from the Nottingham Playhouse tour of Southeast Asia in 1966, had set up a rep company in Palma, Mallorca. He was planning for the latter part of the present season and asked if I would like to play Cliff the friend to Jimmy Porter in *Look Back in Anger*, and possibly be in two other plays. I wasn't too keen at first as Geoff was playing all the major roles. But with his work load running the company, he panicked at the enormous task of learning the lines, backed down and offered me Jimmy Porter plus the others he was going to play.

21

Rep in the Mediterranean

If you end up not going back into rep again, where better place to close the curtain on that part of your career than Mallorca. Geoff Kenion had set up London Mediterranean Productions to present plays during the tourist season. Our theatre was the Sala Mozart auditorium underneath the main stage of the Opera House on Paseo Maritimo in Palma. It was built and run by Marcos Ferragut and latterly by his son Raphael. Geoff had little trouble getting good actors to do the odd play. Harold Innocent, the wobbly moon-faced actor from Nottingham Playhouse days had come and gone in *Bell, Book and Candle*. *Look Back in Anger*, *Boeing Boeing* and *The Private Ear/The Public Eye* would complete the season. Our director was the immensely talented Jonathan Hardy, a New Zealander who had begun his career at the Mercury Theatre in Auckland.

Having learnt late that I was to play Jimmy Porter and not Cliff, I had little time to learn the words of this enormously long role. Jimmy rails against the world in long speeches, talking at everyone around him. It was a role I could identify with but it was two grinding weeks of rehearsal and much angst with learning the lines. I would have to wait to be embraced by the sweet air of the island.

I am often asked how I learn my lines. Unless you are blessed with a photographic memory, and very few are, you have to do it in some kind of rote fashion. Basically I take it in sections. In the early stages having learnt what a speech is about, you can stumble through it in your own words for the sense. But eventually you have to learn precisely what the author wrote, which means going over and over the lines. I use a piece of paper to hide what is coming next. Then if time is short I prevail on someone else to read the other parts, cutting to where my cue comes. It is an agonising and laborious task. And I have found that the quicker I have had to learn words, the quicker those words leave the memory box. Within a few weeks I could not remember a word that Jimmy Porter spoke. Most of the time I see the words on the page. The most frightening thing an actor can do, though it is necessary at the highest level, is to empty their mind of any conscious thought before their first entrance, and allow the character they are playing to speak. All actors walk the plank whenever they perform. I remember a director once saying to me: 'Walk off the stage, Ed. I will catch you.' In other words 'take flight'. But that does not mean acting in a vacuum. Learning cues and listening to what fellow actors are saying are imperatives. Re-acting appropriately is vital to make scenes seem real.

I certainly walked the plank playing Jimmy Porter. From all accounts I might have experienced something close to take off on the opening night. I came off stage and broke down with tears of relief from high tension. Jonathan had drilled me hard but given me such confidence that in a later performance I walked on top of the role. In other words I threw out the words as though they were confetti, revealing nothing of what lay behind the words. This occurred after several performances. He was furious and called a special rehearsal.

One other abiding and more pleasant memory occurred towards the end of our run. At one point in the play the audience hears Jimmy blowing plaintive notes on a trumpet. During two performances the Opera House was hosting a concert by the celebrated pianist Arthur Rubinstein. I was waiting to re-enter from a brief moment offstage and nearly missed my cue listening to the exquisite piano playing right above me. I saw him after the show: a diminutive, white-haired, pale-faced gentleman with expressive hands. I remember feeling second rate in the presence of such a great artist.

The opening night of *Look Back in Anger* seemed to go smoothly, though you could feel the audience being slow on the uptake. The play was perhaps a touch confronting for people in holiday mode. The next morning we began rehearsing *Boeing-Boeing*, a more appropriate play for the American and European packaged tours. The original was written by the French playwright Marc Camoletti with the English translation by Beverley Cross.

I played Bernard, a lothario architect living in Paris who is engaged to three air stewardesses. The play is set in his flat, chaos breaks out after his friend Robert arrives, flight times have changed and all three girls are in the flat at the same time. It is the classic farce which features a lot of opening and closing of doors. A relieving contrast to the Osborne play but no less taxing, as playing farce requires both physical and mental dexterity.

What was very different playing on the perimeter of Spain was that our evening performances had to start at 10.00 pm to fit in to the Spanish working day. We would begin the day's work with warming up exercises based on Tai Chi and Kendo. Rehearsals would go from 12.30 pm to 5.30 pm, then we had our main meal and a rest, did the performance at 10.00 pm after which we would restore our equilibrium in one of the many nightclubs and rarely get to bed before 3.00 am. It took a while to get used to a very different routine and it meant that we had less time to come down from the over-energised state actors are in after a performance, but we were all young and adaptable.

There wasn't much opportunity to socialise outside our group. We were interviewed by Ricky Lash, a local radio celebrity, and met a few locals. But we were fortunate to meet and be entertained by the most celebrated resident of Mallorca.

For almost 30 years Robert Graves had been living in Deya, nestled in the hills west of Palma. He was one of the great literary figures of the 20th century: a world authority on Greek mythology, he wrote one of the seminal accounts of the First World War in the novel *Goodbye to All That* and became more widely known through the BBC television adaptation of his Roman novel *I Claudius.*

Robert and his wife Beryl had come to the opening night and after the show invited the whole company to spend the day at Canellus, their home in Deya. Cradled in a mountain range, Deya was a hauntingly beautiful village where many artists lived.

On arrival in Deya we were greeted by Beryl and her samovar. Tea was always on the go, facilitating easy conversation. It was a lively gathering with about eight of us as well as their family. They were the most wonderful hosts. It turned out for me to be one of the most stimulating days I have ever spent. We were in the presence of a great man of letters. Robert Graves with his white hair and patrician features looked like a Roman emperor. What charisma. He held us in thrall with his erudition and curiosity, but what stood out was his humility. He was genuinely interested in what we all had to say and the road we were travelling. Whenever the conversation ran into foggy territory, Robert would leap to the bookshelf to nail what we were guessing at. I have found that people who are remarkable, highly talented and successful are invariably easy mannered and humble. He would be so excited telling us the stories behind some of the objects he had collected on his travels.

The day was long and rarefied. The conversation during that evening came round to poetry. Robert asked me if I had ever written a poem that I was proud of, I said only one. He asked why only one. I replied because I had to: it flowed from my pen, without me changing anything. He asked to read it, so I left a written copy, having declined to speak it (God knows why, being an actor). A few days later I received a letter from him. He was curious to know what drove me to write this poem with such compulsion and asked me to forgive his impertinence but he felt it needed to be filled out, and so he had enclosed his version.

The two poems are as follows:

'Hollow Shoes'

by Edmund Pegge

I walked in hollow shoes
My heart hung loosely by my side
Down the ghostly neoned street
There was nothing in my mind

Only my thudding feet booming off dead walls
A newspaper nudged by the silent wind
Follows my shadow as it crawls.

(written in a country town in South Australia 1960)

'Hollow Shoes'

by Robert Graves

In hollow shoes long before dawn
My heart swung loosely at my side

I know no more a chill and glaring street
For I have nothing left to hide.

And though this thud of hollow shoes
Comes booming back from high dead walls,
A newspaper nudged by the wind
Sneers at the pace my shadow crawls.

Whose was the fault, poor strangled heart,
That hung you here in a black bag?
Who hurled me from that bed of beds?
Why should those shoes clatter and drag?

(Deya 11 November 1970)

At the end of Robert's letter he threw out a challenge to decide whose poem it was, no doubt enjoying the Greek idea of weighing up the words. I took up his challenge to toss for it, which we did by the statue of a Greek poet in the foyer of the theatre. I won and he declared that he would never publish his version. His letter has been my treasured possession.

There has, however, been a very recent follow-up to this story. Robert never did publish his version and it had left a curious blank in his papers. In 2011 I was visiting my very good friends Adrian and Rita Moore who live in Battersea and met one of their neighbours. We happened to be talking about poetry and somehow Mallorca was mentioned and I told the story of my poem. It turned out that this lady's brother was Professor Dunstan Ward, a don at Oxford who happened to be a recent President of the Robert Graves society. After Robert's version was sent to him, I heard that a puzzle had been solved. They had found in his papers scribbles and references about a poem called 'Hollow Shoes' with my name attached but no copy of the poem that he wrote. He was a man of his word. I duly sent a scan of the letter he wrote as I had the only copy of that poem.

The mini saga of a lost Graves poem was finally put to bed when I visited Deya in September of 2011. I went to the house, now a museum. Standing in that room where we had been entertained, a strange remote feeling came over me. I could hear the laughter and smell the samovar but it was far away. I was able to speak to Robert's son William while visiting. He had been there at our original visit and delighted to learn that this had been resolved. He now has a copy of the letter and the poem.

Private Ear/Public Eye was our next production, written by another occasional resident of Mallorca, Peter Shaffer of *Equus* fame, whom we didn't meet. All three plays were well received but there was never a full house. The financial support promised by the Lions Club failed to materialise and Geoff eventually had to scuttle the enterprise.

For me it was one of the most rewarding and enjoyable work periods in theatre. We were a company of actors performing different roles with a director who knew how to get the best out of us in exotic surroundings. An added bonus was access to one of the world's leading singing teachers. Margaretta Kraus had retired to Mallorca. Jonathan knew her in Sydney and was able to persuade her to give some of us lessons. My speaking voice greatly improved with a greater vocal range and a richer tone. More than anything else, however, I think I learnt about my limitations as an actor. I found it difficult to maintain energy and concentration playing such a large part as Jimmy Porter. Maybe it was due mostly to the short period of rehearsal. But the remark that my drama coach Tom Brown made at NIDA that he thought my acting was shallow came back to haunt me; that although I had the attributes to be a leading actor maybe I lacked the mental and emotional capacity. I think the credits in my career indicate this.

On my way to the airport, after my brief visit in 2011, I called in at the Opera House, now mostly taken over by seminars, lectures and film shows. After looking around I tried to find the statue where Robert and I had tossed for ownership of my poem but no trace could be found. I was sitting having a coffee in exactly the same cafe as in those days, when I saw a grey-haired gentleman walking towards me from the theatre. He had been told someone was looking for a statue. Marcos Ferragut introduced himself to me. He had been the prime mover in creating the theatre, now run by his son. It was 41 years ago when we were there, but he remembered very well.

*My father, Cyril Cuthbert Colbeck
Pegge, born Ahmedabad, India, in
1883, died Old Windsor,
England, 1952*

*My mother, Evelyn Hill Birch, born
Perth, Western Australia, 1899, died
Adelaide, South Australia, 1998*

*My parents and their retainers in India,
circa 1929. My father worked for the Indian
Imperial Police Force in the 1920s*

*With my parents in the garden of our
house in Old Windsor, 1951*

Scrawny me (far left) aged 10 with my friends at Upton School near Slough, 1949

Already clowning around, with a friend in Old Windsor, 1950

Julian Rees (left) as Luiz and me playing Casilda in a St Paul's production of The Gondoliers, *1953*

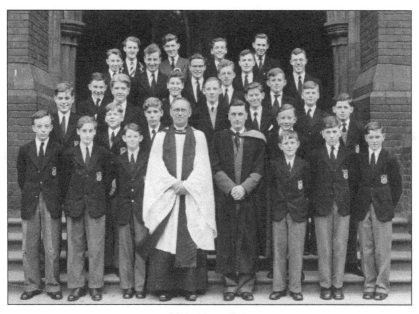

St Paul's School choir with Reverend Chris Heath and Ivor Davis, 1952

*Maggie Barr, our movement
teacher at NIDA, circa 1960*

*Doug Craig (Laertes), me (Horatio) and Alan
Hannam (Hamlet) in the Adelaide University
Footlights Club production of* Hamlet, *1958*

My first Young Elizabethan Players tour with (left to right) Mark McManus,
Peter Couchman, unknown, Janice Dinnen, Doreen Warburton and
Tony Gould, 1962

School fans, Young Elizabethan Players tour of NSW, 1963

Young Elizabethan Players tour of NSW with (back, left to right)
John Maxim, me, Andrew McLennan, Geoff Rothwell, Alan Lander,
(front) Alison Bauldt, David Capstick and Lyn Wright, 1963

Playing Lieutenant Dawes to Rick Hutton's Captain Tench in the
ABC's Prelude to Harvest, *1962*

As Paul in the ABC's My Three Angels *with Anna Volska, 1964*

As Ferdinand in the ABC's The Tempest *with Joan Morrow (Miranda) and Max Oldaker (Prospero), 1963*

The ABC's My Three Angels, *with (left to right) Laurie Langer, me, Owen Wiengot, Murray Rose, Dickie Davis and Gordon Chater, 1964*

As Horner in The Country Wife *at Ipswich Repertory Company, 1965*

As Verges in Much Ado About Nothing *for the Newcastle Playhouse Company, 1967*

As Joey in The Homecoming, *Newcastle Playhouse, with (left to right) Geoffrey Beevers, Andrew Dallmeyer and Harold Innocent, 1967*

In Ye Wor a Canny Fella Will, *Newcastle Playhouse, with (left to right) Trevor Martin, Terence Tapley, me and Andrew Dallmeyer, 1967*

In Hay Fever, *Theatre Royal, prior to the American tour, with (left to right) Michael Malnik, Linda Marlowe, Jenny Counsell, me, Mary Kerridge, John Counsell, Shirley Caine and Peter Gale, 1968*

22

Waiting for the Phone to Ring

One should not try to save money flying on cheap charter flights. The flight from Mallorca was delayed six hours. I arrived at the Finchley Road terminal at 4.00 am on a cold November morning. I was amazed when I found my flatmate Judith Thurman waiting for me. She suggested we have breakfast at Billingsgate fish market and then walk along the Thames Embankment to Tower Bridge. I was truly back in London in the midst of its timeless bustling atmosphere and familiar smells.

It was the beginning of the 1970s and the fashion was still tight crutches and thighs in flared trousers. I had a groovy outfit made in Mallorca, light brown suede leather trousers and jacket, and a pair of high boots made of soft Spanish leather. I completed the outfit with a visit to Mr Fish, the patterned shirt and tie shop in Beauchamp Place. With long hair and a Viva Zapata moustache I looked the part of a Kings Road/Carnaby Street poseur.

The old saying 'changing agents is like changing deck chairs on the Titanic' is mostly true. It can give the career a fillip but unless you are with one of the major agents, it is unlikely that you can crack the big time. I was briefly being considered by Chartwell Artists, a large American agency that handled the likes of Richard Burton. I did, however, eventually join a new agency called Marklew and Hunt. It was necessary as I wanted to move more into the television/film world and they were two young men keen to succeed with wide contacts.

It is one thing getting interviews for roles in television drama, another getting the part. I went up for a substantial part in the police series *Softly Softly*, then for a good part in a new television series starring Tony Curtis and Roger Moore called *The Persuaders*, then met an American producer at

Pinewood studios and read for a part in another new television series starring Shirley McLean. None worked out, though some compensation came from being offered a smaller part in *The Persuaders*. It was only two days playing an arresting cop but it was great fun working with Curtis and Moore, who was yet to play Bond. They were both absolutely charming and helpful and doing that job has paid little bits ever since. In fact I have only recently received in April 2013 a series of payments for overseas sales of the series, which added up to the princely sum of £4.

Apparently, residuals are based on how many television sets in each country the series is sold to. I once had a payment for two pence, which must have been for a castaway on a desert island. Each actor gets a proportion according to their original fee. Those who had ongoing parts in series like *Dr Who* and *The Bill* would hardly need to work again. However, doing what I call consolation parts has probably not been good for building up the career. One should hang out for better offers, but you have to eat and you could die waiting in the wings.

My next brush with a star was rather sad. I was cast in a sketch on a Frankie Howerd show at Thames Television. Having rehearsed a scene with the lugubriously camp Frankie Howerd, I found him hovering over me in the canteen. He asked me if I would like to have a drink with him in his dressing room. I remember being apprehensive but I was probably flattered and went down. As soon as I entered his dressing room he tried to put his arms around me. I gently removed them and assured him I was not inclined that way, which he accepted. He then told me the sad story of his life of which I remember nothing. It was a firsthand experience of 'the loneliness of the long-distance clown'.

So many like Frankie and Tony Hancock suffered hyper anxiety and manic depression. Most straight actors live within the parameters of their psyche. Comics live in a world full of bubbles. They have to keep blowing them with their jokes and frenetic energy.

I have always thought it most important for actors to have outside interests that are nothing to do with acting. Mine were landscape gardening and sport. I played soccer, cricket, golf and fencing. Many famous actors were members of the Stage Golfing Society. I was once asked to move on by an irascible Sean

Connery at Wentworth. Our HQ is at Richmond Golf Club and on most days of the week you will find a chatter of actors looking for a game. This is due to that simple and fairly constant out-of-work statistic. Over a period of three-and-a-half months I did two jobs: a hand commercial for Nescafé and standing in the rain outside Westminster Abbey in a commercial for women's tights. 'Mock not' as Frankie Howerd would say. Then suddenly the drought breaks and you get jobs on top of each other.

I did a sound recording of a Sherlock Holmes story playing the juvenile lead with Robert Hardy and Nigel Stock. I went up for parts at the BBC for *Troubleshooters* and *Paul Temple* and was offered both, which I couldn't do as dates clashed, so I chose Paul Temple – worth three times more. Also I would be directed by Lennie Mayne from Australia. But what was galling about this job was that it was another example of coming second. I would have got the guest lead had not John Gregg bounced into Len's office looking like Rod Laver. It was an episode based on an Australian tennis player. It was an ideal part for me as I am a reasonably good player. John must have lied about his ability because I ended up being his stand-in for the tennis shots. I had to play against Ken Fletcher (the Aussie professional) who was cast as himself. The difference in ability was immediately palpable. Ken was kind placing shots I could return.

I spent two days filming *The Protectors* starring Robert Vaughn (*The Man from U.N.C.L.E*) on a dis-used airfield. Robert Vaughn wasn't friendly. I never met him. He would retire to his caravan and eat on his own. After my first shooting day I was asked to stay on. I ended up never being used again over the next five days but was most grateful for the enormously increased fee.

Generally, 1971 was a bad year for many actors, so much so that a certain group were plotting to storm the West End theatres. It was more like a storm in a teacup. They were officially known as the Workers' Revolutionary Party. Vanessa Redgrave was the standard bearer. Actors would hang around outside the Labour Exchange in Chadwick Street listening to Tom Kempinski sprouting agitprop.

Part-time work and sport kept me from ever sniffing the 'black dog'. Many I knew suffered from depression. Hence alcoholism and drugs are professional hazards of the whole entertainment business.

I had been going out with Carol Cusimanos whom I met through my cousin Marilyn in her coming-and-going flat in Kensington. Carol was Belgium and a high-powered interpreter. Somehow she was interviewed for a magazine called *Romance* on what it was like to live with a 'beautiful man'. Now my friends reading this will be throwing up. I had no idea this was happening but I suppose looking as I did – the Kings Road poseur, with long hair and a Mr Fish shirt – maybe the point was not too stretched.

Injury in a game of soccer led me to my next affair. Di Broklehurst was the physiotherapist who treated me at St Stephen's Hospital, as it was then, in Fulham Road. We were together for the next five years.

Time limped towards Christmas of 1971. I had been up for several commercials with no luck. I remember there was one period during these years when I went up for 30 commercials without success, then I got the next three. Most of us agree the average is one out of ten interviews.

My first job in 1972 was a commercial, a tricky action sequence for car insurance. I had to drive a car to a mark on the narrowest part of Sutton High Street. The never-ending stream of traffic had to be held up by police every time I did a take. The camera was on the other side of the road beside a great arc lamp. There were hundreds of people watching, it was pouring with rain – on arriving at my mark I had to say some boring, difficult lines in exactly eight seconds. It took 15 takes to get it in the can, despite doing it perfectly on the third take, a barking dog making it unusable. The highlight was trying to reverse carefully up the street, half on the pavement to my mark. Because of the rain I could not see clearly out of the rear window and I very slowly but surely crunched into a lamp post, much to the delight of the crowd and great applause. Needless to say I did not get out of the car and bow. I sat behind the steering wheel frigid with embarrassment.

Then, for the first time, I landed an ongoing part in a television series taking seven weeks at the BBC studios in Birmingham. It was a children's television series called *Escape into Night* with a young girl playing the lead. I was playing the family doctor.

Actors often moan when they are in work: having to drive up to Birmingham – staying in musty, care-worn hotels with fading wallpaper, soft mattress and the smell of disinfectant – playing a boring part in a children's television series which nobody will watch and so on. At least out of it came more than one further job from the director Richard Bramall.

My new relationship was blossoming. Di's mother and stepfather lived in a haunted thatched cottage in the quaint village of Ebbesbourne Wake in Wiltshire. I was very lucky to have such an idyllic escape at weekends. I was all in love and sort of proposed to Di on the banks of the river Thames. Two months later we were talking of splitting up with her concerns over money and security. But then we had a wonderful holiday in a cottage in Galaxides on the west coast of Greece. The scent of thyme hung around us as we walked to the beach, which we had to ourselves. Boldly we swam naked. The local shepherd paid little attention but his sheep were curious. The local taverna where we ate every night was run by a gay couple from Melbourne.

There was a wonderful theatrical moment when we visited the ancient theatre of Delphi. I stood in the centre of the performing area. Di went to the top tier. I performed a monologue from Shakespeare. Di heard every word even though I was not declaiming. One night we were roughly awoken by a tremendous thunderstorm. The lightning was frightening and one could understand how easily the ancient Greeks could think that the Gods were angry.

On return I got a good theatre break: the part of Hercules in *The Fifth Labour of Hercules* by Friedrich Durrenmatt directed by Fredrick Proud at the Soho Poly. It was a tiny basement theatre off Regent Street run by his wife Verity Bargate and became a leading off-West End venue.

In the cast were Paul Freeman and David Leland, whom I had met at Nottingham Playhouse. Further on in his career David directed part of Spielberg's film *Band of Brothers*. *The Fifth Labour of Hercules* was most successful, receiving terrific notices from all the main critics. Michael Billington said of the production in *The Times*:

> I've nothing but praise for Fredrick Proud's wittingly, ingenious production and for an acting standard as high as anywhere on the Fringe with David Leland's accident prone Polybius, Edmund Pegge's musclebound Hercules and Juliet Aykroyd's memorably fetching Deinira taking the honours.

I really thought this would move my career along but alas nothing much came of it except another play. Thereafter I rode the 'dark night of the soul' wave.

There was a lot of self-analysis as to why I wasn't doing as well as I felt I should after such a promising start. In the letters I wrote there were these kind of comments: 'Don't worry, I'll achieve some degree of success eventually – a bad period was bound to happen – I'm at an awkward age and not easy to cast – a change of luck is all I need – too versatile for the screen – never had good photographs taken – face too mobile – it doesn't follow that you get work after a good performance in a leading role recognised by the critics in a popular off-West End theatre – nothing necessarily follows on in this business – perhaps I'm not ambitious enough, too lazy, not pushy – agent isn't working for me, need to change.' And that is what I did but the Hazel Malone Management were not into waving magic wands.

Now the idea of going back to Australia for a period of time began to take shape. Before the end of the year a couple of non-paying performances restored some faith. Jerome Willis gathered actor friends to present scenes from Shakespeare's *A Midsummer Night's Dream* which were parallel scenes to an oratorio performance of Purcell's *Faerie Queen* in St Margaret's Church, the chapel opposite Westminster Abbey. It was a gloriously uplifting thing to do. Then my friend David Pinner and I were invited to present a recital of poetry for the Francis Thompson Literary Society in Burgh House, Hampstead. I retrieved some belief in my ability after receiving compliments for my reading of Oscar Wilde's *Ballad of Reading Jail*. These occasional recitals were the beginnings of what would turn out to be another string to my bow.

During the summer of 1972 I joined a small group who had established exclusivity in being used as stand-ins and crowd control on *Top of the Pops*. There were about eight of us in this pool, which was comprised of actors, playwrights, a theatre director, drama teacher and an opera singer. Our job from 10.00 am was to stand in for the pop singers during camera rehearsals when they were late, which was frequent. In the evening during the taping of the show we would be crouching just in front of each camera brushing aside the dancing teeny boppers. We came across many big name pop singers: Suzi Quatro, Barry Manilow, Hot Chocolate, The Sweet, Ray Davis and The Kinks, Small Faces and The Jackson Five. This became a regular, rotational job every two weeks run by a Mr Castle at the BBC booking office. We received £15 plus a National Insurance stamp.

Probably the most significant aspect of this job has come about very recently. This roller coaster witch hunt to expose sex offenders and paedophiles finally caught Jimmy Savile, though too late to punish him. Everyone knew it was going on in the basement dressing rooms at the BBC Centre in White City. Not all disc jockeys were involved but Jimmy was certainly 'leader of the pack', closely followed by the notorious Gary Glitter, often on the show, whose hit song was called just that. Girls in their teens were besotted by pop stars. Jimmy would have suggested they come down to the dressing rooms after the show. Years later I would more closely witness his creepy behaviour.

After the taping of *Top of the Pops* we usually had a drink in the BBC bar. For an actor it was an ideal place to be seen. It was frequented by most BBC television directors. One night towards the end of 1972 I bumped into Bill Hays who had been a director at Newcastle Playhouse. He was in pre-production for a BBC 'Play of the Month'. I had joined him at the bar. He greeted me warmly and as he turned with his drinks he said, 'Get your agent to phone the production office in the morning. There'll be something we can find you.' That something was three small parts in a unique production of Brecht's play *The Caucasian Chalk Circle* over a five-week period starting in February 1973.

Before rehearsals began on *The Caucasian Chalk Circle,* I saw a riveting performance of *A Long Day's Journey into Night* directed by Michael Blakemore for the National Theatre at the Aldwych. The cast was led by Laurence Olivier with Constance Cummings, Denis Quilley and Ronald Pickup. It is interesting to reflect how well Olivier plays failure. Tyrone in *A Long Day's Journey* can't cope with being a failed actor and Archie Rice in *The Entertainer* can't see how bad he is. It was such a strong cast and with another mesmerising performance from Olivier, it is not surprising that the power of the play is still with me. There was one wonderfully apt piece of business by Olivier. He was up on a table changing a light bulb with plenty of dialogue about his acting ability and remarks from the family on how he hides his meanness. He alights from the table and bows to the family – ever the actor.

I doubt that a television adaptation of a Bertolt Brecht play had been done before outside Germany. What is more, the production style was faithful to Brecht's philosophy. The audience was aware that it was staged in a television studio. There were some well-known actors among the cast. John Thaw

(Morse), Robert Powell, Max Adrian, Sarah Kestleman, Bernard Hepton and the principal part of Azdac the judge was played by Leo McKern (Rumpole).

This was the time when I found out that Leo was one of few actors who have a photographic memory. At the end of the first read-through Leo was walking out of the rehearsal room when I saw he had left his script behind and called out. He casually said he didn't need it. I was told he knew his lines from just reading it.

Leo was a trickster. He would often do dreadful things with his glass eye. If he wanted to shock someone he would squeeze out his glass eye, pop it in his mouth and make out he had swallowed it. It was always difficult for actors playing opposite him to know which eye was the seeing one. He wouldn't help – a very Aussie sense of humour.

We had a tragic death early on in rehearsals when Max Adrian died suddenly. Max was the original Dr Pangloss in the Broadway production of *Candide* by Leonard Bernstein. This was the production for which our drama teacher at NIDA Tom Brown had been stage manager and, incidentally, for me one of the greatest musicals ever written. Max had been rehearsing the part of the narrator. This was taken over by Patrick Magee, a hard drinking, well-known Northern Irish actor with an Irish butter voice. He was very different from Max who was short, neat and tidy, very English, with a beautiful-sounding voice.

The production was high quality. There was one shot that took my breath away. The city is under siege, and the Governor and his wife hurriedly escape the city leaving behind their baby. It is found by the servant girl Grusha, played by Sara Kestleman, who nurtures it. Bill Hays, our director, had a cherry picker in the studio. There was a magical sequence done in one continuous take that lasted about five minutes. The camera began low on the baby and you see Grusha's hands lift it up. The camera very slowly follows Grusha's dilemma and movements that cover the whole night. Over this continuous shot which depicts a sunset and sunrise shown on the cyclorama, you hear the narrator's soft voice telling the story. There are very few long one-takes in any kind of filming. It is very difficult to get everything synchronised. It was one of those few tingling moments of beauty and truth.

However, the recording of the play was cut off due to the producer, Cedric

Messina, not allowing any further overtime. This caused an almighty row between the director and the producer, resulting in Bill never working for the BBC again. The recording only went to air once, unfinished, and in the end the tape was wiped.

Plans for returning to Australia were firming up. Di had gone to work in Canada and we agreed to meet up again in Sydney in October 1973. In the meantime I was sent to Coventry; not in the sense that people wouldn't speak to me. I was cast by Warren Jenkins who ran the Belgrade Theatre to play Hardy in *Bequest to the Nation* by Terence Rattigan, a play about Horatio Nelson, to be played by Charles Kay. Also in the cast were the soon-to-be-noticed young Robert Lindsay and Simon McCordindale.

The play is set over the few weeks before he set sails for Cadiz and the Battle of Trafalgar and his final hours on *Victory*. It mostly covers how he handles his affair with Emma Hamilton with his family and friends. It was a thoroughly English play exuding stoicism and 'Pomp and Circumstance'.

It seems this was not a happy period for me. I was standing still, over concerned about money rather than quality of work, wondering how I could sustain a relationship with a career that wasn't progressing. I had had several knockbacks for good parts. A leading casting director called Tony Arnell was always keen to get me work, but in the end never did. I was even knocked back by Ridley Scott who was directing a butter commercial. Despite many rejections I kept believing.

Supportive friends helped. During the summer of 1973, through my good friend and very successful actor Tom Georgeson, I met James and Emma Scott. I was invited to a house party at their place in the Cotswolds. Emma is now married to James Lamb and they have been so supportive in down times. Solid friends outside – but connected to – theatre and acting have been deeply important in my career. For now though it was farewell to the 'Scepter'd Isle'. It had gone a little septic for me.

Part 3

1973 to 1981

23

Into the Arms of Gough

What a difference a decade makes. It took six weeks to get to the UK from Australia by ship in 1965, compared with 30 hours by plane in 1973. England was in the middle of a political and cultural revolution. It took another eight years for a similar sea change to occur in Australia in 1972, after the Australian Labor Party finally wrested power from the entrenched Liberal Party. The new prime minister, Gough Whitlam, like many left-leaning politicians, was far more inclined to support the arts. He had a profound belief that Australia should tell the world its own stories. I arrived to find the film and television industries far more generously funded. It was the best time to return to Australia, not only because there were more work opportunities but there was a buzz in the air. Australians were beginning to shake off their cultural cringe. There was a new-found confidence in the Australian voice.

My first job within a week of arriving was playing a Scotsman, the offsider to Jack Thompson's leading role in a pilot for a new series to be called *Human Target* (not to be confused with the Hollywood series). Not a part I would have been offered in the UK.

There was considerable kudos in returning to Australia for a visit, providing you had had some overseas success. In the hands of the formidable Gloria Payten and her straight-talking assistant Philomena Moore at International Casting Services (ICS), I landed leads in three television dramas following *Human Target*. Two of them were for Crawford Productions.

Hector Crawford had created a production house that would become a breeding ground for technicians and provide regular employment for actors. It could be said that Hector was, to a large extent, responsible for Australian film technicians earning high reputations. Directors like Peter Weir, Fred Schepisi and Bruce Beresford took their technicians to Hollywood. Actors were able to hone their screen-acting techniques. I played guest leads in *Homicide, Division 4, Matlock Police,* and later on, *Cop Shop.* The *Matlock* episode is worth a mention.

John Orcsik and I played a couple of joking playboy gangsters, trying to be like Paul Newman and Robert Redford in *Butch Cassidy and the Sundance Kid.* Even in the short time we had to rehearse (it was a ten-day turn-around for each episode), we found ourselves changing the script and sometimes improvising on a take. It is a creative situation when two actors click together in their roles. We played the parts through our own personalities, which gave us that freedom to improvise.

On the shoot was David Eggby, our camera operator, who would make a future connection with my family when he married my cousin Elizabeth. Our director was Colin Egglestone (with Eggby and Pegge there was a preponderance of 'egg' on this shoot). He was more than happy we were improvising so freely and became another director I worked for again.

Actors do their best work through directors with whom they are in tune and vice versa. Colin was one of them. His career was forged in the Crawford film factory with police dramas. He went on to make a significant contribution to the television and film industry as a writer-director and producer, his most successful film being *Long Weekend.*

Before the end of my first year back in Australia in 1973 I did my first television guest lead for the Australian Broadcasting Commission (ABC) playing Stephen Hunt in *Separate Ways,* a drama in their series called *Love Story.* The ABC also provided a constant source of work, particularly as radio drama was still going strong. However, by the end of January 1974 I was signed up to play Lieutenant Robarts in *Luke's Kingdom,* a co-production between Channel 9 and Yorkshire Television in the UK. This seemed like a promising breakthrough for me. It meant work for the next five months and being seen in, what could be, a prestigious series shown in other countries.

The series was loosely based on Mary Durack's novel *Kings in Grass Castles* and E.V. Timms's *Pages from a Squatter's Diary.* This 13-part series featured the Firbeck family arriving from England in the 1820s to claim land, tame the outback and establish a dynasty. To produce the series Yorkshire Television sent out Tony Essex who came with the leading actor Oliver Tobias and

Bettina Kenter from Germany to cover a German pre-sale. The only other imports were three UK directors: Peter Hammond, Hugh David and Gareth Davies. All the cast and crew were local, plus Ken Hannam and Peter Weir. Two of these directors I had already worked for: Hugh David had given me my first part on British television for the BBC; Ken Hannam had cast me in the BBC series *Moonbase Three* just before leaving.

A reconstruction of an 1820s settlement had been built at Ingleside on the outskirts of Frenchs Forest 20 km north of Sydney. A crew of top Australian technicians including John Seale and John R. McLean had been hired. John Seal went to Hollywood with Peter Weir. Most of the guest roles were played by well-known Australian actors such as Bill Hunter, Jack Thompson, Helen Morse, Chris Heywood and Max Cullen.

Before the shoot began I had to do a crash course in horse riding. During those hot days in January and February all in the cast who were required to ride had to have lessons at Graham Murphy's stables in Frenchs Forest. Sore bums and thighs, swallowing flies, and frightening moments on frisky horses bound us together. Frightfully proper lessons from a stable in Windsor Great Park were my only previous experience; not the best preparation for handling horses on rough terrain in front of a camera in the heat.

I was given a particularly docile horse as I was seen not to be a natural rider. I had a bad experience early in the shoot when I was required to gallop off. Digging in heels and pressing thighs would not shift her. Peter Hammond, our director, was soon fed up and got the wrangler (horse trainer) as stand-in for me. So many sequences involved riding and there were difficulties with the horses. Our first wrangler had to be replaced. Furthermore, our director became equally fed up with some of our acting. I heard him say: 'I haven't come all this way to teach you how to act'. That comment may have been the bad seed that was sown early in the shoot.

Added to that, the weather was being most unkind. In the heat of February to March we were all in some discomfort – I, in my thick redcoat uniform, others wearing woollen clothes. Then with cooler weather down came the rain. Because of the authentic style we would often be shooting in the rain. Even though scenes were shot while it was raining, the fire brigade would still be called in to give more body to the falling water, so that the camera could read the drops. Whenever you see rain falling in a film sequence, you can be sure there is a fire engine nearby.

All was well in my world at the beginning of 1974, living the good life in Sydney with work for the next six months. My part consisted mostly of short scenes in and out of each storyline, so I had a lot of spare time and truncated lines of acting. You could shoot a scene in the morning and not be used to finish it until the end of the day. When shooting out of sequence the difficulty arises in maintaining a through line of action and attitude – in simple terms, a 'threw line of action' is when a character is driving towards an objective. I was feeling comfortable and secure until the gods reminded me that, at some point, you have to pay your dues. No actor should ever get complacent, even in the middle of a contract.

One day after completing the filming on five episodes, I was called into the producer's office in Cremorne. Tony Essex told me without preamble that I would be written out of the rest of the episodes, as my part was not 'coming across'. I felt as if I had been stabbed in the gut. I later found out that because another regular character was proving weak, the storyline needed a shift in narrative. At least I was pleased that the actor taking over was my lifelong friend Alfie Bell. All actors need armour plates to cover up their egos, and belief in their worth. I eventually appeared in seven out of thirteen episodes, which took me through to the end of August.

In my opinion the series was one of the finest historical dramas to come out of Australia and yet after one showing in Australia, UK and Germany, it sank without trace until it appeared on DVD. In fact I received a strange reaction on meeting Maude Spector at a casting session for Yorkshire Television. I said, with the expectations of a very positive response, that I played Lieutenant Robarts in *Luke's Kingdom*. Her reply was 'Oh, we don't talk about that series'.

Something must have happened financially. We all knew Tony Essex had been under enormous strain. (In fact on arriving home in the UK, he was waiting for his wife to open their front door when he suffered a heart attack and dropped dead.) With *Luke's Kingdom* he had a hard-hitting and realistic re-creation of life in those early colonial days. There were no rose-tinted, chocolate-box storylines, and certainly no avoidance of the violence and harsh reality that must have been commonplace. I have recently discovered the series was deemed too brutal by the programmers of that time. It would not be these days.

Despite this hurtful setback of being written out, I didn't plunge into 'a dark night of the soul'. I've always wanted a degree of success but the height of that degree determines how far you go down when rejected. My overall ambition was to achieve recognition and continuity of work. This was the beginning of a healthily cynical attitude to the acting profession. But getting further work quickly, or immersing yourself in a project of any kind, has always been the best antidote.

Having said that, I did record that I was fed up, as everything seemed to be going wrong: my car blowing up on the way to the Blue Mountains, being written out of *Luke's Kingdom*, not being invited anywhere or seeing any friends and, topping it off, throwing a party at my flat to which nobody turned up. The violins were hard at it. At least I could let it all out with my girlfriend. Di had joined me in October of 1973 and we were renting a spacious modern apartment with plenty of light on Edgecliff Road, Woollahra. So it didn't take me too long to snap out of this 'poor me' state. Sydney Harbour itself is a massive tonic. You can get on a ferry and have your blues blown away by an exhilarating ride to Manly.

I was still under contract but not being used when further work came along. Radio was still a dominant medium, particularly because it could reach every corner of the vast continent that is Australia. I picked up where I had left off eight years previously. Most of the radio drama directors were still working for the ABC. It did my ego no harm playing two leading roles. *The Year of Living Dangerously* was a major radio drama series which was very popular. I played Guy Hamilton, the journalist, played by Mel Gibson in Peter Weir's movie. In every way I was dead right for that role in the film and Peter agreed, but he needed a star to get the money. I also played the leading role of Scott in *Fire on the Snow* by Douglas Stewart, about the famous Antarctic expedition. The role Peter Finch played in an early radio production after the war.

Acting in radio dramas does require a specialised ability that not every actor has. The primary facility is to be able to sightread. Rarely do you receive a script before the studio day; it requires a very fast absorption of your character and what the play is about, but all you have is your voice to convey all that. Radio acting requires clear and expressive speech. Over-realistic mumbling actors would not get employed. You have to have sharp diction speaking consonants, for they convey the meaning of the word; emotion and attitude are conveyed on the breath through the vowels.

Depending on the nature of the character and the scene being played it is necessary to be fast, to listen intently to the other actors and to pick up the cues. Listening to actors you are playing with is one of the fundamental principles of acting. This means that much of the business of acting is reacting, being aware and exercising your sixth sense. In the theatre every performance is unique for this reason. For the screen you do take after take until every nuance that the director wants is captured. Sadly there is very little radio drama these days.

What I did next during this period was profoundly important for my development as an actor. The famous teacher/director Stella Adler had come to Australia to conduct a series of master classes in acting. We all thought we were going to be instructed in the Method School of Acting, from the Actors' Studio in New York, associated with the great Marlon Brando.

The Actors' Studio was co-founded by Stella Adler, Lee Strasberg and Elia Kazan. Stella broke away from Lee Strasberg's teaching method after visiting Moscow in 1934 and taking private lessons with Konstantin Stanislavsky. The great teacher had written what became regarded as the bible for actors – *An Actor Prepares*. As Stella found out he claimed only to have codified what every first-rate actor does instinctively. One of his tenets had been taken up by Lee Strasberg and taken too far. 'Think of your own experiences and use them truthfully' had become the central teaching system called the Method. It meant that actors over-personalised every role they played. Stella directed us down the path of deeply examining the text to find 'the emotional origins of the script and to build the character around them'.

Her workshops took place in the Bondi Pavilion Theatre in Sydney. Thirty professional actors worked on set scripts in two-hourly sessions twice a week for four weeks. The sessions were open to the general public and once the word got around there was always an audience. I teamed up with Carmen Duncan, from my year at NIDA, who had already made a name for herself. We prepared scenes from Chekhov's plays, and finally concentrated on the last scene from *The Seagull*.

Stella was very demanding; there was nothing democratic in the way she worked. We would dissect every line of the play. It was more like digging to unearth the reason why characters said what they said. In other words from the text we had to build a physical and emotional world that our character inhabited. Initially this would come out of information that was both said by and inferred from other characters. Then we were encouraged to pose questions, to use our imaginations in how the character not ourselves would behave or react in every moment of each scene.

Having got under the skin of our characters and thoroughly rehearsed, we were told to stop thinking of what we were doing or what was coming next and to let ourselves go. Stella had really understood and put into practice Stanislavsky's most profound observation: that he was providing a route map for exploring what he called 'that conscious road to the gates of the unconscious'.

Carmen and I gave our final performance on the last night. There were 300 in the audience. What happened is what keeps you being an actor. Carmen took off playing Nina - acting from her sub-conscious - being Nina, and I went with her in my role. She gave an astonishing performance in the very difficult last scene of *The Seagull*. The audience rose as one giving us a standing ovation, Stella was in tears saying that she had never seen Nina 'played so right'. She was most complimentary to me, saying that I had made a breakthrough, and that we were two of the few who had really understood her interpretation of Stanislavsky's method. She had given me a very hard time in another scene from an American play I had worked on with another actress. After what happened on *Luke's Kingdom* it was a huge boost to my confidence.

The essence of what she taught continued for some time after. Carmen Duncan, Lex Marinos and I gathered local actors to work in the Stables Theatre. We were tutored by Bryan Syron and Henry Bannister, who had worked with Stella in New York. The playwright Alex Buzo became involved with his play *Wentworthville*. It was developed on Stella's guidelines, which resulted in a stunning performance by John Hargreaves, acclaimed by the critic Katharine Brisbane. The project lasted until the group gradually dispersed.

24

On the Road and Then Some More

After Alfie Bell and I had completed our contracts on *Luke's Kingdom* at the end of August, we took off with our partners for a well-earned holiday.

We did a round air trip to Townsville via Adelaide and Alice Springs, dropping down briefly at Tennant Creek. It was hot, flat and dusty. The vista reaffirmed my lack of any affinity with the Australian outback, probably seeded from those hard years of touring. I have never quite understood where the beauty lies, as the outback seems so featureless. The lush green fields of England are in my bones like the 'good yeoman whose limbs were made in England'.

From Townsville we hired a car and drove up the coast road to Port Douglas. I can appreciate the beauty of tropical Australia and back then there was minimal tourist development. We stayed in a boarding house on Trinity Beach for $12 a night each and virtually had the whole beach to ourselves. We spent most evenings in the undiscovered haven that was Port Douglas. It was a seaside village nestling in the bosom of the hills behind, which had attracted interesting people from the cities. It was like an artists' colony and despite a small population boasted five top-class restaurants. One of them, the Nautilus, is still there and serving good food. It was in the hills and as we walked up the steps I espied a recognisable figure. It was the ebullient John Heywood, who had been in the second intake at NIDA.

He was a boy from the country, full of fun and ideas, and had been to agricultural college. During those days at NIDA I was most surprised when I found John climbing from the roof into my attic flat one night to proposition me. I had no idea he was gay, nor had quite a few girl students who were most disappointed.

Now here was John nicely partnered with Bill Austin running a restaurant miles from the gay capital, in the north of the redneck state. Bill had been a very successful stage manager with J.C. Williamsons, the long-established family company of theatrical entrepreneurs. Then he and Bill had taken over the restaurant from our NIDA speech teacher Joan Whalley.

We discovered that John had not entirely given up acting. In this tropical world he was inclined to play different roles with us, which made us think he had gone a bit 'troppo'. He was the oyster fisherman – the pirate chef – the event creator – the tour guide and the hurt, sensitive soul at the end of an empty glass late at night. He wore different clothes to suit the activity.

We happened to be there after he had caught an enormous fish and had invited the hippie tribe down from the Atherton Tablelands to partake of a feast. He had caught an eight-foot Maori Wrasse, gutted it, filled the belly with tropical fruit, wrapped it in what looked like hessian, laid it on coals in a huge pit and covered it for eight hours. Inland from the beach, we were in a large hollow which slightly resembled an amphitheatre. There must have been a gathering of about fifty. Among the smoke and the gentle infusion of strumming guitars, John in his bandannas conducted proceedings in Christ-like manner. It was a truly biblical scene.

John as tour guide took us to the first lighthouse to be built in the far north of Queensland. We were greeted by a spick and span dapper little man and his good wife who came from the Home Counties in the UK. Many years later I was accompanying a friend delivering something to a neighbour in a village in Surrey. The door opened and there stood the dapper little man from the lighthouse. The best of the many coincidences in my travelling years.

The rest of 1974 up to early 1975 was a period of lean pickings. The coffers were helped by shooting a commercial for Swan Lager in Perth. Beer ads paid well. The job enabled me to attend a huge family gathering from my mother's side. In 1841 the Birch family, having arrived in Bunbury down the coast from Perth, had gone forth and multiplied. I must have been introduced to a hundred cousins.

In February 1975 I successfully auditioned for a touring production of *Male of the Species* by Alun Owen starring Edward Woodward of *Callan* fame and Michele Dotrice, who had played Betty in *Some Mothers Do 'Ave 'Em*.

The director Val May, from the Yvonne Arnaud theatre in Guildford, was impressed with my work in neighbouring Farnham. The tour took us to New Zealand, Melbourne, Adelaide and Sydney, finishing in July.

Our producer was Maurice Binder whose claim to fame was being responsible for the titles and credits for most of the early Bond movies. The tour was promoted by Wilton Morley who turned out to be Robert Morley's son. The cast included Lorraine Bailey, well known for her part in the Australian television series *The Sullivans* and a 'slip of a gal' called Louise Ogle-Rush with whom I kept in touch for many years.

We opened in Wellington, the capital of New Zealand, on 18 March after three weeks' rehearsal in Sydney. On our first day off we went horse riding along a narrow peak between the coast and the mountains. It was exhilarating; you could taste the clean air. The following Sunday we went on another car journey out of Wellington. Our end point for this journey was an invitation to tea with the formidable and wonderfully eccentric Davina Whitehouse. She was an English actress who had emigrated to New Zealand in 1952 after considerable success in the UK. We were late due to driving on a very winding road cut into a mountain range that became a pathway through majestic fir trees. These two main volcanic islands that make up the country are not very wide, but you cannot do any journey in a rush. One is continually amazed at the spectacular scenery.

Davina's house was built on the rocks at the foot of a mountain on the west coast. Here is how I described the scene in a letter:

> Soon after we arrived her neighbours turned up with their goat and they all came into the sitting room. Her neighbours were hearty hikers smelling of sweat and earth – there are a lot like that in NZ. It didn't take long for the goat to misbehave, obviously not used to sitting rooms.

Through Davina I was able to get some radio work. Local producers always grabbed the opportunity to use visiting artists. I did a couple of voice-overs and a small part in a radio play for the long-serving drama director at the NZ Broadcasting Corporation with the memorable name of Fergus Dick.

There was a lively arts scene centred around the Downstage Theatre where many well-known NZ actors cut their teeth such as James Laurenson, Jonathan Hardy and Tim Elliott. But the funding axe has fallen. The final curtain came down on 21 September 2013. The Downstage Theatre Company had been the cultural hub for 50 years. Mind you, it is more important to fund the building of a yacht for the one-off America's Cup, which incidentally NZ lost after being 8–1 up. An example of the economic rationalists severing the cultural arteries of the body politic.

Edward Woodward, whom we all called Teddy, was a collector of rocks and precious stones. He wanted to visit the famous Greenstone factory in Hokatika on the west coast and invited a few of us to go with him and Michele. Here is how I described the journey in a letter:

> We sped across the fertile, billiard-tabled Canterbury Plains, famed for racehorse breeding, to the foot of the Southern Alps crowned by the snow capped Mount Cook. This huge mountain range had a narrow opening gouged out by the running waters of the Waimak River over billions of years. We drove for three hours in pouring rain along precipitous roads. Sometimes we would be within a few feet of a 400-foot drop to the rapids. All along on both sides of this gaping ravine waterfalls sprouted, sometimes cascading on to the road as we drove along. It looked as though these huge granite rocks, bearded with trees, were bleeding white blood. Our progress went though areas reminding us of Scotland, North Wales and Cornwall. Some treeless rock ranges with great craggy boulders had been fashioned by the winds into weird shapes. It looked like a perfect setting for the Druids to perform their mystic rites.

At the factory we watched the entire process of how large pieces of stone are cut, shaped and polished into jewellery. I got caught up in the thought that in your hand you could be holding something that was formed a billion years ago. Afterwards, we took jet boats 40 km up the winding river Waimak, hemmed in by sheer rock faces, and returned, bucking the river horse, over rapids in large inflatables. It's a hard life being an actor.

Christchurch was a nice provincial town that had a similar ambience to Adelaide with a touch of Stratford-upon-Avon. We hired bikes to ride around a town so flat it reminded me of Noël Coward's singular comment about Norfolk being 'flat' and New Zealand 'shut'. It was not unlike that in those days. Trying to find a restaurant open after the show was nigh on impossible.

It has always been the way among most actors in the theatre; you cannot act on a full stomach and most need to wind down after the show with a light meal and a glass or three. The stage director of the theatre, Alan Babbage, whom I knew from my early amateur days in Adelaide, helped us find our way around. We had a very pleasant time in New Zealand. The audiences were warm and enthusiastic, but as Teddy and Michele observed, slower on the uptake compared to London audiences, where attending the theatre is a cultural habit.

Theatre actors have to exercise their sixth sense in every performance and more so when touring. It entails: being aware of the audience's reaction while you are performing, not speaking through a laugh and allowing sufficient time for high emotional moments to resonate. Timing is the essence of comedy. The basic principle is that you come in with your line as the laughter subsides. An important part of an actor's craft is to have highly tuned antennae, to quickly gauge audience reaction.

Melbourne audiences were quicker. The season at the Comedy Theatre was most successful and financially rewarding for me as I was able to fit in an episode on *Homicide* and *Division 4* for Crawford's, plus radio dramas at the ABC.

We had a two-week season in Her Majesty's Theatre, Adelaide. Many friends and family came to see the show. After returning to Sydney by car through the vast plains of the outback, I found myself yearning for the green fields of England and my English friends.

During the tour we felt there was something in the air between Teddy and Michele. We knew he was married with a family and we thought nothing of him and Michele spending a lot of free time together. Stars of any show are, and in a way have to be, slightly apart from the rest of us. Not only are they on stage most of the time but a lot of their spare time is taken up with publicity. However, our suspicions were never quite confirmed until we got back to the UK. There on the front page of the *Evening Standard* was a picture of Teddy's wife Venetia who had threatened to commit suicide if Teddy didn't come back to her. Apparently it was not the first time. I do think this time was different, that he had fallen in love with Michele on that tour. Nevertheless, Venetia's threat seemed to work as Edward and Michele were unable to marry until 1987, but they stayed together until he died in 2009.

25

Home Sweet Home

I arrived back in the UK on 1 September 1975 to a warm welcome from friends and within four days I was in work. Three years previously I had played the doctor in an ATV children's series *Escape into Night*. The casting director at ATV happened to phone my agent and offered me a part in the soap opera *Crossroads* just as I was returning, having not known I had been away for two years.

There was a stigma attached to being in a soapie. Being identified in one part for many years could jeopardise your career once out of it. What is more, you were unlikely to be regarded as a serious actor. The compensation of course was constant income. In those days the acting profession was very snobbish and more so in England than in Australia. Actors the calibre of Mel Gibson, Guy Pearce and very recently Chris Hemsworth began their careers in *Home and Away*. So, as it was a UK soapie, it was probably fortunate that I only appeared in five episodes. I played Mr Jessel, a probation officer-cum-social worker for Benny, a popular character who had learning difficulties.

On return I had bought a 1968 BMW 2002 with an eight-track cassette system for £550. In modern parlance I was cool, bombing up the M1 in my BMW with the eight-track blaring out Neil Diamond. I was not seen as so cool on the first day when I accidentally sat in Noele Gordon's seat in the green room.

Noele Gordon was a major television star and let everybody know it. She had created the character of Meg Richardson in 1964 and ended up playing it for 18 years. I walked into the green room and sat on an empty chair. There was a silence, actors' eyes were upon me as Noele walked in. She stood there looking at me. There were other chairs available. Sue Hanson nudged me, whispering 'That's Noele's chair'. I stared at Sue in disbelief but arose in suitable Uriah Heep manner.

I then committed the cardinal sin of stopping in the middle of a take when clearly hearing a baby cry. Apparently under no circumstances do you stop when the cameras are running. Soap operas are run on very tight schedules. Three half-hour episodes were shot over a ten-day slot. That is well over one hour of actual screen time. It was probably as well that I was to be in only five episodes. I did three then and another two early in the following year.

Actors are cast to type in soap operas. There would be a few lines describing the part. Because I had played a kind and friendly doctor in ATV's *Escape into Night* series, they must have thought that quality was what they needed in the part of Mr Jessel. In other words, the casting department would not have put out that part for tender. They would have phoned up my agent and asked if I was available and then offered the role. This was not common practice, unless you were in the A-list of actors.

The old 'casting couch' is a cliché and a myth. It probably happened in the old days of Hollywood and in theatrical circles in England during the 1920s and 1930s. There is, however, a case to be made for favouritism. It is easier to land roles if you are on what I call the roundabout, i.e. often seen going from one job to another. In more recent years we often see the same faces in the many different series on British television.

During my time on *Crossroads* I visited the Dotrice family home in the Cotswolds. Poor Michele was in an emotional pit. Her mother Kay had phoned me to ask my opinion of Edward Woodward and invited me to call in. Michele's well-known actor father Roy Dotrice was away. Edward did have a reputation for liaisons with young leading ladies. Kay was certainly like the lioness protecting her cub. I helped to console Michele during my visit. She needed to unfold her memories of the tour, presumably to sort out her feelings. She needed assurance as to whether he was genuine.

A sharp memory I have of this visit is being greeted by three ferocious Doberman Pinschers as I arrived and noticing the long swan-like neck of Michele's sister Yvette. I can see an Hieronymus Bosch painting in those images.

A few years previously Roy Dotrice's awe-inspiring one-man show, *Brief Lives*, had reinforced my earlier ambition to do something similar. *Brief Lives* is based on John Aubrey's diaries, which were observations of life and times in

17th-century London. His performance was notable for his staying on stage for the entire two and a half hours, feigning sleep during the interval. I stayed in my seat watching him. Stillness is such a powerful force. He achieved entry into the Guinness Book of Records for the most solo performances – 1782.

Soon after returning from Australia, Di and I moved into a one-bedroom basement flat in Chelsea owned by Dougal Rankin, a film producer. The house was near World's End, a pub on the Kings Road. We were lucky to get it as Mrs Rankin chose us out of 30 applicants. Our rent in 1975 was £24 per week; in 2013 it was around £500 for a similar flat in Chelsea.

Work was scarce. My photo had gone to Paramount Studios followed by an interview for a small part in the film *Black Sunday* starring Robert Shaw to be directed by John Frankenheimer (*Birdman of Alcatraz*); the phone didn't ring. It was back to landscaping and *Top of the Pops*, and nothing came from our landlord being a movie producer. Then, through my Australian actor friend Nick Tate, a connection was made to another source of employment in the territory of the South London crime world.

Tommy Mulholland was company director of The Hygienic Decorating and Cleaning Company situated in Peckham. He enlisted me on a £100-per-month retainer to get big cleaning jobs from which I would receive five per cent of the contract. I got the job mainly because I was on *Crossroads* and also 'cos I spoke proper'. He already had a cockney actor on his books but he wanted to go more up-market. Tommy was not a typical *sath* London working-class lad made good. He had inherited the company from his father who had sent him to a private school. He was not a loudmouth with bimbos confetti-ing largesse. He was thin with spectacles, but he did have one trait of that ilk – a wad of notes in his back pocket which he fingered with his thumb, and he did mix in the boxing world.

I often accompanied him to the Thomas à Becket, a famous boxing pub in the Old Kent Road, run by Beryl Cameron-Gibbons. She was well-known in the boxing world and had the distinction of being the only female boxing promoter in Europe. She was charming and attractive but you wouldn't want to go one round with her in the verbal ring. All the famous boxers had trained there, including Muhammad Ali and Joe Frazier. Eventually Henry Cooper (British heavyweight champion in his day) took over from her in 1983.

One evening stood out. Firstly I was surprised to see that Dennis Waterman's brother was one of the fighters; perhaps that accounts for Dennis looking like a fighter. Secondly, I was astonished by the very funny but highly racist after-dinner speech concerning a Pakistani batsman, given by one of my cricketing heroes Fred Trueman. He got away with it then with his North Country straight-talking manner, before the days of political correctness.

Although I cannot remember witnessing any criminal activity, it was going on. I was told if I wanted anything I just had to put in an order. The source was euphemistically described as 'orf the back of a lorry', and what's more they said 'you get a staff discount'. The location was near the areas where the two famed London gangs operated – the Krays and the Richardsons. I did hear of a few shootings. It was very useful for an actor to mix with real-life characters.

During most of the middle of my career, I seemed to be in a state of high concern over not climbing the ladder and earning more. I certainly went through many periods of depression – not the black dog, more 'down at winged heel'. In a sense I had arrived at a crossroad. Perhaps being in a soap opera of that name prompted the idea that I had taken the wrong turn earlier and was now in a stalemate. I had hoped at this point in my career to have some control; to be in a position to choose what I would do next – to be sent scripts for consideration. Despite looking the leading-man type and often playing guest leads in a one-off episode of a series, I was rarely auditioned for an ongoing role in a series. I was never out of work for too long, because I accepted everything I was offered.

Playing Mr Buell in an episode of *When the Boat Comes In* starring James Bolam was typical of one of these guest leads. All the other work during this year was also typical: four other BBC plays playing supporting roles, four documentaries, three commercials and a lunch-time play at The Old Vic. The gaps were never more than a few weeks but it was never quite enough. I was always hoping, and had expectations, to win more significant roles, be more in demand. That belief was probably essential to keep going as an actor. Many I knew gave up. The compensation for being a supporting actor (a Horatio) was the diversity of work and the many and varied people I met. Life was never dull and I was able to ride out those periods of slough along the way.

One of the documentaries I did was for the Royal Navy in Portsmouth, and it gave me a James Bond illusion. I was filmed giving a lecture on comparisons between the British and Russian navies. I had to learn text describing the technical comparisons of the ships and their armaments between the opposing fleets. I should have had an autocue as it was incredibly difficult to learn. It also sounded top secret. I had the fanciful idea I might be captured by the Russians to divulge the information from this lecture.

In those days autocues were very primitive. Someone would be standing next to the camera with a stand rolling down the text written large on cloth. The actors eyes would always be slightly off from looking directly into the lens. The craziest job I had involving an autocue was in a field somewhere in Cambridgeshire delivering a talk on weed killers. The wind was up and the poor person operating the autocue was behaving like a manic scarecrow.

At least filming documentaries and commercials was interesting and often fun to do. They were also remunerative and sometimes meant travelling to exotic places. The next one I did was purely because of my fencing and fight-arranging abilities. I played a medieval knight in a sword fight on the battlements of Bodmin Castle in Kent for a history programme.

The more strings actors have to their bows the greater the chance of keeping in work. These days every actor needs to be trained in martial arts, be able to sing, play an instrument, dance, ride anything that moves, be an acrobat and a juggler; in other words, jump through flaming hoops for demonic directors.

However, I still believe the most important element in a stage actor's training is speech. It seems to be seriously neglected these days, as often I cannot hear clearly what many actors say. Increasingly, live performances and film are dominated by visual and physical effects. Text-based plays are almost becoming a thing of the past. Shakespeare will last because arrogant directors can muck around with his plays. I was thrilled recently when I went to see *Hamlet* at the Yvonne Arnaud Theatre in Guildford. It was a traditional production set in Elizabethan times with Ed Stoppard, Tom's son, playing the Prince. I heard every single word. It felt as though I was hearing the text for the first time.

Hobbies and specialist abilities are always mentioned in CVs. Cricket is a sport I play to a reasonable standard and I love everything about the game. I was approached by Robert Fleming, a producer at Thames Television whom I had met socially, and who knew I played for the Stage Cricket Club. He was producing a wonderful series on the history of sport called *This Sporting Land*. He asked me to raise a side to re-create how the game might have been played in the 18th, 19th and 20th centuries. In a way we became professional cricketers for a few days. We were animating the old cricketing prints. It was a good position to be in as I was able to get my friends some work.

Clive Graham and his offsider improvised the birth of cricket. Playing shepherds, they wonder what to do when one of them rolls up a sheep turd and looks at the other who has a stave. It would have been a smelly beginning. We were all dressed in Restoration costumes to play an 18th-century match on a field in Hertfordshire. It was a very leisurely game bowling underarm at two sticks with a bail, to a batsman with a bat shaped like a hockey stick. The Victorian era game was nearer to that of the modern era. The bowling action had become a sling with a straight arm. Some sport historians suggest it was due to women being allowed to bowl. They had to throw sideways to clear their bustles. It was a fun job.

Being a sporty person, I have played a lot of charity golf and cricket matches with famous people. A charity match at the Maidenhead and Bray Cricket Club was stacked with names, including the club's president Michael Parkinson, but for me there was one other more important person.

She was a bright young thing (to use a 1920s phrase) called Linda Barr with whom I had a strong relationship for five years and who remains a friend to this day. Linda was a budding actress and understood the insecurity – the ups and downs – of the profession.

The next memorable person I met was John Cleese. The Barclay brothers were making a comedy film notable for its lengthy title. It was called *The Strange Affair of the End of Civilisation as We Know It* starring John Cleese and Arthur Lowe (Captain Mainwaring in *Dad's Army*). My old friend from Sydney Nick Tate and I played a couple of Aussie characters. I happened to be reading the *Guardian* (which actors were supposed to do, being traditionally left wing), waiting to be called on to the set, when I came across the most bizarrely amusing court report. It came from York Crown Court under the heading 'Glass-eyed Burglar Advised to Retire'. This burglar had a deformed hand, one leg and had lost an eye when a woman assaulted him. The judge told him he was a rotten burglar and to give up as he was always being caught. I showed the article to John Cleese who immediately rushed to the phone. I don't know whether any sketch came out of it, but I am sure if it had people would have said that it was far-fetched.

I experienced a very low period during my 37th year and so did the country. The economy was stagnant. It was in the thrall of Arthur Scargill and the striking miners. Even though I was not having a bad year financially due to repeat fees from commercials, my career was stagnating.

I had been considering buying a flat, nudged by a female prod. But the idea of a mortgage felt like having a yoke thrust around my neck. It took another two years and a more persuasive female to remove that fear. Renting was much more common and had no stigma in those days. But it was money going to someone else for the privilege of having a roof over one's head.

This fear of ownership and responsibility maybe was seeded during my upbringing. My parents had led a dull, routine-bound, bourgeois life. I had come through the post-war free-thinking, sexual revolution led by the likes of Germaine Greer. I was seduced into thinking money was not important, that ideas and fun were; that meeting interesting people and being led to the fountain of knowledge to achieve self-fulfilment was the path to take. Certainly I sought the company of people who had a way at looking at things that made me laugh and think. 'Those were the days my friends' – and we really thought they would never end.

And so my search for any old golden fleece continued.

26

Scoring a Few More Goals

The year of 1977 began well and got better. It began with that job on the John Cleese/Arthur Lowe film and was followed by an ongoing role in a lightweight television series called *Follow Me*. It was a six-episode series shot on location around Bristol for HTV, a South West station. England had area television stations like Anglia, Yorkshire and Granada in Manchester, which had independent budgets for drama. The series for HTV was directed by Peter Graham Scott for whom I had worked before in a BBC drama called *The Expert*. He had an unusual second-string occupation: he was a pig farmer in Berkshire. He had no trouble taking home the bacon.

Follow Me was filmed around the docks (which smelt of history), the local airport, and over Clifton Bridge, where I was chased down and had to fall off a bike. I played the part of a nervous, easily led boffin involved in a gang of hijackers. I am obviously awfully good at playing weak characters.

This job took me towards the end of March, then a familiar circumstance immediately followed. An actor had dropped out of an episode of a comedy series called *Miss Jones and Son* being directed by Peter Frazier Jones at Thames Television and I was asked to replace him. This was rapidly followed by being cast in a role that would have reverberations for many years. The part of Meeker in a *Dr Who* episode called 'The Invisible Enemy', with Tom Baker and Louise Jameson. The part came about through the episode director. Derrick Goodwin had first directed me at Ipswich Rep in 1966. I had become one of his stable of actors.

This particular episode was noted for being the first appearance featuring K9, the computerised robotic dog. Because this episode introduced K9, much anxiety pervaded TCN1, the huge studio at the BBC Centre in White City. K9 kept breaking down. Plays were still being video recorded, which meant long sequences being recorded by cameras on gliding podiums. This was great for our pockets as we earned heaps of overtime. I can easily recall the joy and pain in the basement makeup room. I had to be in at 6.00 am to have the scales attached to my face. Meeker had returned to earth contaminated. The pain came later getting them off.

At the time none of us had any idea of the potential magnitude of *Dr Who*, and the extent to which the radiophonic workshop would become a template for future sci-fi films and series. There was a saying going around the acting fraternity in London at the time that if you hadn't done at least one episode of *Dr Who* or *The Bill* you weren't a proper actor. There were hardly any actors I knew who hadn't been in *Dr Who* at some point in their careers.

Up until 2013 I had not been invited to partake in any fan club conventions. I knew that some actors were almost making a living attending them. I used to play cricket with Anthony Ainley, who played the Master. He told us that with appearance money and residuals from sales throughout the world, he hardly needed to work. For the past 37 years, I have regularly been sent small cheques for sales and repeats from just that one and only episode. Recently I received a cheque that was many times more than my original fee. You may try to imagine what all the Doctors earn. The BBC paid a very low upfront fee but with this huge capacity for selling programmes worldwide, residuals kept being paid for many years.

I had only one experience attending a London *Dr Who* convention. Toby Hadoke, an actor and an aficionado of *Dr Who*, invited me to a signing in a Chiswick pub. There were about eight signing tables but there were only three actors, the others were technicians and anyone who was vaguely connected to any part of any episode. I did catch up with an old acting friend from my Newcastle days. John Leeson was the voice of K9. His voice remains but sadly he has departed.

It seems an industry has been created with currency for any kind of memorabilia. A compulsively obsessive worldwide fan club has evolved. One fan came to my table with an enormous poster, crab-filled with autographs, there was little space for my claw. And every fan wanted a photo taken, so we looked like old buddies. God has been supplanted by Celebrity.

Because in 2013 there was a 50-year celebration, the fan club in Adelaide had found out I was in town. They enticed me with a small fee to give an address on my experience of being in an episode of *Dr Who*. I was astonished to find at least 100 fans had gathered. I was gazed at in a kind of adoration.

After my address I was interviewed and asked some very modern questions:

How did you approach your part?
Probably learnt my lines and hit my marks. It was along time ago.
What did you think of being in Dr Who at the time?
Nothing, it was just a job.
How did being in Dr Who affect your career?
It didn't until now.

When I told the assembly that I had never seen the episode, and only recently found out how I was killed, there was a kind of gasp. I said it was from watching a BBC documentary about a television series Louise Jameson and I were in. In one clip there was a brief glimpse of Meeker falling past the camera with a dagger in his back thrown by Leela.

Apart from a radio play I was out of work for 10 weeks after *Dr Who*. Doubt can eat away at your confidence. If it isn't confronted and banished it can become a cancer of the ego. I threw myself into buying a flat. Not dwelling on negative thoughts allows unexpected things to happen. Also I do seem to have timely luck for survival. This time, it came from being cast in the BBC series *Secret Army*, playing an Aussie airman, which covered a seven-week period of intermittent work. It could not have been better as I was on a retainer.

My tally at the end of the year was not as bad as it seemed at the time: a guest lead playing an Australian soldier in an episode of *It Ain't Half Hot Mum*; a part in an episode of *The Saint*, 'Secret Army'; a voice-over for an Australian documentary on the Faraday children kidnapping; an all night kitchen clean; bought a flat and auditioned for a season of plays at The Old Vic, for Prospect Theatre Company. It was lean pickings for that period of four months but I was hardly on my uppers and doing nothing.

Besides, my relationship with Linda was blossoming and I had my friends in the country I could visit at weekends. In the old days of Bertie Wooster and Jeeves, weekends outside London were called 'cuntry hice' parties. That is literally how the toffs pronounced them.

To stand on the stage of The Old Vic on which so many great actors had performed was an awesome experience. I had recently been thrilled at a production of *Royal Hunt of the Sun* with Robert Stephens playing Atahualpa and a famous production of Seneca's *Oedipus*. This production was directed by the great Peter Brook with John Gielgud and Irene Worth. As I walked into the dress circle I found an actor colleague from Australia, Neil Fitzpatrick, seemingly tied up to a post. When I asked what the hell he was doing there, he said, 'Don't talk to me. I'm in the production.' It was an all-round production with the chorus dotted in different parts of the auditorium. Breaking out from the proscenium stage had become fashionable.

A famous incident occurred at an audience-invited dress rehearsal when an enormous phallus was rolled on to the stage. There was a silent gasp during which the outrageous Australian actress Coral Brown turned to her friend saying:, 'Nobody I know'.

Waiting in the wings before auditioning is the worst part. Fear and trepidation are your enemies. You try to push down on the rising panic in your gut with deep breathing. You keep going over the first line and quietly hum to relax the voice and keep it forward. The call comes: 'Next!'. It is a day of judgment. You enter from the prompt side on to a bare stage with a work light.

'What will you be doing, Mr Pegge?' says the darkness.

'Sir, one of the choruses from *Henry V.*'

'Very well. Proceed.'

You turn and walk upstage, standing for a moment letting the tension slip away, releasing the breath. Then turning to the front with a deep breath, you stride downstage with arms apart speaking the opening few lines, hoping to get to the end of the speech before hearing the familiar words: 'Thank you, Mr Pegge. We'll let you know.'

That is how impersonal the auditioning procedure is. In the auditorium that day were Toby Robertson and John Dove, very personable people as I was soon to find out. My agent phoned within a few days to say I had been offered the parts of the Duke de la Trémouille and the executioner in *St Joan,* and Agrippa in *Antony and Cleopatra.* I always try to sound cool on hearing I have got a job and immediately ask how much they are paying. I was told by an older actor not to be too excited on the phone to one's agent. After all they haven't got you the job. But on putting down the phone I would have yelled 'Yes!', then a warm feeling of relief and security would rise: respite for a while.

Initially the contract would end on 16 April 1978 but Prospect Theatre was a touring company with their base at The Old Vic. It was decided that St Joan would be retained in the touring repertoire. My contract was extended to the middle of July, with the possibility of an American tour. The other plays were Derek Jacobi's *Hamlet*, Barbara Jefford and her husband John Turner in *Antony and Cleopatra*, and *All for Love*, a Restoration play by John Dryden on the same subject. *Twelfth Night* was added later with Jacobi playing Malvolio. It was all very exciting to be acting with stage royalty, and the prestigious Old Vic stage attracted very strong supporting casts.

There were two connections from my Adelaide background working in and around The Old Vic and the National at the time. Lance Campbell, a feature writer for Rupert Murdoch's the *Advertiser*, was in the UK at that time furthering his career. He landed the job of publicist with Prospect Theatre Company but was also required to be an ASM (Assistant Stage Manager). He said it was so frantic running around he hardly remembered doing the other job. He ended up becoming a fine journalist and many years later wrote an article on my career.

I was surprised to find another backstage connection from Adelaide. John Rothenberg began his career as a stage manager during the early amateur theatre days. He left before I did and soon reached what could arguably be the pinnacle job for stage managers. From 1967 to 1984 he was principle stage manager at The Old Vic and the National, working with world-renowned directors and actors of that era. It is doubtful that this is known by many or that his achievements have been truly recognised.

There were three memorable incidents during the season at The Old Vic. The first occurred during a matinee performance of *St Joan*. Eileen Atkins playing St Joan was kneeling in prayer towards the end of the play, before she is burnt at the stake. I was the only other actor on stage playing her guard. Suddenly we noticed a man ascending some central steps from the auditorium. He came beside Eileen and knelt in prayer. I moved to remove him but Eileen gestured me back. She kept her eyes on him and at the end of her prayer speech she raised him up and gently led him back to the steps. Nothing was said as he walked back into the auditorium. Eileen was motionless, staring into the dark whence he had come; the audience were transfixed. It was a rare moment in the theatre when an intrusion was incorporated into the performance so well, thanks to the brilliant, fast-thinking Eileen Atkins. There was no applause, as there often is when something goes wrong of which the audience are aware. It was a spine-tingling experience. We found out he was a psychiatric patient. I recently discovered he had been a director at the Royal Court Theatre and was known to Eileen.

The second incident was mightily painful. I was standing in the wings with a dresser doing a quick change in *Antony and Cleopatra*. The dresser had handed me my sword and buckle upside down, and the brass knob of the hilt fell directly onto my big toe. This may well bring a wry smile. I went on and Doctor Theatre made me not think of the pain. Afterwards, I was taken to a nearby hospital in Westminster where I was given the standard treatment for such an injury: a Bunsen burner, a stretched out paper clip and a large nurse. The end of the paper clip was held over the Bunsen burner, a strong nurse held me round my shoulders, the hot end of the paper clip was plunged into my blackened big toe and my screech was heard across the Thames, as a spurt of blood gushed up like an oil strike.

The third event happened outside the theatre but connected to it. I had given a fellow member of the cast a lift to his home in Redcliffe Gardens, Earls Court, in my BMW. He had bought a bottle of whiskey. He kept feeding me capfuls while driving. We finished off the bottle while throwing a frisbee in a side street which attracted the attention of two policemen on the beat. As I was about to get into my car those policeman suddenly appeared, asked me to walk down a white line and then arrested me under the suspicion of being over the limit. Eventually I was escorted to Chelsea police station by five policemen, one to drive my car and four in the car with me to make sure this criminal didn't escape. By the time they breathalysed me I was only just over the limit. I did make the observation that their manpower for my arrest was definitely over the limit which they didn't find amusing.

I was supposed to go for my court hearing at Horseferry Road during the time I was touring and managed to get it postponed until just before my return to Australia. I was gazing full of trepidation at the magistrate who fined me

£50 with a licence ban for a year. Then it dawned on me. I would be away for that period and driving on my Australian licence. I remember saying to myself:

> My lord, you have no need to fine me and ban me. I am removing myself to the penal colony of New South Wales, surely that is punishment enough?

That would have gone down well, declaimed in theatrical style. It would take another 35 years before having another experience of that kind.

Also in the company was a very young Oz Clarke. He began his career as an actor but ended up being an international wine guru. I was most amused watching his wine versus beer journey with James May. May would often raise his eyebrows when Oz was banging on about the virtue of wine. He had an endearing pompous manner even in those early days.

Rarely in the theatre does an actor pull out of a performance. But Bernard Lloyd came down with shingles and was replaced for a few performances by George Baker with script in hand – some understudy. George Baker was already a major actor with many film and television roles. Ian Fleming wanted him to play Bond but the part went to Connery. He famously dubbed George Lazenby's voice in a sequence in *On Her Majesty's Secret Service*. He later became best known for playing Inspector Wexford in *The Ruth Rendell Mysteries*. He was a friend of Toby's and happened to be free.

Our tour was an A tour, the top level, which meant major companies appearing in large theatres in cities and cultural centres with hotel accommodation and a limited season. B tours might last six months playing in towns and seaside resorts, staying in theatrical digs. They usually featured a television star in a comedy. My girlfriend Linda Barr did a couple of these kinds of tours; one was with Colin Baker who had just finished his time as Dr Who.

Most actors on tour would use their spare time during the day to explore places of interest or pursue a hobby. Colin Baker's hobby was searching for Victorian rubbish dumps. Linda, who helped him, would often come home with dozens of pharmaceutical bottles caked in mud. These dumps were often found in car parks, like where the recently discovered bones of Richard III were found.

My contract ended mid July. I was in work for six months just when I had bought my first flat (which incidentally cost £10,000 in an up-market area of Wandsworth, despite being not far from the prison). During this period of work I had been able to do two commercials and a day's work on a movie, and I had received residuals from the BBC, a commission from a cleaning contract and holiday pay from Prospect. Looking back, I wonder why I was moaning so much about not making a decent living.

It didn't take me long to decide to return to Australia after having lunch with Jack Thompson and Peter Sumner. They urged me to go back, saying the film industry was buzzing. The absolute clincher was being banned from driving. The other factor in those days was keeping the multi-purpose visa going. I had to renew it every three years. This would be resolved in 1979.

27

Following the Sun

My departure was timed very well. Not only would I not be inconvenienced with loss of licence, but I was fortunate to get a commercial and play a cricket match at Lords before leaving.

The commercial was for Tia Maria and was being directed by the well-known Cliff Owen, much loved by actors due to a likelihood of overtime. He was also great fun to work with and liked a red or two over a long lunch. The overtime came to eight hours, which tripled the day's fee and would then produce residuals that would drip feed my bank account while being away.

Every boy cricketer dreams of playing cricket at Lords. The Stage Cricket Club played a match every year on the Lord's Nursery Ground against the Cross Arrows (made up of young and past professionals from Middlesex Cricket Club). I was never quite good enough to be an automatic choice for this tough fixture but was chosen this year, which did wonders for my confidence. There has, for many years, been a strong relationship between actors and cricket; perhaps because it is a team sport consisting of 11 individuals.

Within a week of arriving back in Australia in 1978 I was in rehearsal for Shakespeare's *Cymbeline,* with the added bonus of the production being in Adelaide. The reason I was in work so quickly was familiar; the part had been turned down by another actor. That actor happened to be one of my best friends, Alfie Bell, who had recommended me to Colin George, the then director of the South Australian Theatre Company.

Colin had built a highly respected reputation in the top repertory circuit in the UK, based on a small company of actors on contracts for a season of plays. This ensemble structure was begun by his predecessor George Ogilvie and over the next 15 years rivalled the Melbourne Theatre Company. Colin was able to attract Australia's top actors, including Colin Friels, Brian James and Michael Siberry.

I felt very much at home with the way Colin George worked. There was just enough practical discussion of the text with strong imaginative ideas for staging. *Cymbeline* is not often performed. I suspect it is difficult to make relevant, modernising being the fashion these days. It does have some magical song lyrics, as in the much quoted 'Fear no more the heat of the sun'.

I played Belarius, an old banished Lord with a beard. During rehearsals I was made aware my voice was not in the right place, that it was too far back in the throat, lacking forward resonance. This made me very concerned and self-conscious. I had always thought that was the character of my voice, as it was often mimicked. Charles Collingwood (Brian Aldridge in *The Archers*) at Stage Cricket Club matches would put on my voice. A slightly foghorn tone was probably caused by smoking. I did some intense voice work. Playing Belarius in *Cymbeline* turned out to be the last appearance I would make in a Shakespeare play, which looking back I regret.

People often ask how I learn the old-fashioned lines and whether I find Shakespeare difficult to understand. It can be hard work in the rehearsal period, dissecting meaning. Once words and actions and all the elements of the play are brought together, it becomes a joy. His great plays are a symphony of words. The characters, the structure of sentences, scenes and acts once woven into a whole become so much more than the pieces in the visual and aural mosaic. Shakespeare's writing and vision have a fundamental musical base. From his iambic pentameters to his codas in the final acts, the actors are swept along. As in many great works of artistic expression, musical terms are often used to define their inner meanings. Art critics use words like rhythm, tone, line and harmony. I have found performing in a modern play, like those of Osborne or Pinter, to be more taxing and bumpier. Acting in Shakespeare's plays is like catching a wave. You ride on the internal rhythms.

It had been a good year, and 1978 ended with an episode in *Cop Shop* for Crawford Productions in Melbourne. However, a slightly unusual air journey was required to get to the job. Tony Barr, a fellow actor and I, were booked to fly to Melbourne from Sydney on a regular airline. But sometimes during these periods, like in this instance, pilots would go on strike. Crawfords arranged for us to be flown on a private two-seater light aircraft. We were farewelled in a terminal shed by our agent and the well-known Aussie actor Bill Hunter, who had brought us a bottle of whiskey to allay any fears.

Our pilot was a middle-aged ex-RAAF officer who had flown sorties in Papua New Guinea. He regaled us with hair-raising stories of flying over mountainous ranges, which actually made us feel safe in his hands. Mind you our in-house beverage did enhance a feeling of euphoria as it became necessary to finish the contents, it being a very long flight with no toilet facilities.

The sight of two gentlemen taking turns to kneel on their seats trying to aim into the neck of a bottle in bouncy conditions accompanied by ribald comments, must have provided our pilot with another crazy story to tell. Towards the end of the flight we were sitting there wondering what to do with the recycled whiskey.

The first six months of 1979 was an acting drought. I spent most of it erecting circular stairs in homes on the north shore of Sydney. Then the gods decided to give me a break. It began with an interview in June with a top-flight sitcom director from the UK, Michael Mills, and his scriptwriter Vince Powell.

They had been invited by the ABC to guide local talent towards the high standard of sitcom for which the British were noted. John O'Grady was the ABC co-producer. The series was to be called *Home Sweet Home* about an Italian immigrant family. John Bluthal had been signed up to play the lead. I was up for the part of Father Murphy and heard very quickly that I had got it. There was a reading with the cast of the first episode in July but it took until February 1980 for the first of six episodes to be recorded.

In the meantime Anne Peters my local agent in Adelaide found a suitable part for me in a series to be shot in Melbourne for the ABC. *Lucinda Brayford* was a period drama based on the Australian novel by Martin Boyd about the life and loves of an Australian lady in Australia and England in the post-First World War era. With Wendy Hughes playing Lucinda, I found myself co-starring with a fellow English actor Barry Quin and the yet-to-be discovered Sam Neill. I was to play Pat Lanfranc, an emotionally retarded English gentleman, an important role for which I was interviewed, not screen tested.

Interviewing for a part was standard practice through to the 1990s except for commercials. Now everybody is screen tested because that is the way the Americans do it. Increasingly it seems most projects are creatively strangulated by budgets worked out by producers and accountants, who have little imagination but a strong say in the casting.

With increasing trips between Australia and the UK on a British passport, it seemed wise to acquire dual nationality. So I found myself among many southern Europeans being naturalised in a ceremony at Mosman Town Hall. It was conducted by the Mayor of Mosman, Barry O'Keefe, whose brother Johnny was an Australian pop star. Apparently, after several toasts, I talked loudly in the presence of the Minister for Immigration (Michael McKellar) about my family having founded the colony of Western Australia.

The traditional wishes for good fortune in the new year certainly worked for me in 1980. It could not have happened at a better time. My girlfriend from the UK had arrived and we were talking of marriage. I had a long period of fairly constant work from 14 January.

The first episode of *Home Sweet Home* had been completed in the third week of February 1980 while I was still working on *Lucinda Brayford*. Throughout February and March I was flying back and forth between Melbourne and Sydney. My agent, David Brewster at Kevin Palmer Management, relished the nightmare scheduling. He was the best agent I ever had but sadly slipped away 'to the undiscover'd country' too soon.

I somehow managed to fit in a feature film during an eight-day break before starting on another *Home Sweet Home* episode. I had heard about it previously, as the script was being written by Colin Eggleston, the director on *Matlock*. I held very little hope for the shoot dates to fit in but this time they did, even though the movie was being shot in Melbourne.

The film was directed by John D. Lamond, well known for his lightweight sex movies like *Felicity* and *Pacific Banana*. It was initially called *Stage Fright* but it was changed later to *Nightmares*. It was a horror movie and I had the doubtful distinction of being killed while standing naked. I was repeatedly slashed from a shard of glass after making love in a dressing room! The story was set in the theatre. I was playing a coarse actor who was having more success with women than with his career. The part, perhaps, could have been seen as being close to the bone, but it certainly seemed to herald a pattern in my career – of being killed off in so many storylines. Notable in the cast was

Max Phipps and John Michael Howson. There was also a claim that it was the first time in Australia a steady-cam or pan-glider was used. It felt strange at first to see the cameraman walking away with his back to you.

Each episode of *Home Sweet Home* took about five days to rehearse and two days in the studio. This contract would turn out to be the one and only time I would have an ongoing role in a series, being in 18 episodes out of 24. I had to miss out on the third series due to an offer no actor would refuse. There were six-month gaps between each of the four series, which spread over a two-year period.

Home Sweet Home appealed to the immigrant population. It featured an Italian taxi driver who refused to adapt from his traditional ways, with his young family who had rapidly become Australian. In the hands of Vince Powell and Michael Mills, the plot ideas were beautifully structured and very funny with sparkling dialogue.

Vince was given a team of local writers who ended up writing most of the later series. Similarly, Michael Mills was given the young Geoff Portman and another to take over from him. It is my conjecture that because of this brief to mentor and take over, the series never received the recognition it deserved. There was an increasing inbuilt resentment in Australians against being told how to do things by the English. In 1981 the Logie award went to the locally made and very Aussie *Kingswood Country*. There was little doubt for many that *Home Sweet Home* was superior. In my opinion *Home Sweet Home* left a benchmark in scriptwriting and direction. The influence was there in the next very popular ABC series with Ruth Cracknell and Gary MacDonald in *Mother and Son*.

John Bluthal was a Polish immigrant to Australia and had become a very high-profile comic actor in the UK. He had starred in the acclaimed comedy series *Never Mind the Quality, Feel the Width*, written by Vince Powell, then had worked on Spike Milligan shows, before he more recently was a regular character in *The Vicar of Dibley* starring Dawn French. He hadn't worked in Australia for a long time and found the standard wanting. He would often stop, rant and rave about things not being right. Nothing rankles Australians more than someone who comes back from overseas and carries on about how much better it is done there. I had some sympathy for his frustrations but it was early days in the company's learning process.

I made a mistake on camera (something to do with a champagne bottle and Jill Perryman playing a nun, though I can't remember the details), which was bought by Dick Clark Productions in America for their blooper programme years later. The first I knew about it was when a cheque arrived from my London agent.

It was most enjoyable playing Father Murphy and I sensed I had made a good impression on both Michael and Vince. This was the beginning of a significant period in my career. I was being recognised in the street. The Italian stall holders in the market would ask me to bless them. Even after the turn of the century I was hailed by an Italian cafe owner in the outback. It was reported that in 1983 *Home Sweet Home* was the top-rating show in Belgium, beating *Dallas*. My profile was rising.

For the first time after meeting a director, I was invited to take away a script and, if I liked the part (which was a co-lead with Michele Fawdon), it would be mine. Michael Carson, one of the drama directors at the ABC in Sydney, was directing six original plays about social problems in our urban communities. The play was called *Silent Cry* in a series called *Spring and Fall*. A far cry from what I was doing. Somehow the scheduling worked out. It was recorded just in time for me to fly to Melbourne to complete the final shots on *Lucinda Brayford*. I was on a plane for London on 1 May.

I had done four different television jobs in three months. *Silent Cry* received critical acclaim, with Michele Fawdon, playing the wife, winning an award. I had a very warm feeling about this solid period of successful work plus a strong indication for another six episodes of *Home Sweet Home* next October.

But there was a dark shadow in my personal life.

28

Back and Forth

Within two weeks of returning I was off to Madrid to shoot a commercial. I found myself in a run-down complex of famous film studios in the foothills above Madrid. It was where Clint Eastwood's spaghetti westerns were made.

I walked down the dusty street, rolling the Stuyvesant cheroot from side to side, hands ready, eyes squinting, looking for movement. I have always admired Clint Eastwood's acting. One might think it isn't acting because he does so little with his face, but his inner force and presence are spellbinding. It is a feline quality. He responds rapidly to a situation, but most of the time he is in a state of readiness. And that is compelling. He has refined minimalist acting to the ultimate.

On return I was back at my old hunting ground, the Theatre Royal, Windsor, in *Alphabetical Order* by Michael Frayn, one of Britain's leading playwrights. During the run of the play I was able to do the part Vince Powell had suggested me for at ATV. It was in an episode he had written for a sitcom called *A Sharp Intake of Breath* starring David Jason. It was being filmed at Elstree Studios, north of London, which meant a lot of angst travelling. When you have a performance in the evening, there is always a knot of worry doing anything during the day. It has always been an absolute rule that actors should be in their dressing room by the half, which is actually 35 minutes before the performance. This time I managed to avoid cows on motorways.

I had a couple of scenes with David Jason. He was so easy and helpful to work with, despite seeming to be in a state of high anxiety. It is in the nature of comedy to worry over whether something works. It is much harder than straight drama. 'Comedy is a serious business' was originally coined by the great 18th-century actor David Garrick and added to by W.C. Fields with: 'A serious business with only one purpose – to make people laugh'.

The cost of living had doubled from 1978 to 1980. This was an early indication of the pressure-cooker economy which eventually exploded in 1987. I resisted the easy advice from well-off friends to climb the mortgage ladder and I still have the one and only property purchased in 1978.

At the beginning of October I was winging my way back to Sydney to do the second series of *Home Sweet Home*. It was to be over a 10-week period with a 50% fee increase. This augured well for further series. I was lucky to be in work. My good friend who had settled in Australia had a lean time in Sydney during 1980. That brought home to me the advantage of having a career in two countries. Any performer is more likely to get work in England, purely through the huge volume of product that is needed to supply a worldwide audience. Australian television dramas, and to some extent movies, are hamstrung for investment, as they need to be initially secured in the local market.

I made a habit whenever I arrived back in Sydney to call up my close friends and tell them to join me in the queue at Doyles Restaurant on the foreshore of Watson's Bay. This was well before Doyles became commercialised for tourists. We would sit outside the original stone cottage, washing down a dozen rock oysters with Seaview riesling. This would be followed by John Dory fish with chips while watching the sun descend through the great arch of the harbour bridge. That was one small reason I loved Sydney in those days. For me the harbour makes Sydney one of the most bracing and embracing cities in the world. It has character and history through its higgledy-piggledy streets. Walking through the Rocks area you can feel the past under your feet. Robert Hughes captures the essence of early Sydney in *The Fatal Shore*.

I was probably more content than at any other time in my life. I was in work, with a further series in the pipeline. Linda and I had planned and booked a skiing holiday in the Austrian Alps over Christmas. She was appearing in a play for the English Speaking Theatre in Vienna. This was another avenue of work for English-speaking actors. Other capitals in Europe had similar companies, Vienna and Stockholm being the best known.

I was soon bumping over the Bay of Bengal to Delhi on a Philippine Airlines DC10. The door-to-door journey took about 30 hours. Two days later I was on a British Airways flight to Munich, where I boarded a train on a four-hour journey to the mountain village of Steyr.

It was dusk and snowing. I looked out of my window expecting to see a station and platform where Linda would be waiting. There was no platform. I saw a lone figure running towards the old train as it crawled to a standstill. There was a drop of three feet to the ground; throwing out my bag it crunched on the snow. Linda was several yards away. I was transfixed. It was Julie Christie from the film of *Dr Zhivago* running towards me. I hadn't quite gauged the distance between the train step and the white-shrouded ground. As I was declaring Linda's name my leg went from under me, and I landed face-first into the snow. Bang went what could have been a beautifully staged romantic moment. Instead of playing the part of Omar Sharif I looked like an understudy for a snowman. It was better really; we had a helluva laugh rolling about in the snow.

Another train journey the next day took us to the enchanting village of Radstadt. The Sports Hotel where we stayed overlooked a typical Christmas card scene. We were gazing through the gently falling snow to a brightly lit Christmas tree, a path leading to a church with a steeple and beyond – the lights of a faraway town.

What happened next resonated with me. We were drinking in the bar after a traditional fish meal when someone quietly began singing *Silent Night*. Everyone joined in singing the English words. Then an eerie moment in time when at the end someone began singing the carol again this time in German, which gradually picked up to full voice. It was spellbinding, as it evoked that famous occasion during the First World War when both sides emerged from their trenches into no-man's-land after the carol was sung in a similar way. The music and the peaceful words called them together. A perfect example of how the arts bring people together, whereas the pursuit of power flings them apart.

On our way to midnight mass, we walked through the graveyard of the church, illuminated by the local custom of placing lighted candles on every grave. It was a hauntingly beautiful scene.

We had a memorable holiday. I found skiing frightening, all arms and legs. More to my liking was careering down a windy mountain track under a full moon on a toboggan, fortified with rum and tea.

A gentle chug-chug train took us to Salzburg for a few hours on our way to Vienna, Linda had booked tickets to the Kaiserball. We wandered through the bustling alleys of the old town, lingering in the newspaper-stick coffee houses on the main square, but avoiding commercialised Mozart.

The Kaiserball, now called Le Grand Bal, held in the Vienna Hofburg Palace every New Year's Eve, was beyond expectations. We climbed a grand marble staircase overhung with enormous chandeliers, passed a statue of Kaiser Wilhelm on the way into the main ballroom. There were altogether three vast ornately decorated ballrooms, shimmering with chandeliers, with an orchestra in each. One could briefly experience the joy and excitement of those gala balls of the empire days. We waltzed our way into the second year of a decade that would see a lot of changes, with the early part taking me to the highest point in my career.

29

Tenko

Tenko is the Japanese word for 'roll call' and in a way there comes a time in an actor's life when you need to be called. Are you present and correct in the division you find yourself at 40 years old? My answer would have been yes even though I never seemed to be satisfied.

Inevitably the euphoria from our holiday in Austria was short-lived. I returned home to a large tax demand with no immediate prospects. Had I known what was in store I would not have needed to write:

> ... have just got to get through this bleak period ahead, try to survive until next September, when I shall more than likely be engaged for a further series of *Home Sweet Home.*

It didn't last too long. Not only did I get two small film jobs while landscape gardening during an extremely mild winter, I was also up for a part in a new series for the BBC.

Actually it was Linda who was up for a part in *Tenko.* This series was an original idea developed by Lavinia Warner. Stories and details were gathered from reminiscences and letters of women who were captured and incarcerated in camps by the Japanese during the early part of the Second World War.

Linda sadly didn't get a part, but while being interviewed suggested to the director Pennant Roberts that I might be suitable to play the Australian journalist. I had met Pennant before at a wedding and he duly called me in. After a second interview with the producer Ken Riddington, my agent called to say I had got the role.

At the same time my Australian director friend Ken Hannam wanted me for a part in *Day of the Triffids*, also for the BBC. At one point I was able to do both as it fitted in with a week out on *Tenko*, but then a day was changed and I couldn't be available. However, that was not the end of it.

Before rehearsals began for *Tenko* I was able to slot in 10 days on the popular series *Angels*, again for the BBC. The director was Patrick Tucker who, with his wife, established the Original Shakespeare Company that beckoned me later.

All this activity certainly shows how quickly fortune can change from an anticipated 'bleak period'.

Although getting a part in a female series was unlikely to propel me into becoming a noted television actor (meaning regularly being considered for parts), it did raise my profile. It also added mileage in my travelling career. After two weeks rehearsal nearly all the cast were flown to Singapore for three weeks of filming.

Filming abroad is like being on a big school outing. All travel and accommodation paid for, our BBC per diems of £26 were sufficient for an evening meal. It was cheap to eat in an open air market like Newton Circus. An evening meal for three cost £17. It was an exotic experience eating on the streets of Asia. You sit on plastic chairs in 32 °C and high humidity in a playground for cockroaches and your nose twitching at the pungent smells of Asian cooking. Somehow, from tiny kitchens delicious food appears served on plastic plates by an impassive Chinese face. Our headquarters were at the Equatorial Hotel on Bukit Timah Road.

The old part of Singapore had not been developed in 1981, though I fear it may have been destroyed since. Chinatown was where many street scenes were filmed, having hardly changed since the Second World War. My main scenes from the first episode were filmed on the terrace looking out onto the garden of Raffles Hotel. This famous hotel had also hardly changed since the days when Noël Coward sat at the bar, sipping his Singapore Slings in between slinging his wit. The other major location was on the tiny island of Kusu, a forty-minute ferry ride from Singapore, where we filmed the shipwreck scene.

There were three well-known actors in the cast and one who became a television star later. She was Stephanie Cole who is still featuring in series such as *Doc Martin*. Anne Bell was a leading actress in the theatre and television, as was Stephanie Beachamn (*Dynasty*). The late Bert Kwouk, who was the leading Asian actor in London, played the Camp Commandant. He was best remembered playing the beleaguered assistant to Peter Sellers in the

Inspector Clouseau film *The Pink Panther*. Daniel Hill (*Judge John Deed*) also made a name for himself.

I was playing Bernard Webster, an Australian journalist sent to report on the situation in Singapore in 1941. My on-and-off girlfriend was Rose Millar, played by Stephanie Beacham, who came with a reputation for being difficult. She was certainly feisty, had a sharp tongue, and her acting was precise and fast. I was in awe of her. Her manner made me feel inferior. After all, she had acted opposite Marlon Brando in *The Nightcomer*. I had never acted with anyone quite like her before. She was very demanding in the way she wanted to play scenes but eventually she came round to working with me. I got on well with her in the end – in a working capacity!

The scenes of life in Singapore were of an Empire community completely unaware that the Japanese forces could land on the east coast of Malaya and make their way down the peninsular to Singapore. It was regarded as impregnable, a fortress, but the guns were pointing out to sea. Dances, tiffin, parties and gossip were the order of the day. The situation lent itself to high drama. After Singapore was bombed on 8 December 1941, there were rapid preparations to leave by ship. There was a very jolly but doomed New Year Eve's dance party, which we filmed in the BBC studios. The scene was reminiscent of Lord Byron's poem '*The Eve of Waterloo*' from the *Childe Harold* collection, when Napoleon's troops were on the outskirts of the city: 'On with the dance! Let joy be unconfined.'

Boarding the last ship to leave the war zone was also filmed in a studio back in London. The ship was torpedoed off the North Borneo coast and we were filmed scrambling ashore on the Singapore island of Kusu. The location could almost have been where it had actually taken place. The shipwrecked group were all seen crawling out of the sea, gathering together and moving inland to find shelter. The film shows us staggering up a jungle path until we find a hut, which in reality, was by a pig farm. We were then filmed lying around exhausted trying not to react to the awful smell. Then without warning or rehearsal we hear the sound of a vehicle. There was a camera taking a wide shot of our group as we tentatively rise in the hope of rescue. The truck stops and out poured Japanese soldiers, jabbering and pushing. Acting was not necessary, it was frightening. The Japanese were mostly Asian students employed as extras. But we had a few extras in our group, including an old Singaporean couple who were petrified. It was too real for them. They had to be comforted. Our wily Welsh director Pennant Roberts achieved a moment of real truth.

The shipwreck and capture took three days to film. The scene on the beach alone took 14 hours in one day. I spent most of the day in wet long trousers and shirt. At one point I am seen limping hurriedly along the beach looking for Rose (Stephanie), finding her trying to save clothes from a smashed-up soaking travel bag. She was standing knee high in the sea, her wet clothes clinging to her voluptuous body. I think my wide eyes caused the rebuke 'Are you going to do that on your close-up?'.

There was a dramatic photo taken with my arms round Stephanie and Anne Bell, having just emerged from the sea, which appeared on the front cover of the *Radio Times*.

The view on our return journey by ferry to Singapore Harbour was equally dramatic. A storm was brewing as we approached. Great black clouds were rolling up. The sharp lines of the tall buildings with great ships in the foreground gave the impression of a theatrical backdrop. There were hundreds of ships in dock and anchored out at sea, Singapore being the second busiest port in the world.

Singapore under Lee Kwan Yew was a well-ordered clean city but it retained something of its romantic past from the time when it was the hub of the Empire in the East. An example of this was when I went to find Mr Chan. He was a very well-known bespoke tailor. I called into his shop to order my suit, trousers and shirts, which would all be made within 24 hours. I was somewhat surprised when he told me that Lord Mountbatten was one of his clients. For some reason he wanted me to have a copy of his last order. It was on Broadlands headed paper (his stately home). It proved to be most poignant. The order requested: three dozen underpants, 16 shirts, a double breasted blue blazer and two pairs of flannel trousers. He obviously expected to live for a good while. The letter was dated 2 August 1979. Two weeks later he was blown up on his boat by the IRA.

There was a further connection to my career in Singapore. A friend, Liz Perry, had married Philip Johnston who was the Secretary of the Singapore

Jockey Club. They were fairly typical of an expat couple living the good life in one of the last bastions of the Empire. They had servants, amahs, chauffeurs and entertained people in high places. I, in turn, was entertained royally by them. The Japanese bombs could not obliterate the deep legacy the British left behind. It prevails with so many expat Aussies, British and Europeans working with many staying on.

Soon after returning to London, during the period of rehearsals for the studio scenes, Ken Hannam, directing *The Day of the Triffids,* called me at home on a Friday night. He asked if I could take over the role of Walter (the part I was originally offered) at short notice. Sound familiar? He told me the actor cast in my place was not up to it. His producer, who also knew me, agreed. At this point on *Tenko* we were filming the ship-sinking scene in the big tank at Ealing Studios. Pennant Roberts had no problem letting me do it.

It was only one scene, as he is the first to be killed by a triffid. The first episode was booked to be recorded the following Tuesday night. I received the script on Saturday morning and learned the lines that day by constant repetition. On Sunday morning I was off to the BBC rehearsal rooms in Acton to work the fairly wordy scene with John Duttine who was playing the lead. On the Monday morning I was picked up and taken to Ealing studios to be filmed leaping off the ship's side into the sea. (A portion of the side of a liner had been painted on a backdrop next to the huge tank.) At the end of the day's filming a car was waiting to take me to the BBC Centre.

My character was in the first scene, so I had to be ready by 7.30 pm to do a one-and-only rehearsal with cameras. In the next episode I appear as a dead Walter, for which I received a special separate fee of about £15. The BBC decrees that £15 is what you are worth dead. The same procedure the next day, except it was the final recording. It was heady stuff, racing from one studio to another playing two different roles with minimal rehearsal.

I had never seen that first episode of *The Day of the Triffids* until 2007 when I was visiting a school in South Australia. I found on arrival they were studying the novel and had been watching a video of that BBC production recorded in 1981. I sat and watched my performance and was amazed how fluid and totally convincing it was. I had quite a lot of chat but didn't seem to falter. It felt like watching someone else. Well, I was the 'take-over kid'.

30

More Heady Days

By the end of June 1981, I had been in almost constant employment by the BBC since the beginning of the year. The fourth production was in a strange sci-fi series called *Code Name Icarus* in which I played a piddling little role in a control room with a lot of technical lines. These kind of parts give more grief for an actor than most other kinds of roles, because lines are difficult to learn and you have no scope to play a character. At this point in my career, looking back, I should have started turning down these jobs. In a sense you are a glorified extra, but I was paid for a whole week's work when I only worked one day, and I kept receiving lots of repeat money. It would be another six months before *Tenko* was shown, which was probably why I kept accepting anything offered.

Agents are like fishermen on a river bank, casting the line into the stream. The float with bait on its hook is your name. An appropriate part comes along, the casting agent takes a bite. Your agent is phoned and an appointment is arranged. I was sent to the celebrated Blake's Hotel, founded by the actress Anouska Hempel in South Kensington, to meet a director and producer from Hollywood. This interview was for a part in an epic television series being made all over Europe and America by Paramount Studios. They were looking for an actor to play Air Commodore Lord Burne-Wilke in an adaptation of Hermon Wouk's two novels about the Second World War, *The Winds of War* and *War and Remembrance*.

Gathered in the lobby of the hotel, waiting to be called, were a number of familiar faces, including Christopher Cazenove and my friend Ian McCulloch, who was a higher profile actor than I. The moment came to take the lift to the top floor. In the lift on my way to the interview, I was preparing for the meeting – taking deep breaths; checking the tie, hair and fly; trying to think of some jolly off-hand remark to appear at ease – but knew all along I had another wait before the meeting. Imagine my stunned look when the lift door opened and there they were, the interviewing heavyweights from Hollywood. Nobody had said anything about the lift opening straight into the room. After a brief panic I relaxed, thinking I hadn't a hope in hell of getting this part. Dan Curtis was the director and Barbara Steele the producer. I cannot remember what I was asked and what I said. I walked out of the hotel and cast it out of my mind.

I was very consumed by my relationship with Linda. We were hardly ever together for any length of time. Plenty of money was spent on phone calls. She always seemed to be busy being busy, and was having understandable doubts about getting married. And it followed that I continued to be plagued with the idea of seeming never to move up the earning ladder. Despite the recent constant work, I was still struggling to pay bills, in particular a three-year tax demand. All actors are paid weeks after working in television and film; theatre pays weekly. You have to be pedantically disciplined to put money aside, and actors in their private lives are, generally speaking, neither pedantic nor disciplined.

During the month of July, I was spending a day at Lords Cricket Ground. Sitting there watching England play the West Indies, I could not have imagined that a short scene on the phone had taken place in the Members' Pavilion which concerned me. Later at home, my agent June Epstein told me she had phoned the Secretary at Lords in the afternoon. She had tried to persuade him to put a call over the loud-speakers for me to call into the secretary's office to receive an urgent message. The secretary politely asked June if it was a matter of life or death. June replied, 'When he hears what I have to say, he will have a helluva lot more life in him'.

The secretary was apparently amused but declined the request. I had got the job in *The Winds of War*. I was dumbfounded. It took a while to sink in. My only little regret was that my name did not caress the air waves over the hallowed turf.

There are two dreams most actors cherish: to see your name in lights in the West End and to land a part in a Hollywood movie. This was nearly there, with a good support role in a Hollywood television series and an appearance off-West End at the Soho Poly basement theatre and at the nearby Old Vic.

This was what I had won: a significant support role in four long scenes with Robert Mitchum, a major Hollywood star, in an epic blockbuster for Paramount, a major Hollywood studio. I was being paid a hugely inflated fee compared to the BBC, and was to be flown first class to Seattle plus handsome per diems. But I only found out we were going to America during a wardrobe fitting at Bermans. My initial booking on *The Winds of War* was to finish on 20 September in UK. At one point it was going to be possible to do the next six episodes of *Home Sweet Home*, which was due to start in Sydney on 21 September.

Often technicians, and particularly wardrobe personnel, know before you do what you are doing. I definitely couldn't do the next six episodes of *Home Sweet Home*, which concerned me. There was talk of a further series next year, so feared I might be written out. In the end they wrote in another priest who had taken over while Father Murphy was on leave. I would be brought back for the final series.

June Epstein (no relation to the Beatles' manager) was naturally delighted. She was becoming annoyed with my going backwards and forwards to Australia, saying she couldn't build a career for me if I kept disappearing. That has probably been the crux of why I didn't make more of my career in both countries.

I was on a good run and it continued. Maybe my stars were in alignment. I had an interview for a commercial to be shot overseas somewhere and another for the BBC series *Bird of Prey*. I heard about getting the BBC job just before leaving for America.

The commercial was to be shot in the Maldives for Abbey National Building Society. The brief to agents was 'an average couple to be seen running along a beach hand in hand having a holiday of a lifetime'. I said to my agent it would be pointless going to the interview. They would be looking for a male model, there was no dialogue. How wrong I was. Typically, I had to turn down two other jobs, one ironically being for Woolwich Building Society. But it turned out to be a fantastic paid holiday.

We were flown to Colombo on 2 September and stayed for two nights in the famous Galle Face Hotel. It was a wonderful relic from the days of the Raj, with ancient waiters in white jackets serving tiffins and teas. We even saw a performance by the Sri Lankan Army Dance Troupe in the vast ballroom. The streets of Colombo displayed a different story. The city was very run down and polluted, with beggars everywhere. Many had limbs purposely removed in order to beg from what looked like skate boards.

We flew on to Malé, the capital of the Maldives. This spindly country is comprised of over 1000 islands in a double chain of 26 atolls formed in the middle of the Indian Ocean 1000 km from Sri Lanka. Our island was a further 65 km boat ride.

We arrived at a jetty that led into an open air dining area. Our accommodation was basic. Circular huts made of bamboo on a concrete floor with a bed, table, clothes-hanging space and a divided-off shower and loo. A small veranda looked out on to white sands, palm trees and an aquamarine sea. You could walk round the island in 10 minutes. There was little else to do other than read, swim, snorkel, windsurf, fish and walk hand in hand along a beach into the sunset – yucky stuff. And this is what we were filmed doing.

Being on a tight schedule has not been a common occurrence in my career. I had to be back in time for my first day of shooting on The *Winds of War* by Thursday 10 September. Having just got sufficient footage for the commercial after a whole week there, I left the middle of the Indian Ocean on Tuesday 8 September. A speed boat travelling at 40 mph over choppy seas got my all-shook-up body onto a plane to Colombo, where I arrived just in time to take another flight to Bombay.

Arriving at Heathrow early Wednesday morning, I heard my name over the tannoy system. My agent instructing me to go straight to Bermans for a final wardrobe fitting. My head was in a spin, I felt very tired and worried. I had been going over and over my lines on this trip, the environment of which was out of kilter with the world I was about to enter. By 6.45am on Thursday morning I was ready, with twitching nerves, to be picked up.

In the car was a familiar face. I had been Patrick Allen's offsider in an episode of *Troubleshooters*. He was playing Air Vice Marshall Sir Hugh Dowding. We were being taken to the actual RAF ops room in Uxbridge that was used during the war, now a museum. Within 48 hours I had travelled from a tropical paradise location in the middle of the Indian Ocean, to a room deep in the bowels of West London.

By 7.15 am I was in make-up, by 8.00 am in uniform and descending the same steps taken by those men 40 years ago. We were walking in their shadows. It was an eerie experience being in the actual operational room used by RAF Fighter Command, from where the Battle of Britain had been conducted, which we were about to re-create. The scene was shot in the narrow ops room that was used then. It looked over the huge table maps upon which girls were pushing the aeroplane counters. Above them were the boards for each aerodrome, indicating numbers of aircraft. Among the girls below operating the tables was Victoria Tennant playing Pamela Tudsbury, the love interest in the story who becomes engaged to my character in *War and Remembrance*, the sequel.

I sat in my position in a state of nervous anticipation, waiting for the big man to arrive. He came through the door and there was a kind of hush. You could immediately sense the man had charisma. Robert Mitchum shook my hand, greeting me warmly and in so many words said to the director, 'Let's run the scene a couple of times so Ed can get into it'.

Dan Curtis, our director, was a man on a mission. The film had a huge budget of $63 million, but it was very tight. He wanted to shoot every scene in one take, which of course was impossible. He certainly didn't want to waste too much time rehearsing. This is what I wrote in a letter:

> I had all the dialogue, Mitchum said three lines. It was very difficult to maintain concentration being filmed in the actual control room where the real officers at the time would have been. It was hot and crowded. I had to say my lines over and over for the various takes at different, impossibly tight angles. After a while I began fluffing (*stumbling over the odd word*) but not disastrously. It took 10 hours to complete which left me pretty bushed. The director came up to say not to worry about the fluffing and that I was marvellous – mind you Americans throw out superlatives like ordering coffee. However, the production office later confirmed that he must have been pleased as he didn't complain about me. He had a reputation for being difficult and complaining about everything.

That last comment would prove to be all too true.

By any standards it was a difficult scene for any actor to do on his first day with a major star on a Hollywood epic. Mitchum was understanding and generous. I spent most of the day in his company. He told some wonderfully funny stories about famous people he had worked with. These stories would be further embellished later with the help of vodka, his favourite tipple on location in America.

My schedule was crazy. I only had a day after that exhausting shoot to get things together for the train journey the next day to Vienna. Linda was working there in the theatre again. I was dashing over trying to save our relationship. Linda wanted out – just when I was about to earn lots of money. In typical female form she wanted to see me earlier but by the time I got there it was too late. She was over her crisis and still wanted to break up.

The gods love dishing it out when things are going well. At least we visited a few places of interest which we had missed before: the Spanish Riding School and the Pummerin Bell in St Stephen's Church, and we rode the Great Wheel, which featured in the film *The Third Man*. I think she wanted me to hover unseen in the background of her life, as Orson Welles did in the movie. The train and boat journey home were miserable and exhausting. I had a week to lighten the heavy, lovelorn heart, which must have succeeded because I wrote in a letter: 'Oh well, such is life. At least it isn't boring.'

On 3 October I boarded a flight to Seattle and was shown into first class. That helped.

31

An American Dream

Being the first time for me in first class, I had the feeling of flying on a magic carpet. We were in the front of the plane in large bucket seats that only tilted backwards. Champagne was on tap and it was the one and only time I ever tasted Beluga caviar. The only niggle, as we winged our way across the Atlantic and northern America, came from Howard Lang in the bucket next to me. It was a long flight and in that time he told me his life story until he nodded off snoring.

Howard, playing Churchill in *The Winds of War*, was known for playing Captain Baines in *The Onedin Line*, a very popular series in the 1970s. Alan Cuthbertson was the other actor on the flight, cast as a British army officer. He was well known for playing English gentlemen. I was surprised when he told me he came from an early settlement family in Perth, Western Australia.

Our location for the week was in Bremerton Harbour, Puget Sound, a short ferry ride from Seattle. It was the HQ of the US Strategic Arms in one of the largest naval bases in America, where the Polaris missiles were developed. Also many naval vessels from the Second World War were mothballed in the harbour. Our location ship was the mighty USS *Missouri*, being refitted. It had been decked out to look like the British battleship *Prince of Wales*. We would be filming the famous, crucial meeting between Roosevelt and Churchill for America to be persuaded to enter the war.

This shoot was big stuff. Another ship, carrying the President in his wheelchair with his entourage, manoeuvred beside the *Missouri* to allow them to cross over. President Roosevelt was played by that fine actor Frank Bellamy, with Roy Poole playing his Secretary of State, Harry Hopkins. The scene ended on the bow deck below where we were filming. After the agreement had been reached, the hymn 'Onward Christian Soldiers' was sung by the men who had formed a three-quarters square. The actual event was being re-created. It was mighty stirring.

What was also mighty stirring were the butterflies in my tummy. This was my first day, the schedule having been affected by constant rain. I had been waiting to be called for four days. At last I was called on deck to film another big scene with Mitchum. Alan Cuthbertson was also in the scene but hardly said anything. The three of us stood in front of Dan Curtis before going to where it would be shot. This was roughly the dialogue:

> Dan: Okay Ed, you stand there. Bob, you stand here, Alan, the other side of Bob, just do a few lines for me ... okay! Ed and Alan swap positions ... say a few lines ... right that's it, let's do it.
>
> Ed: Excuse me Dan, I thought it would be appropriate for Burne-Wilke to smoke a pipe in this scene.
>
> Dan: Okay fine, let's do it.

And that was the only rehearsal we had. There was no chance to practice with the pipe. It didn't matter to Bob so much, he had little to say. So there I was on the top deck of the USS *Missouri* in the rain – a thousand US naval ratings acting as extras watching – dozens of technicians rushing about – three cameras operating at the same time – huge arc lamps lighting the scene – loudhailers squealing and a manic director shouting.

The master shot that filmed all three of us in long shot went well. I had lit the pipe and puffed out the smoke through my dialogue, like I had seen so many film actors do in those war movies. We were half way through shooting my close-up when the camp continuity man leapt up, flapping his hands saying: 'You caan't use that Daan, the smoking's out of sync'.

Without rehearsing pipe business it was going to be difficult maintaining continuity from the master shot. It took another four takes for the continuity guy to stop yelping. Dan seemed okay but I sensed he wasn't. It was costing $2000 per minute to shoot on this location, with two battleships and a thousand extras. He expected not to be held up by actors, only by technical problems. Bob's close-up took one take.

Robert Mitchum had not said anything while I was struggling through my close-up. He waited until the shooting wagon had moved on. His slightly slit eyes looked at me kindly and in his inimitable laid-back manner said: 'Well Ed, you've learnt something today. Never use a prop in a close-up'.

That story has been handed down to all the actors whom my great friend Greg de Polnay has taught at RADA over his period of time teaching there.

It was exhilarating being on a big Hollywood shoot: I signed autographs for extras; I had my own caravan and personal assistant, Pamela Grant. Her official, somewhat over the top, title was 'the second assistant to the second assistant'. She was at hand all the time and even invited me to stay with her in LA after the wrap in Bremerton.

During the evenings in the Hilton Hotel, groups would gather, but rarely did the crew mix with the actors. After a 16-hour day the crew were exhausted and hit the sack early. Mitchum liked a drink and a chat and a whatever else might 'happen along'. One night his son arrived with supplies. Rumour had it that Mitchum was an early pioneer in the private cultivation of the fun weed. I spent most evenings in his company with a small group of other actors. To keep up with big Bob was way beyond my drinking capacity. Consequently, I cannot remember any of the dozens of wonderful stories he told. One event belonging to this 'happen along' outlook alarmed me. Lack of privacy would be a huge downside of stardom.

During the shooting of the scene I have just described, someone had noticed a mark on Mitchum's face, and we heard make-up had taken awhile to repair it. Rumours abounded, but it wasn't until the evening when Bob told us the whole story. He had arrived at his hotel room after leaving us, to find three woman waiting with autograph books. He duly signed, said goodnight and opened his door. The three women pushed past him, slammed the door shut and tried to rip off his clothes. While he was bundling them out, one of them managed to scratch his face badly enough to bleed.

Mitchum explained there was this subculture of women who would find out where famous people were staying on location and then try to seduce them so they could claim to have slept with so-and-so. Mitchum called them 'Mexican star fuckers'. I would describe the pursuit as 'cunting for trophies'. For him, I suppose, it was all in a day's work.

Paramount, at my request, had booked my return to London via Los Angeles and New York. On the flight to LA we had a spectacular view passing over Mount Shastri and the still smoking volcano of Mount Saint Helena. The year before it had erupted to the extent of affecting the weather patterns of Europe.

My lovely assistant Pamela Grant met me at the airport and drove me straight to Santa Monica, where groovy people were parading themselves up and down the famous boulevard on roller skates. She had to go away for the first four days so I spent that time at the Montecito Hotel. It was situated behind Grauman's Chinese Theatre, famous for the hands and feet of stars on the forecourt. I tried a few to see if any fitted, in case I had been a star in my previous life!

The hustling trail had to be hit, to get an agent and see casting people. It was easy to meet Hoyt Bowers, Paramount's head of casting. He opened the door for me to meet an independent casting director called Reubon Cannon, who thought I would do well in Hollywood. Eventually, I found myself in the offices of Paul Khoner and Associates, an agency that specialised in European actors.

I was dealing with Walter Khoner, a kindly Viennese gentleman but it took me three meetings to persuade him to take me on. It was fortunate I was able to get together an NTC showreel. I knew about needing to acquire the green card and a visa, but I really didn't take on board the necessity to live, or at least move there, for however long it would take. James Laurenson, an actor friend, was in LA at this time touring with the Royal Shakespeare Company. He had the time to get an agent and within several months was back in LA with his family. He returned to the UK after a year having appeared in television productions, but said he earned money mostly from doing endless pilots for new shows.

Bad timing meant I was unable to renew the connection with Kirk and Anne Douglas as they had just left for the east coast. At least I caught up with Murray Rose, the champion swimmer who was now an actor and a sports promoter/commentator in LA. We had always kept in touch since meeting on the ABC production of *My Three Angels.* It was a great shock to hear that leukaemia had taken this supremely fit and beautiful man, known as the 'seaweed streak'.

Americans are wonderful hosts. I moved into Pamela's apartment for my last four days during which we did Disneyland and saw Elizabeth Taylor in *Little Foxes* at the Music Centre. On the last night she took me to Hollywood's oldest restaurant, Musso and Frank Grill near Grauman's on the Boulevard, where the stars of present and past have dined. I wrote 'it was a glorious night, like living a movie'.

And so my time in Tinseltown had drawn to a close. I never went back and have no regrets. Many actors over the years have uprooted themselves to chase the hare of stardom in that feckless world. The public only know of the few that succeeded: most go home. Those who stay hover in the myriad waiting rooms of Hollywood, seriously deluded. I was on my way to a much more real city.

32

Home on the Big Bird

I had already lined up to stay overnight with my old flatmate Judith Thurman who now lived in New York. We had shared a house in Barnes in the late 1960s. Judith had eventually succeeded as an author after moving back to New York. Her highly acclaimed biography of the Danish author Karen Blixen (Isak Dinesen) became the hugely successful film *Out of Africa*. On first meeting up with Judith she was very excited that this film was going to happen. The project was in pre-production. We were on a coffee crawl in Greenwich Village when Judith suddenly said: 'Ed, there's a part you could play. He's the lover of Karen Blixen: an aristocratic big-game hunter called Denys Finch Hatton.'

Judith in her excitement had not thought that through. A star was needed. However, although Redford's screen charisma worked well with Meryl Streep's superlative performance, I have always maintained he was miscast. The part should have been played with more bite and toughness by an upper-class British actor. Nothing like me I hasten to add. There are very few American actors who can play English or other accented characters (Marlon Brando as Fletcher Christian was laughable). Meryl Streep, however, was totally convincing as Karen Blixen.

I was booked to arrive back in London late that night. I had arranged before leaving for America to watch the second episode of *Tenko* with the director Pennant Roberts and his wife Betsanne. I was disappointed not to be back in time. 'You would get there in time if you flew Concorde,' said Judith. 'Try up-grading.'

Paramount had paid £2,560 for my fare but I still thought it would stretch my pocket to upgrade. I phoned, and to my surprise they only asked for $140 or £70. What's more there was a seat free that day. I was going on the most beautiful plane ever built, the one Judith and I used to go out to watch ten years previously.

The journey began in the Concorde lounge, with me trying to look nonchalant, as though I was popping over to London for a meeting and popping back. My casual clothes with bits and pieces of hand luggage gave me away among the suited gentlemen with no more than a briefcase. It was not surprising I could get a seat; there were only about 40 passengers and interestingly, no women. Someone asked me later what it looked and felt like from the inside, two metaphors came to mind – like flying in a long cigar tube with butterfly wings.

It was not as luxurious as first class in a Jumbo. The seating was two each side of the aisle and tight with not as much leg room. But it is only three hours to Heathrow. And when you consider that you are flying at the speed of a bullet, at twice the height of Mount Everest, you need to be in a lean machine. I was surprised that I had written: 'the food was very good but not outstanding, however, the champagne flowed all the way'. The most thrilling sensation was feeling the incredible power from the engines on take off, and then the second thrust (the sonic boom that causes the noise) as it goes beyond the sound barrier at about 750 mph (1200 km/h). At top speed we were travelling in the outer atmosphere at close to 60,000 feet (18,000 m) at 1300 mph (2100 km/h). What was mind-blowing was being able to see the curvature of the earth's atmosphere.

I certainly didn't expect to talk to anybody during the flight. The atmosphere was 'gentlemen encased in a vacuum, working'. So I was surprised when the gentleman behind me made an opening remark. He was Richard Bloxridge, the CEO of Wilkinson Sword, for whom I had featured in a commercial, which he remembered. His very good friend Duncan Heath happened to be a top actors' agent in London. Naturally this was followed up but nothing came of it. Connections: some work, some don't.

The captain had come through soon after take-off to individually greet the passengers. Being an appalling name dropper and main chancer, I told him I had just been working with Robert Mitchum in a Second World War series and been playing 'one of you chappies – would awfully like to see how this jolly thing runs'. I'm sure I wasn't quite like a character out of P.G. Wodehouse. Whatever I actually said he seemed amused and immediately invited me to the cockpit. He even allowed me to take a photo of the bewildering bank of instruments and lights.

I then had the temerity to ask if I could be in the cockpit on descent to watch how it was landed at Heathrow. The captain said it was highly irregular, but 15 minutes from landing I was called to come through. I was strapped into the seat behind the pilot with headphones. Just before the wheels touched the tarmac the first engineer pushed a button and the nose dipped, becoming a beak. It was such a gentle landing, like a butterfly on a flower. They had brought Concorde in manually and through that procedure chatted away about what they planned for the evening. I was in plenty of time to get to Pennant Roberts's home. Flying Concorde was a fitting way to end a dream that came true.

As Winnie the Pooh would have done, once home I stepped aside and considered where I had been and did a little basking, but only for a minute. This roller coaster year had not finished. Despite having just come back from Hollywood, the first port of call as an actor in the UK is to sign on at the labour exchange. It is essential to get a franking credit for your pension.

The actors' bread and butter world kept things going. The BBC's television drama school called. I was cast to play extracts from the Michael Caine role in the play and film *Educating Rita*. To my surprise the director was Michael Attenborough, son of Richard and nephew to David. Michael became a successful director in theatre and television but never used me.

Bird of Prey, filmed in Birmingham, would turn out to be something of a cult series. It was a techno-thriller and propelled Richard Griffiths into the top ranks, notably for *The History Boys* and *Pie in the Sky*. There was a strong supporting cast led by Nigel Davenport, but another member of the cast raised a few eyebrows. There, at the first rehearsal, was the infamous Mandy Rice-Davies. She had been at the centre of the Stephen Ward scandal in the early 1960s with Christine Keeler. She had had a few minor credits, but I'm sure the producer Michael Wearing was delighted to have the publicity it would generate. All I remember was her strikingly different outfits every day. She was the owner of a fashion shop in Birmingham.

From 21 November to 23 December I was under contract to the BBC, which meant I had been in work for almost a whole year. I had earned in the region of £24,000, which was a proper, though average, professional salary. I had a truly happy Christmas.

Part 4

1982 to 1992

33

What Next

Early in the new year of 1982 I became initiated into the third degree of Freemasonry. It was an important payback for the fine education I had received, and it afforded me many future connections. A Master Mason is the minimum level that allows you to participate in full proceedings and attend any other lodge, but to rise to that level you have to go through a strange, somewhat mystical ceremony. I had to swear never to reveal any of the inner workings and secret words of that ceremony, but I can outline roughly what happened in my final raising.

In an adjoining room to the Square I was blindfolded with my chest bared and one trouser leg hitched up to my knee. The steward knocked three times and various questions and answers were given requesting entry. Then I was led onto the Square and told to kneel in front of the Grand Master to answer the final terms of loyalty. After the blindfold was removed I was required to make a speech of acceptance. It was nerve-wracking. Even though I am used to performing I have never been keen on making speeches, preferring to hide behind a mask. All the same, my speech went well and I was warmly welcomed into the Brotherhood. I have recently resigned but hope that what I contributed will, in some way, help another young person. The bad press Freemasonry receives is unwarranted. They not only look after those in need within the craft, but also support a wide variety of charities and projects, particularly in cancer research.

Whatever might have happened in 1982 it was unlikely to exceed the achievements of 1981. It had been a roller-coaster ride from Disneyland's Magic Mountain to the gentle landing on the tarmac by the Big Bird. Now it was back to 'bits and pieces' work and healing a 'broken heart'. Linda had finally left and was in another relationship. The gods seem to go out of their way to slap you down when you've been up high but at least I had work to look forward to. I was already lined up for another six episodes of *Home Sweet Home* in Sydney over March/April. There was also a strong indication that I would be brought back for one episode in the second series of *Tenko*, some time in the summer. A couple of features were on the near horizon, and it would not take too long before getting embroiled in another relationship.

Looking back to this point in my career, I probably should have upped sticks and moved to Hollywood. Many others did without having the contacts I had made. However, being an actor based in London is a safer, more diverse environment to gain some success, and the British acting fraternity is friendly and supportive. LA felt like a metropolitan jungle. You needed to have armour around your ego and a very small degree of trust in what people said. It would have been the ultimate risk-take for me and I didn't feel sufficiently confident.

Instead, I was back in familiar territory doing a commercial, an industrial film, a BBC training film and two days on Ronnie Corbett's sitcom *Sorry*. Then off to Sydney with a certain amount of reluctance about playing Father Murphy again – 'not moving my career forward' – which was a dumb remark. After all they could have written me out when I was unable to do the third series. It would keep my face out there with a strong possibility for a sale to the UK. When actors think only from their egos, sensible decisions aren't always made.

Before leaving for Sydney I fell under the spell of a woman struggling to escape from a loveless but well-heeled marriage. There was something bewitching about her, a sense of being lured into a web. She had the kind of quality that lured the Knight in Keats's poem 'La Belle Dame sans Merci'. I was flattered that this comely, elegant lady with warm eyes should entice me into her arms. I knew her inherent sensuality had been neglected. It was hanging in the air on my departure so I returned to London with eager anticipation. But in this fervent coming together again lay the seed of distancing, calculation and ultimate hurt. I described the state of the affair in a later letter:

> The saga continues. I am actually living a BBC Play of the Month – a common theme being the break-up of a middle-class family and the hovering triangle. I have had to fade into the background as she is trying to re-kindle a flame from the embers of her marriage.

We did have a summer of love: she came to cricket matches even in the rain, she brought her children to watch me filming *Tenko* on location, and her cooking had the sensuality of Nigella Lawson. Finally she achieved uniqueness by falling asleep while I was performing. I was reading her my short version of *Under Milk Wood* from a cottage that looked out on to the Black Mountains in Wales. Perhaps that is all we should hope for: snippets of bliss and limited periods of complete happiness. The affair was all over by the end of the year and some time later she ended up marrying someone with more substance.

The lead-up to appearing again in *Tenko* required some disciplined preparation. I needed to look as though I had been incarcerated in a Japanese prisoner-of-war camp for a year. This was not as arduous a task as expected. I went on a simple diet: cutting out sugar and not mixing protein with carbohydrates. In other words I didn't eat meat with bread or potato and only drank whisky, losing about one-and-a-half stone, equivalent to about 10 kg, over a period of eight weeks. After a visit to a Harley Street dentist to have a blackened tooth-cap made, I looked suitably gaunt. The tooth-cap was arranged by the BBC and cost a few hundred pounds, more than my fee.

The scene where Rose and Bernard meet up at great risk takes place in the jungle between two prisoner-of-war camps. We meet in a simple bamboo hut secreted among dripping foliage in a steaming jungle of North Borneo.

The magic of movie-making had us in a gravel pit in Dorset on an unusually cold day in August. In between takes smoke machines and the make-up department worked overtime, pumping mist and keeping us looking sweaty. We also had blankets to stop us shaking from cold. On the screen it cam across as a powerful love scene in a hot jungle setting.

In my estimation it was the best, most convincing screen acting I had done. Stephanie and I worked so well together that we had many a tear among the crew. I had become Bernard Webster, making the part my own. Credit for reaching that depth of feeling must also go to our director Jeremy Summers.

High on success I turned down an offer to be in a play starring John Alderton at the fashionable theatre restaurant in Sonning on the River Thames. In hindsight that turned out to have been unwise as John Dove was directing. He had directed *St Joan* at The Old Vic. I had got on well with him and he was, in a sense, inviting me into the circle of actors he uses. After being unable to take up a subsequent offer to be in his production of *A Month in the Country* by Turgenev at the Bristol Old Vic, I never heard from him again. That has always been a regret. Added to this is the fact that I have never been in a full production of a Chekhov play: an unfulfilled ambition.

Despite the successes I had during the last year and a half, it didn't take me long to be affected by a state of limbo. The latter part of 1982 was a lean period for many. When you get a period of few interviews the agent will say 'there is a low level of activity', which sounds like the Battle of Britain. It was getting me down but at least I tried to do something about it.

A friend of mine put together a voice-over tape – which was hawked around the rabbit warren studios of Soho – and found my Australian accent came in handy. I did a grandiloquent introduction for Dame Edna Everidge in the Russell Harty Show and imitated Paul Hogan in a series of Fosters beer voice-overs.

I have always been aware of a desperate feeling to be liked. Whenever meeting someone new, I have invariably found myself taking on their manner and accent. I was always interested in what people thought and where they came from, in a way trying to be like them. I would always put on a 'yer know wot I mean' London accent when in the company of tradesmen and then be just as toffy among the 'hooray Henrys'. I certainly took the edge off the Pommy accent in Australia.

During the last part of 1982 I got a little work shooting a commercial in Barcelona. After the shoot I met up with a friend who knew the city well. She took me on the funicular to the Miro gallery, then down to Las Ramblas to witness the Festival of the Three Kings and finally to a local restaurant through the winding alleyways of the old city. It was always a great tonic suddenly to be whisked to a European city.

My equilibrium was helped by taking up sessions on the Alexander Technique, used by many performers. After every session I came away feeling taller and buoyant. The technique was created by an Australian actor in Tasmania who had lost his voice, analysed what he had done and devised what has become an internationally recognised system for re-alignment of posture and muscular tonicity.

I walked upright into 1983 with a more positive outlook.

34

Lean Times

Despite my positive outlook, not one acting role came my way throughout 1983, even though I was virtually offered the guest lead in the opening episode of a new sitcom for Granada. At my expense I had travelled to Manchester and after the interview was told by the producer the part was mine. However, he did say the episode required the okay from the Controller (shades of *Brave New World*), but he was confident, as the pilot for the series had been accepted and the set was built. I would know for sure the next day.

Two days later having not heard, a friend of a friend reported that the Controller had pulled the plug on the first episode. The reason given was due to the Australian character having a heart attack, which might offend or upset people watching a comedy programme. Yet another let down. I was becoming very aware that nothing was directly coming from the two best parts that I had played; that my reputation was not based on a particular genre of part; that my versatility was working against me for developing a career. Of course, through this lean time my current affair began to fade. No drama, just a cool shunt.

Being cast in three commercials for Europe eased the ennui. The first found me on a tennis court in Barcelona for a mineral water commercial, playing an exhausted tennis player. The next was in Madrid for a cigarette commercial in which I had to learn a line in Spanish. I had enough spare time to linger awhile in Botins – the oldest restaurant in the world, from 1725 and still operating – made famous for being the writers' restaurant, frequented by Ernest Hemingway. I was able to spend much longer visiting the Prado Museum and Art Gallery. I got very excited looking at Botticelli's painting called *The Story of Nastagio degli Oresti (first episode)*. This title could be loosely translated as 'The story of the naked girl being bitten on the bottom by dogs with huntsman chasing'. I spent some time looking at that.

My trip to Milan was most enjoyable and even better paid. I was cast in a toothpaste commercial in which I was required to speak directly into camera. I had to mime speaking cod Italian so that a local actor could dub his voice-over my lip movement. What was interesting about this shoot were the personnel and an amusing evening out. I was directed by Justin who was at Oxford with John Cleese, Peter Cook and Dudley Moore. He was a charming gentleman with a dry wit. The cameraman was English, the make-up lady was from Cookham in Berkshire and the costume girl from New Zealand. I was not linguistically isolated.

After the shoot Justin took us to the famous Indian restaurant in Milan called 'Binares', like the one in London. We were greeted at the door by a very dark Sudanese gentleman speaking immaculate English. He took us to the cellar to wait for a table.

We were soon joined by an American couple, a whiz-kid record producer and his earnest Jane Fonda-styled wife. Then the sound count rocketed as down came a bunch of American jewellers. They kept introducing themselves with bone-crunching handshakes:

'Hi, I'm from Chicago. My name is Baab and yaors is?'

'I'm Ed.'

'Great to meet you, Ed. What brings you to Mylan, Ed?'

'We're shooting a commercial.'

'Oh, really? You in the movies, Ed?'

'Well actually I've just been working on The Winds of War *with Robert Mitchum.'*

'Oh my god, did ya hear that, Jess? Ed, say hello to my wife. Jess this is Ed, Ed this is Jess. He's a movie star.'

Dale Carnegie would have been proud of him, my name mentioned at least five times on meeting. Needless to say this encounter marred what would have been a very European experience. It actually felt like playing a part in an awful American sitcom.

I was compensated the next day. Having bought the obligatory umbrella, Milan being famous for umbrellas, I hailed a taxi for the airport. I had sufficient time to take in *The Last Supper* by Leonardo da Vinci in the monastery of Santa Maria delle Grazie. It was in the early days of restoration.

You could see the beginnings of its resurrection, but most of the figures were faint and scaffolding prevented any kind of experience.

It would have been silly not to take advantage of these trips. To those in the profession, snooty about tarnishing their image and talent, I would ask: did you get paid to see *The Last Supper*, visit the Rijksmuseum in Amsterdam, the Prado in Madrid, have a meal in the oldest restaurant in the world and have a holiday in the Maldives?

The height of tarnishing my acting career fell through eventually and probably just as well. I was suggested for being the presenter on a new magazine-style programme for long haul flights on Qantas planes. They couldn't afford David Frost so the agency handling the project were considering me. Like the object it was intended for, it hung in the air for a while but never landed.

The best way to attract more work is to commit to an outside project. I took on a landscaping job on my own. I experienced deep satisfaction from building two walls which reminded me that I shared something with Winston Churchill. I am sure he mused, as I did, that the wall would still be standing long after he ceased to be upright.

Of course, immediately after commencing this job three interviews came good. I was able to juggle them all and ended up earning one third of my year's eventual income in two weeks. One of these jobs was a commercial with Ronnie Corbett in which I had the experience of being ignored. We were filming in a shop in Barnes. I was part of the main action and spoke a line to him. I was not an extra. Extras do get ignored. Not once throughout the day did he say anything to me, nor look at me, nor in any way acknowledge my presence. Charlie Drake behaved similarly, I was told. Unlike Frankie Howard who wanted to do much more than acknowledge my presence!

There have been two occasions since then that my path has crossed with Ronnie's. Once on the golf course and the other was backstage, visiting Judi Dench in her dressing room after her performance in *Hay Fever* at the Haymarket. I was able, in a way, to get my own back. Ronnie was dominating the gathering standing next to Judi. I managed to butt in moving next to Ronnie and relate how I had played Sandy Tyrell three times and even performed the play in the open air Greek Theatre in Los Angeles. Ronnie kept looking up at me with that astonished look of his, as though I had committed an impertinence. Poor chap, Judi had arranged a seat for me next to her secretary right in front of him in the stalls.

Despite the paucity of acting work I was able to change agents and this time there was no changing deck chairs on the Titanic. Scott Marshall & Partners have looked after me ever since. Through them I landed a lucrative ongoing sales training film for Volvo cars, and after handsome repeat fees for commercials, having done eight during the year, I wasn't penniless.

Being very much on my own and not poverty stricken, I was a good candidate for a hasty plunge into a new relationship. Friends of mine had brought along a friend of theirs to a cricket match I was playing in. She was an attractive country girl from Warwickshire, living in Alcester near Stratford-on-Avon, not far from her parents farm. I did some chatting up but as she was somewhat GI (geographically impossible) living in the Midlands, thought no more about her. However, another sales training film was taking me up to Birmingham, so I phoned to say I would be passing through. She offered to put me up, so I suggested she book somewhere for a meal the following Friday.

The evening progressed easily but somehow came to a radical conclusion. It must have been the wine, the romantic surroundings and gazing at this comely, rosy-cheeked English country girl, because I asked her whether she would consider marrying me. She immediately replied in the affirmative with a four-week deadline to make up my mind. I was taken aback at her directness and her saying she always knew from the moment we met that we would be together.

Always one to go with the flow, four weeks later we were engaged with instructions given for buying the ring. A friend of hers was a Jewish jeweller in Birmingham. A beautiful sapphire and diamond ring set in gold was purchased at the trade price of £275. It was worth £600. Champagne corks popped with parents and friends, and a date for the wedding discussed.

Annabel came from a family who owned a well-known brand of jam, still available. Her parents also owned 800 acres of prime Warwickshire farmland. I was introduced to the formidable aunty who seemed to hold the purse strings. She interviewed me rather in the manner of a North-country version of Lady Bracknell. I was asked what my prospects were. With a smile I replied,

'I haven't a clue'. She thought what I did for a living was more of a hobby. I am sure she tried to persuade Annabel against this union. But Annabel would have none of it. She began planning my life with hers; worrying what she would do with her dogs and her cottage when we were visiting Australia – she had two enormous Irish wolfhounds and a dachshund. She insisted I would have to sell my flat and invest the money.

A marriage juggernaut had been launched and I began a slow retreat. Mind you the idea of living near Stratford did appeal so long as the Royal Shakespeare Company wanted me. Nesting on farm land near the great man's birthplace had a nice historical feel about it. But the reality of spending the rest of my life with a girl quickly showing more interest in her dogs, who slept with her, and where to live, was giving me rapid retreat fever. Perhaps it was my flirting with 'country matters' that had blinded me. Mind you, if I managed to climb over the wolfhounds to talk of 'country matters', I would be just as likely get a nip on the ankle from the dachshund.

My concern was to let her down gently. The friends who had introduced us were amused by the unfolding drama. But they did warn me that she had had a three-month nervous breakdown after the last boyfriend left her. The poor girl was obviously desperate to get married. I must have played the mea culpa role well because I was able to persuade her to give me back the ring. It wasn't thrown at my feet. With all this to-ing and fro-ing and being out of work, I needed the money.

Her dogs, her car and her possessions were all she ever talked about. She bored me witless. I believe she ended up in more appropriate company by marrying a Texan oil millionaire and living in America. And so the curtain came down on yet another attempt at being conventional.

35

Escape

Escaping to the Antipodes when things got tough in UK was starting to become a habit. My great friend Susie Maizels in Sydney was putting me up for filming projects and I knew that Ken Hannam would try to find me a part in a remake of *Robbery Under Arms*. He and Don Crombie would be co-directing.

Whenever I flew back from the UK, Sydney would normally be my base, Melbourne and Sydney being the centre for most things. But through Don Dunstan, the premier of South Australia in the 1960s, the South Australian Film Corporation had established a firm foothold in the movie-making landscape. It has a long list of credits including *The Breaker, Stormboy, Sunday Too Far Away* and *Shine*. Now it was to be a remake of *Robbery Under Arms*.

Luck was not running my way however. Both Ken and Don wanted me in the production but they couldn't find a decent-sized role. So they came up with a proposition: would I take the small part of a banker and be in charge of organising the cricket sequence? I would be Assistant to the Director for that period of filming and receive a separate fee.

The actor playing the Peter Finch role of Captain Starlight was Sam Neill, with whom I had co-starred on *Lucinda Brayford* in 1980. My job included coaching Sam to be able to look as though he could play well. My main task was to choose the cricketers and organise the match. Fortunately the main oval at my old school St Peter's College had been chosen for the shoot. I had been playing for one of the old boys' sides and was easily able to enlist a team plus the headmaster, and one other rather special member of staff.

Sam Neill could not have had a better stand-in cricketer than Paul Sheahan. He had opened the batting for Australia in the Ian Chappell era and was regarded as a fine strokemaker.

Wind and rain greeted us on the shoot day but one of the team had influence with a local television station. Their helicopter hovered over and blow-dried the pitch. Time was saved a little by having an ex test batsman. Paul was required to hit the ball on top of a marquee at deep mid-wicket. It didn't need faking; he managed it twice.

The whole shoot went on for almost 12 weeks, longer than normal. The reason was that they were making a television series and movie at the same time. It never really worked. The television series did well but the movie was disjointed and sank without trace. I was cast in another big television series later in the year called *Anzacs*, which gets an annual showing in Australia on Anzac day. Sadly, being on a film contract, there are no repeat payments.

During those few months before the *Anzacs* shoot I spent time with my mother, who had turned 85. She had just had a successful second exhibition of her paintings. A tradition had grown whereby I would invite my friends to her cottage to celebrate and they would always persuade her to recite the monologues she had learnt from Lionel Logue's elocution classes. Mother declaimed her monologues with grand gestures, immaculate diction and serious humour. She loved performing.

Anzacs was shot on farmland outside Melbourne by Burrows/Dixon Productions. They had mashed up a vast paddock into a first World War battlefield. In one sense they were lucky to have a lot of rain, though fire engines were still needed. The whole area felt close to how it must have been; mud everywhere and sodden trenches. Good for actors but not for crew moving equipment around.

I was cast, without a screen test, in a difficult role. Captain Young was an overbearing stickler for doing things by the book but a coward in the front line. It is much harder to play an anti-hero, particularly when you don't have a sufficient number of scenes to illicit any sympathy or understanding. It was written as a foil for Paul Hogan's character to show off his larrikin one-line put-downs. Not that Paul was playing anyone else but himself, as he did in his *Crocodile Dundee* movies. The coward element was to enhance the hero played by Jon Blake who knocks out Captain Young, crumbling with fear, unable to lead his platoon. In other words I found myself playing those two elements of the part, with no canvas to find a third dimension. I was told that what I did with the role was what they wanted. However, I was very unhappy with my performance. It felt stilted and superficial to me.

I arrived back in England in the cosy time of the year when summer wanes and the evenings close in. Autumn is the smell of burning leaves and log fires, the smooth feel of brown conkers and contemplation among the lengthening shadows. Keats called it 'the season of mists and mellow fruitfulness'. Something of that can be found in Australia, but it is never quite the same.

My agent suggested me for a couple of Hollywood movies but the one project I thought I had more than a chance of landing was the sequel to the *The Winds of War*. *War and Remembrance* was definitely going ahead. My only worry was hearing that some major parts were being recast. With Lord Burne-Wilke becoming more central to the love storyline, my fears were well-founded. I was devastated when my agent said that Rose Tobias Shaw, casting the series in UK, was instructed to recast it. It was galling to see an actor I knew play my part. Was I pushed because of the pipe? At least I had some satisfaction when seeing it. The part had been cut right down and marginalised. I certainly had the lion's share of the role in *The Winds of War*. That disappointment could have seriously affected me but fortunately I was not living on my own. My new partner Jenny had flown to London ahead of me.

It was hardly compensation but I was cast as a pilot in a new television series called *One by One*. The director was Richard Bramall whom I had worked for six years ago. The series was nothing to do with Noah and his ark but it was to do with transporting animals.

The shoot took place on an RAF airfield somewhere in Surrey where a Boeing 707 was in dock for repairs. I mention this because I was taken by what I had written in a letter about the scene in front of me from the cockpit where I spent a long time waiting. It is a tiny sketch of winter and gave me a Vivaldi *The Four Seasons* feeling.

> It was bitterly cold. The beginning of a very cold spell. The sky was black and the red sun on the horizon seemed to burn through the skeletal trees as I watched the gliders being towed down the airstrip and rise into the silent sky. It was eerie in the white landscape with gently falling snow on the ghost aeroplane.

The year ended in a jolly Christmas dinner with Australian friends. You can always pick up a stray Australian around Christmas in London. I literally bumped into Paul Bertram, whom I knew from early Sydney days, as I turned a corner. He was visiting with his girlfriend and would have had Christmas in a hotel. Many years later we would be in a play on a long tour.

Seven of us had dinner then went to midnight mass at St Paul's Cathedral. Somehow we all piled into my car with Paul in the boot of my hatchback. We were part of a congregation of about 3000. I am not sure how spiritual the experience was, but it was certainly high church theatre. I did, of course, imagine, during moments of silence, that I could just hear the faint echo of a certain 13-year-old boy's voice among the angels of the whispering gallery. I had sung solo all those years ago on St Paul's School Founders Day.

36

A Missed Chance

The year began well. I was cast as a millionaire Irish business man in an afternoon series for Thames Television called *Gems* about the rag trade. I was in several episodes over a period of four weeks, playing a smooth, dominating role. There was talk of my part being brought back but that fell through. Wardrobe were allowed to spend £400 on buying an Astrakhan coat from Acquascutum in Regent Street for the role – more than my fee.

At the end of 1984 I had been considered for one of the leading roles in a new BBC series. It was the part of Tom Howard in *Howard's Way*. Pennant Roberts, who had cast and directed me in *Tenko*, wanted me but Gerald Glaister, the producer, wanted Maurice Colbourne. Producers having more say, Colbourne got the job. I was given a consolation role in one episode, playing an accountant called Basil. It was bad enough playing an accountant – but to be called Basil! The series would have given me work over a period of five years. More importantly it would have lifted my profile to greater recognition within the industry and the public. It was a pivotal point in my career.

As things so often turn out though, when one door slams in your face another opens – well, more like a hatch. I bumped into Michael Mills while recording *Gems* at Thames Television. He was the establishing director on *Home Sweet Home* for the ABC in Sydney, now directing a sitcom called *Chance in a Million*, starring none other than Simon Callow and Brenda Blethyn. It was only to be a one-off part in one episode but it eased the disappointment soon after completing work on *Gems*.

A short holiday over Easter in Copenhagen staying with friends suspended any further self doubts. It was refreshing being in a Scandinavian country: visiting the viking ships in Rosskilde, the Little Mermaid (looking tiny and forlorn) and Elsinore Castle (looking for the ghost in Hamlet); wandering through a quaint 15th-century village, all clean and tidy in yellow ochre; eating Danish ice cream; riding bicycles around the old city; and taking in the castle guarded by a paltry number of lacklustre soldiers (Denmark never spent much on defence).

All artists need their champions and in this profession they are the directors who keep using you. Jeremy Summers, who had directed that love scene in *Tenko,* must have known how disappointed I was about *Howard's Way* through Pennant Roberts. Jeremy was kicking off another new series for the BBC called *Big Deal.* It was to star Ray Brooks, who had made his name in a movie of the play *The Knack.* He played an East End 'likely lad' called Robby Box: a petty criminal with an eye for the main chance, a gambler and a loser. I would be in four episodes at different times, ending in September. It was a very cleverly observed series, rich with cockney chat and I thought it had the potential of being as popular as *Minder,* but it didn't seem to register. I am fairly sure I never received repeat fees.

It was fun to be in but again I had reservations about the part I played. It was created primarily as a foil for the Ray Brooks character to put down or send up, so the part was not fully developed. It wasn't dissimilar to the functional part I played in *Anzacs.* Jonathon was a successful Australian businessman keen on Robby Box's girlfriend, but out of his depth among these low-life characters.

My final scene was shot in the rooftop restaurant of the old Derry & Toms building in Kensington. It happened to coincide with my niece and nephew's first trip to London. They came to watch their uncle play this tongue-in-cheek scene of pathos. Having been stood up by the girlfriend who has gone back to be with Robby, he sits on his own in this empty restaurant drinking into his cups, talking out loud to the non-listening waitress saying lines like: 'I am the most eligible man I know. Why has she chosen this waster? Women, they lose me.'

Grant and Linda thought this hilarious, having some knowledge of my track record with women. It occurred to me later that there were echoes from the first professional role I played. I was very good playing Andrew Aguecheek in *Twelfth Night* who had the immortal line: 'I was adored once too'. Have I been playing this part in real life, I ask myself?

A door that had opened in 1983 opened wider in 1985, becoming lucrative and more frequent. Michael Bosely and Lynda Wolfe's company had the Volvo car manufacturer company's sales training contract. They had cast me as the official trainer for Europe in a series of videos giving instructions on selling techniques. It was lucrative and ongoing over a three-year period.

Industrial films were a big earner for actors. John Cleese had a separate company and made training and information films that were sold to many international corporations. The 'Two Ronnies' feathered their nests with them. Latterly, role-playing in live sessions or being filmed in them can keep nagging partners quiet and bank managers happy (if you can find one these days).

Around this time I met Bob Kingdom at the Chelsea Arts Club, which was frequented by all kinds of artists but was originally established for painters and sculptors. Bob Kingdom was one of a number of thespian members. He spent many evenings there and was known for his mimicry, writing skills and voice-over work. At the time I met him he seemed to have lost his way. Like me he was a disciple of Dylan Thomas. I told him how I had put together a one-man show of *Under Milk Wood*, and that I had sat on the stool of the tavern bar Dylan frequented in Greenwich Village where he had drunk his last. I owned the vinyl record of Dylan's poetry recital in New York called *A Few Words of a Kind* and invited Bob back to my flat to hear it. Looking at him totally absorbed, I saw a strong likeness. He was Welsh, a little flabby with chubby cheeks, liked a drink and with his sonorous voice I suggested he might get together a one-man show of Dylan's life. His eyes brightened and I could see that I had perhaps sown a seed in his mind. With help from fellow Welshman Anthony Hopkins, *Dylan Thomas: Return journey* was finally premiered at the Edinburgh Festival in 1985. Since then he has developed one-man shows on Truman Capote, FBI boss J. Edgar Hoover and Edward VIII, performing in many parts of the world. I don't know exactly whether he would recognise that night as the beginning of the turn around in his fortunes. It makes me feel good to think I might have lit a spark that changed his life.

The Chelsea Arts Club was good, but Joe Allen's was my favourite restaurant for taking friends and overseas guests after a show. It is secluded in a basement on Exeter Street off the Aldwych, frequented by performers from West End shows. One of the great delights when you descended into the basement was to hear the ivory sounds from Jimmy. He wasn't quite Billy Joel but he was 'The Piano Man'. His gig lasted 37 years.

The year ended on a sad note – saying goodbye to my landscaping employer. Patrick and Mary O'Grady were off to live more amenably in the Algarve. However, that was not the end of my landscaping. Another actor I knew had been recruited to help out with big jobs and I suggested to him we keep going. Luckily he was more competent than I on technical matters. His name was Richard Kettles. Kettles and Pegge had a solid sound and we dug and built well into the 1990s.

37

Back and Forth Again

Unless you become a name, trying to move your career forward in countries that are at opposite ends of the world can feel like chasing the source of a rainbow. It was easier in the 1980s as there was more work, but the boom was beginning to sound hollow. Only a few Australian Hollywood stars can go back and forth now. For the majority of actors you have to be on tap. Perhaps if I had remained in the UK my career may have firmed up at the level of being regularly used, but I would have missed out on a variety of acting projects and many rewarding experiences in Australia.

I was lucky enough to be in Adelaide during the festival of 1986 in which I experienced a thrilling performance. It was the legendary production of *Richard III* by the renowned Rustaveli Theatre Company from Georgia. I was overwhelmed by the intense power of their acting, even though they were speaking Georgian. The abiding memory came mostly from their leading actor Ramaz Chkhikvadze, described by Festival Director Anthony Steel as 'the Olivier of the Caucasus'. It was not unlike the experience after seeing the film during my student days of that other great Russian actor Innokenti Smoktunovsky playing Hamlet. Like the country, Russian acting is monumental but believable. The Russian voice is big, deep, rich and thrilling.

I also attended a poetry performance in Melbourne by the great Russian poet Yevgeny Yevtushenko. Despite speaking his poems in Russian he was able to communicate the basic ideas and feelings through the musicality of his voice. He was performing his poems, not just speaking them. Many years later I developed this idea in my own rendition of his breathtaking poem 'I Would Like'.

Before returning to the UK in March 1986 I did a job for a small company selling farm products, information and ideas through a library of videos.

The company was called Avid and was run by Dale Kelly. Dale had been an Olympian, in the same swimming squad as Dawn Fraser and Murray Rose. I had fronted her promo tape. This job spawned a working friendship which would lead to other projects and more, over the next eight years.

It was a not an unusual March greeting for the first month back: cold, wind, rain, thunder, sleet, hailstones and no work. However, on meeting up with my cousin Phyllis from Zimbabwe, a story about my father lifted my spirits. She related a remark he made at a dinner party in Poona, India. The wife of a district officer was claiming to be a ballet dancer and proceeded to climb on to the table to demonstrate. No sooner had she done a few pirouettes than my father was heard to say: 'She maybe a ballet dancer but she's got no bally knickers on!' It was only hearsay for me that he had a sense of humour. It filled a tiny gap in my heart.

The spirits were also gladdened by the arrival of a new member of the family. Katharine Elizabeth Devereau Lambert became my first cousin twice removed, her actress mother Marilyn being once removed. It was also good to have my sister over, for to be sure Murphy's Law activated work. Within a week of her arrival my agent was on the phone with interviews and availability checks, even one from Australia.

The first was a six-day shoot in Spain for Peugeot. I was asked if I would be confident driving fast along mountain roads. I would be playing a doctor visiting a patient in a remote pueblo to deliver her baby. I said 'of course' and put on my quiet, reassuring doctor's look. Two days after the interview I was flying to Granada where the crew hired cars.

We drove that evening to Bubion in the heart of the Sierra Nevada Mountains where we stayed for three nights. Further up the mountain was the picturesque pueblo of Campaneira, the doctor's destination. I had to drive the Peugeot through the narrow, steep and windy streets looking for the patient's house. Time seemed to have stood still in this remote village, but there was a very agreeable tavernita. Many years later I visited Campaneira and was greeted almost like family by the owner. Nothing had changed.

The difficulty was adjusting to Spanish time. Scenes were shot early in the morning to catch the dawn light and late evening for dusk. At least I was able to catch up from only four hours sleep at night with a siesta midday. Then we did travelling shots higher up the mountain just below the snow line. It was hair-raising driving fast along windy, bumpy, dirt roads etched into the mountain side, with precipitous drops and snow-capped peaks just above. I ended up waiting on my own at the top for the crew to join. The scene was primordial: so quiet and peaceful, with no evidence of civilisation.

I had been travelling with the director who was looking out for locations and saw so much of this vast, spectacular range that few Spanish people, let alone tourists, would see. On the last day of filming we moved towards the town of Guadix, famous for its cave-dwellings, where we filmed my leaving home. On our way we stopped off at a tavernita in a very remote pueblo where I had the most extraordinary experience.

We walked into this small bar and as we were ordering something to eat and drink, the barman kept looking at me in a funny way. He pointed to a big television screen behind me. I turned and there I was, a big close-up playing Lord Burne-Wilke in *The Winds of War* but speaking Spanish. There were many double takes and astonished sounds in Spanish by the locals. Needless to say the landlord was magnanimous.

After the shoot we travelled by train from Guadix, which we left at 1.30 am, arriving in Madrid at 9.00 am. It felt like being on a long-retired Orient Express. The cabins had the aroma of vintage claret. One was soothed by the sensuous feel of the oak panels. The train gently rocked me to sleep as it ambled its way to Madrid, from where I flew to Barcelona in order to catch a connecting flight to Nice.

Tessa Kirby, a close friend of my cousin Marilyn, was living in Monte Carlo and had invited me before to visit. This was the perfect opportunity. No time to take in the Cannes Film Festival but Tessa was able to book a table at a very famous restaurant.

La Colombe d'Or, in Saint Paul-de-Vence, is renowned for its cuisine and art gallery. The haunt of many famous artists, actors and writers over many years, it is set in the picturesque walled hilltop town, one of the oldest on the French Riviera. There are many paintings by famous artists, some left in lieu of paying for a meal. There was a story told of some elaborate April Fools' Day prank, whereby many paintings were stolen and returned on on the same day the following year.

It was also the home village of one of my favourite French actors, Yves Montand. I watched him playing boules in the village square. This rounded off a week in which I packed a heap of memorable experiences, in addition to earning £1000. Not bad for a virtual holiday.

No sooner had I returned to London than I was off again to Adelaide. It would be a two-day shoot filming a series of commercials in which I had to learn about six slightly different scripts speaking direct to the camera without autocue. It was the one and only time I have flown across the world just to do a job and flown back.

Financially I was doing well again but the actor's ennui was seeping into my psyche. I had not played a role since the previous summer on the BBC's series *Big Deal*. Again I was at a reckoning with where I stood in the profession. My main source of income came from commercials and training films and I was increasingly missing out on significant roles. Taking an overview of my career so far, I would have to conclude that I projected an affable, charming front with little depth and no lingering power.

There is one physical factor that I can do nothing about which may have a bearing. The camera reads the inner thoughts of a character through the actor's eyes. I would say all stars and most leading actors have large, wide and expressive eyes. Mine are too close together and not easily readable. I believe it makes a significant difference and has limited my progress.

A sprinkling of bread and butter jobs gave me enough to buy the jam, indeed more so than roles for the BBC. I travelled up to Manchester to be in a promotional film for Boddington Brewery and was taken aback when introduced to Billy Beaumont. Billy had been captain of the English rugby union team that had won the Grand Slam in 1980 and he was now deemed a celebrity. He was a great rugby player and a charming man but no performer. Perhaps all those years with his head in the scrum damaged his short-term memory.

I had an amusing incident after filming a commercial in Glasgow. I was waiting for my flight home at the airport when suddenly I was confronted by a very excited Scotsman: 'Excuse me, laddie, but were you in *Big Deal*?'

I nodded. He turned and walking back to his mate, saying: 'There y'are. I told ya so. Y'owe me.'

I had become public property in that instant. He had won his bet.

After playing a role of 'insulting brevity' (as described by my agent) in *The Mistress* starring Felicity Kendall, I went to RAF Wittering in Lincolnshire to shoot an instructional film. It was about detritus left on runways called FOD, which can get sucked up into jet engines on take off. Pity this was not seen by the Paris Concorde people.

I also got a role in a Channel 4 re-creation of the famous 1986 legal case brought by Britain's MI5 against Peter Wright in Australia. He was being defended by Malcolm Turnbull QC, who later became Prime Minister. I was asked to voice Turnbull's image.

All these kind of jobs are interesting to do, and far better than sitting around waiting for some plum part to turn up.

Cast of the Theatre Royal tour of America
with Kirk and Anne Douglas at their home
in Los Angeles, 1968

'El Lawrence' Pegge with Blanche D'Alpuget
by the pyramids outside Cairo, on an
excursion from the ship Flavia, 1965

As Sandy Tyrell (for the third time!) in Hay Fever, Marlowe
Theatre, with my cousin Marilyn Smithwick, 1970

As Luther in The
Daughter in Law, Castle
Theatre, with Christine
Welch, 1969

As Jimmy Porter in Look Back in Anger, *London Mediterranean Productions, in Mallorca with Liz Hughes and Malcolm Ingram, 1970*

As Lieutenant Robarts in the Channel 9 and Yorkshire Television co-production Luke's Kingdom, *with director Peter Hammond, 1974*

As Meeker in Dr Who *episode 'The Invisible Enemy', 1977*

As Father Murphy in the ABC's
Home Sweet Home *with Roger*
Ward and John Bluthal, 1981

Playing Bernard Webster in the BBC's Tenko, *with Stephanie Beacham (Rose) and Anne*
Bell (Marion), 1981. Above right: Rose and Bernard watch the bombing of Singapore.
Bottom right: the shipwreck scene, with director Pennant Roberts

*Playing Air Commodore Lord Burne-Wilke in Paramount
Studios'* Winds of War *with Robert Mitchum, 1981*

As Constable Bagley in Anglia TV's Cause
Célèbre *with Helen Mirren, 1987*

*Working as Assistant Director for the
cricket sequence with Sam Neill and
Paul Sheahan in* Robbery Under Arms,
*filmed by the South Australian Film
Company, 1984*

The cast of Fallen Angels *with Hayley and Juliet Mills (centre)
on tour in Australia and New Zealand, 1993*

The cast for Travels With My Aunt,
*a London Full Circle Production,
consisting of (back) Nigel Miles-
Thomas, Natalie Bohm, (front) me
and Roger Lloyd Pack, on tour in
South-East Asia, 1998*

*'Friends, Romans, countrymen' speech
in* Shakespeare's Greatest Hits
*performed in the garden at Glen Ewin
Estate, Adelaide Hills, 1993*

*Lunching with Suzie Maisels at the Cruising
Yacht Club in Sydney, 2003*

*With Richard Potter after we created
the Informing Performing Company
in Adelaide, for touring poetry
performances and writing workshops
to schools, 1998*

*Kenneth Branagh, with Bill and Wendy Wauchope, visiting Glen
Ewin during the filming of* Rabbit Proof Fence, *2001*

Our family house in Old Windsor, 2014. We lived in the right-hand side; the house was later enlarged

Adrian Horton, founder of the Gentlemen of Old Windsor Cricket Club

Old friends from Nottingham Playhouse days. In 2014 Judi Dench invited Alfie Bell, Jan Craig and me to lunch in her ancient thatched cottage. She cooked us a fish pie.

My 'lady beyond compare', Annie Green, 2004

*My sister Eunice Warnes and me with our mother at her art exhibition
opening in Greenhill Galleries, North Adelaide, 1989*

38

'My father! – methinks I see my father'

I had returned from a nothing-much-happening break in Australia to a nothing-much-happening period from February to the end of March 1987 in the UK. I was also back to an empty flat. Jenny had moved out, but it was the beginning of many more ins and outs.

Then fortune's wheel began turning again. The sequence of events over two weeks went like this: two voice-overs in Soho – drove to Marlowe to interview for a training film – on to Daventry to front a script on autocue – back to London flat late on a Sunday night – re-packed suitcase ready to get to Gatwick to leave on a flight to Malaga – shot commercial following morning – flight back to Gatwick – re-packed ready for a three week location shoot in the Lake District – returned to find Jenny back in the flat.

I had worked for Laurence Moody in a small part a few years previously and his promise to find me something better came good. He offered me the guest lead in an episode of another new BBC drama series called *Truckers* about the life of truck drivers (similar to the recent series made in 2013).

It was another Aussie character but fun to play. He was an excitable con man called Denzil who rushed about in a smart suit trying to impress his girlfriend, played by Sharon Maughan, saying 'pardon my French' all the time (which was also the name of the episode). Sadly, like *Big Deal*, it was never shown again.

I had been staying with my old friends in Northumberland after the shoot when a call came to be interviewed for a part in *Cause Célèbre*, a television adaptation of a play by Terence Rattigan. It would be rehearsed and recorded by Anglia Television in Norwich. After a four-hour dash I arrived just in time at the offices of *Spotlight* in Leicester Square. John Gorrie and his producer John Rosenberg were interviewing me. We somehow discovered we all had parents who had spent time in India. This completely dominated the conversation. The reason I was there seemed quite incidental, but at the end they mentioned there was actually a part that they thought I would be suitable for.

It turned out to be a not-insignificant policeman's role in a star-studded cast that included Helen Mirren, David Suchet, Harry Andrews and Oliver Ford Davies. There was a one-on-one scene with Helen Mirren, where you can see me being clutched by her in a photo, and nerve-wracking scenes being cross-examined by David Suchet, which took a whole day to shoot in Twickenham studios.

The part did belong to the genre of police constables in all those Agatha Christie plays but it was better written. The part also required me to have a Hampshire accent. Apart from having the sound of John Arlott, the great cricket commentator in my vocal memory bank, I was able to raid the BBC voice library at Portland Place.

A long rehearsal period was booked at the Duke of York's army barracks in Chelsea. The room where we rehearsed was at the top of some very steep stairs which Harry Andrews had great difficulty climbing. He had bad emphysema and I found myself obliged to assist from behind. He was a big man. It was sad to find this giant of a man whom I had seen playing tough characters in war films like *The Hill* reduced to such weakness. I was also surprised to discover he was gay.

Sometimes an actor can feel a shudder when playing or preparing for a role that evokes someone close to you. It was said that it happened to Daniel Day Lewis when playing Hamlet on seeing his father as the ghost in Act I. I believe it was more than a shudder. He had to leave the stage. Something of a shudder for me happened when in make-up before recording.

I was in my policeman's uniform, brilliantined, looking into the mirror. I turned away to have my moustache attached, turned back to the mirror and there was my father. It was the strangest feeling. It was not like seeing a ghost but more a reincarnation and a comforting sensation. Even though the uniform was different, my father had been a policeman in India; the hair and moustache had brought us together.

Anglia had a very generous budget. A half day's rehearsal was spent at the Old Bailey by those actors whose characters were to be cross-examined.

The court hearing we witnessed was mind-boggling. The evidence and cross-examination centred on graphic sexual descriptions. If my memory serves me the case was about incest. I thought that only happened in Greek plays. I've obviously led a sheltered life.

This generous budget reflected in our fees. For playing the guest lead in the two-week shoot on *Truckers* for the BBC, I was paid a special high rate of £450 per week. On *Cause Célèbre* I was paid £610 per week over a period of six weeks in a supporting role with generous expenses. I was able to save over £4000.

However, from the end of the contract I had no work for three months, and Jenny had crept back into my life. She persuaded me to take a short holiday on the Costa del Sol, which I hardly needed. We headed for the hinterland after escaping the playground of the rich in Puerto Buenos. Driving through the mountains was an exhilarating experience, eating in humble local tavernitas on our way to Rhonda. This ancient town, famous for having the oldest bullring in Spain and a bridge that spans the deepest chasm, commands a 360-degree view over the surrounding countryside. The buildings seemed to have grown out of the rocks at the top of this little mountain. How it could have changed hands so often seems a mystery. It looks impregnable.

The next day we went up through the mountains again, noticing how similar the landscape is to Australia with the predominance of eucalyptus trees. We had booked to view the Cuevas de Pilato – the Caves of Pilato, only discovered at the turn of the 20th century. This is how I described the visit:

We met the local Spanish guardian and guide on a ledge at the opening of the caves overlooking his valley. It was so peaceful, the view so majestic and ancient. You could feel history all around. We were the only two there until an American middle-aged couple joined us. He looked like James Stewart but he was deaf. He was keen to show off his Spanish, which he spoke very loudly, and they took very little notice of us. We were escorted into the cavernous gloom lit only by lanterns made in Belfast, which I thought quaint. We weaved our way through these truly magical caves, carved out by water over millions of years. The shapes were spellbinding, identified with modern names such as the Michelin Man. Great blocks of rock had been carved by nature to look like Indian temple figures and primitive carvings of fish, horses and bulls on the walls overhanging remnants of pottery. All this among a hanging forest of stalagmites and stalactites. There was evidence of the beginnings of civilisation from the Neolithic period, all revealed by just a lantern and a guide who knew his history. It was a memorable experience.

We headed East along the coast road to stay over in the Salobrena Hotel where Jenny's friend Martin lived. After driving for three hours we stopped off at a pleasant looking restaurant near the town of Nerja. It was set back with an open car park in full view from the highway. As we walked towards the car after only a 40-minute break, I could tell something was wrong. The rear triangle window of our Seat was smashed and all our baggage gone – passports, tickets, wallet, all in my Concorde bag, cameras and both suitcases, but my diary with all contact numbers had been left on the seat.

I regaled the proprietor who suddenly could not speak English. We rushed down to Nerja, found the Municipal Polizia and tried to report that everything was stolen from our car. They could not have been less helpful. Eventually we found the Guardia Civil (the national police force) who were most helpful and gave us the report for insurance.

Luckily I had the phone number of Martin's friends whom we were to meet as he would be away. It was strange checking into a hotel with no luggage and only the clothes we had on. We were so relieved when Bill and Cora-Lee Measden arrived at the Salobrena Hotel with basic necessities. Bill paid for everything and had the car fixed. I was able to repay the loan later in London. He was a most interesting man, a commander on destroyers in the war, and he knew Lord Mountbatten. I must have had good karma to have found such a kind and generous couple. They alleviated not only the extreme inconvenience but also that hollow feeling when stranded. Useful for the actor's memory box.

After immediately returning to Malaga to deal with passports, tickets and buying a few clothes, we at least had a pleasant few days watching a fiesta parade and a bullfight. Our besmirched feelings towards Spanish people were greatly repaired by sitting next to a Spanish gentleman who, in immaculate English, explained the finer points of bullfighting.

Again, after a good start to the year, drought set in – no work for three months but at least it was summer. Many agents throw an annual summer party where actors, casting agents and directors are in the mix. I caused an incident when holding a leading casting lady over the edge of the swimming pool in Fred Astaire fashion. An actor passing gave me a nudge. It was a very wet way of getting noticed. Sometime later the wife of that actor cast me in *The Bill*. She had been standing nearby. Perhaps it worked.

Not long after returning from the stolen holiday I was off to Rome to shoot a commercial in the famous Cinecittà Studios, where I had another chance meeting. John Neville was filming *Baron Münchhausen* and remembered me from Nottingham Playhouse days.

I was surprised to read a vitriolic account of sightseeing in Rome with a fellow actor in a letter to my mother.

> We made perfunctory visits to the Vatican, the Colosseum, the Forum and the Spanish Steps. We walked from the Vatican to the Spanish Steps along the river Tiber, which was filthy, quoting lines from *Julius Caesar*. Was not impressed by Rome, very little art and mostly grotesque, bulbous statues guarding over-ornate buildings, celebrating power and dominance. Spent 10 minutes in the Sistine Chapel with 500 American tourists, all being told to quieten down every five minutes, because it was the House of God and required respect. The Basilica was monumental and totally extravagant. Much prefer St Paul's Cathedral. The square is colossal, so vast – no wonder the Pope can hold sway over so many with such majestic props – rather like Hitler did! Generally I found Rome dirty, busy, noisy and very expensive. We paid £18 for two beers and two double-decker sandwiches. I've had enough of the Continent for the time being.

I certainly had a brusque and arrogant manner in those days, with no pretensions of becoming a eulogising travel writer.

The day after returning from Rome I was at the Riverside Studios in Hammersmith. I was asked to do a play reading for Kenneth Branagh, who had formed the Renaissance Theatre Company. He was fast emerging as the star actor/director he became. He was a friend of my friend Alfie Bell.

I had recently visited Kenneth backstage at the RSC in Stratford where he was playing Prince Hal in *Henry the Fifth*. He remembered that I had played an Aussie officer in *Anzacs* and asked if I would do this reading of a play by Richard Beynon called *The Man with the Donk*. Beynon had written a play about Private Simpson and how he had saved so many lives by carrying wounded men down the slopes of Gallipoli on his donkey. He was well known in Australia for his play *The Shifting Heart*.

The cast included Carolyn Moody (*Emmerdale Farm*) and Amanda Root, Kenneth's partner at the time. But the most surprising credit on the programme was the director, Sam Mendes. It was very early in his career. Only one thing registered with me at the time. He was a seriously good cricketer and I tried to get him to play for the Stage Cricket Club.

That was a good credit but unpaid and I had had only one day's work in four months. This had put on hold any thought of moving and probably contributed to a gradual break-up. I was in a very low state. Rejection is like people taking pot shots with an air gun. It hurts but you don't drop. Six months prior fish had been biting, but now my float was drifting. And then one night a massive event happened that jolted me out of too much self pity.

On the night of 15 October 1987 Jenny and I walked out into my back garden just before going to bed. There was a strange, eerie feeling in the air. It was very dark and heavy and unnaturally warm, as though a great shroud had been thrown over our heads. Neither of us thought any more about it until the morning. Somehow we had slept through the worst storm for 300 hundred years. It became known as the Great Storm of 1987. In three hours it had devastated Southern England, knocking out millions of trees and leaving thousands of homes without power. We took a walk through Wandsworth Common. The damage was awesome. Our first sight was a Porsche crushed by a massive tree, as though a giant had put his foot on a Dinky toy. Everywhere there was debris, with people walking around looking dazed. A great reminder that we are but nothing in the wake of Mother Nature, who had behaved more like a Violent Father.

One, among many victims, was the cricket ground at Sevenoaks where I had often played. The eponymous oaks were reduced to one oak, but the name has not changed. The most unfortunate man in England was the well-known forecaster Michael Fish, who had completely played down its magnitude. He ended up being as eponymous as Sevenoaks, wearing his name on his face.

When you are at the bottom the only way to move is up. Not that I was in any way destitute. Financially I was okay, from my high earnings during the first four months, residuals from commercials, a few small jobs since and landscaping work. Essentially my self-respect as an actor felt it was being surgically taken apart – too many knock-backs. Then, hey presto, within 48 hours everything changed. I found myself on roller skates again complaining about not having any time.

The first bite came from being asked to prepare a series of poems to read on a fairly prestigious, niche BBC television programme called *Five to Eleven*. Forge Productions, run by Ralph Rolls and his assistant Catherine Pinner, were currently supplying five five-minute slots of famous people, mostly actors, being seen reading their favourite poems at 10.55 am every day through the week. It had become surprisingly popular.

The Australian Bicentennial was soon to be celebrated and Ralph approached me to choose apposite Australian poems. Knowing that Laurence Olivier, Michael Horden and Judi Dench had presented, I felt very honoured. What is more he thought it appropriate to include the poem I had written in Australia that had been admired by Robert Graves. The BBC in its benevolent exactitude gave me a royalty payment of £14/6/-. I am not sure if Robert's estate got a cut.

The year closed on a more positive note with a career boost from Australia. A booking for another commercial in Adelaide came through for early in the new year of 1988. At the same time David Brewster, my new agent in Sydney, rang to say my good friend Susie Maizels was offering a very good film role without a test or interview. By this time I had a very good showreel.

It was a television film about the fall of Singapore, featuring Gordon Bennett, Commander of the Australian forces. It was part of the Mike Willesee series about famous Australians. My old friend Bill Kerr was cast as Gordon Bennet. I would be playing Lieutenant General Arthur Percival, Commander of the British forces, the co-lead – at last a role of some substance.

This to-and-fro existence had its advantages when one pool became stagnant. Generally I was getting more educated Aussie roles in the UK, and more upper-class English parts in Australia. For playing Percival I would have to get out the cut-glass accent from the voice cupboard.

A friend happened to phone my mother soon after I had left for Sydney. Mother was so excited she said to him:

'Do you know Edmund has been promoted? He is playing a Lieutenant General. He was only a Squadron Leader before.'

This is similar to my godmother who thought I was the Director General of the BBC. Mothers invented status inflation.

39

Thank God for Crime and War

It sounds an awful thing to say but for actors crime and war are a godsend. So much drama comes out of these two human activities. Of course, out of war comes the most dramatic spectacle and behaviour. Murder, rape, pillage and theft were subject matters in Greek tragedies and continue to dominate today's numerous detective series. Drama needs dynamics – opposites clashing – and the bigger the better in movies. But in Greek tragedy the violence was reported by a messenger. Today blood and guts are shoved in our faces. I wonder how sanitised the next generation will be? I believe the individual stories of overcoming adversity or taking a journey of discovery are just as compelling, like in the films *Billy Elliot* and *Philomena*.

At least 10 detective series were running in 2014 made for television in the UK. These are in addition to the American sausage machine for violent crime, and those grim Scandinavian ones. There would hardly be one actor in the world without a crime or war credit to their name. The only recent relief from dead bodies has been a re-run of *Last Tango in Halifax* with Derek Jacobi and Anne Reid, and thank god for *Miranda*.

The fall of Singapore would be my next appointment with war, which would commence on 4 January 1988 in Sydney.

The central theme of the television film *Gordon Bennett* was about the part Lieutenant General Gordon Bennett played in the fall of Singapore. He was vilified by the press at the time for returning to Australia before Singapore fell to the Japanese, although ordered to surrender and return by Blainey. The film went some of the way to rectifying his reputation, even though he was greeted with white feathers (the coward symbol) as his ship arrived at the quayside in Sydney harbour. The blight of leaving his troops behind was never entirely eradicated.

The wonderful Bill Kerr playing Bennett had made his name in the UK from his ongoing part playing the Australian from Wagga Wagga in *Hancock's Half Hour*. This part made Wagga Wagga the best known Australian town other than the capitals. He was the archetypal Aussie actor: strong and forthright with a great laid-back sense of humour, continuing the legacy left by Peter Finch, Rod Taylor and Errol Flynn.

He and I hit it off on the first day of rehearsal. The cast were all sitting around a table about to do a read-through when the director Stephen Wallace asked us to give a history of our characters. Bill and I glanced at each other. Neither of us had ever been asked to analyse our parts and voice it with other actors outside of a workshop setting. Bill was from the old school whereby you did your homework on your character at home, where you left it. This was methodology used more in the theatre, though not in rep or most television series, where pressure reigns. Some of the younger actors in smaller roles went on and on about their parts.

Bill muttered away briefly about the justification for being recalled by Blainey and virtually said that he had no idea how he was going to play it. I mentioned Alex Guinness's performance in *The Bridge Over the River Kwai*, using the 'poker up the bum' idea from his walk, for this painfully wet General. The constipated Prince Charles look. We had a laugh about that afterwards. There was a terrific bond between us playing these two very opposite roles. How these two may have got on in reality one could only guess at, but I know the scene we had at the end was very moving. It had the ring of truth about it. The dialogue went as follows:

> *Percival:* Your men fought bravely. They gave more than we a had a right to ask.

> *Bennett*: In case we don't see each other again till this is over, good luck and God be with you.

> *Percival:* We'll be blamed for this you know. By God we've done our best.

Disappointingly, this leading role, in which I know I did well, never registered and the film was not repeated, as far as I can find out.

Soon after finishing the shoot, I was lucky enough to be in Sydney for one of the most significant celebrations in Australian history. Australia Day (26 January) 1988 was the bicentennial celebration of European settlement in

Australia. On this day 200 years ago the First Fleet, led by Captain Arthur Phillip, declared the first British colony at Sydney Cove. Embedded in this arrival were the seeds for much drama. Out of just over a thousand who landed, 696 were prisoners of whom 504 were male and 192 were female, and only 348 were free settlers, which included an undisciplined Marine corps. Add those statistics to the soon to be displaced native Aboriginal population and you have a cauldron for drama.

Yet as far as I can recall no major film has been made of those first few years of white settlement. There have been several television dramas, but in a way the story needs to be told by a British production house with modern film technology. After all it is a British story. It was the painful, bloody birth of a nation.

The basis of my knowledge of the early settlement years has come from reading books like *The Timeless Land* by Eleanor Dark and Robert Hughes's *The Fatal Shore*. I recall making notes from the former book, thinking it great material for some kind of play, film script or two-man show with an Aboriginal actor. I suppose there was no big, major conflict, which an epic film requires. The invasion of the land was a gradual, creeping series of small events. It would be hard to film erosion, which is what happened to the tribes. Though Tasmania achieved a final solution, with some exciting skirmishes and a charismatic tribal leader. War in Australia has not been on a sufficiently grand scale for a Hollywood epic.

Australia Day is a two-edged sword. It is a celebration of an incredible achievement in perseverance by Captain Phillip and all the first settlers, but for the natives of the land, a day of great sorrow. Their land and way of life was irrevocably destroyed. This has been more recognised in recent years. In 1988 it was a day for a massive party on the harbour to mark this unique event.

An old school friend from Adelaide had sailed his 55-foot, traditional-looking bowsprit ketch *Cabaret* to Sydney Harbour as part of the Tall Ships Race. Square riggers from all over the world came to the party. Together with other friends, we all climbed aboard not a minute past 8.00 am. Our captain was known by all who have sailed with him as Captain Bligh. He would keelhaul anyone, even his best friend, if they put his boat in danger or disobeyed his orders. All in good fun. Captain Bligh – also known as Alan

Cotton – was a widely travelled and highly respected yachtsman. He survived a 360-degree roll-over in the Tasman sea.

His true colours were quickly witnessed by many when, on emerging out of Darling Harbour to form the line, a 100-foot steel vessel from India rammed his stern. The language hurled at the incompetent idiot who was supposed to be skippering this rogue vessel regaled the ears of many in other boats. It was accompanied with a well-aimed empty bottle of wine. There was one already handy.

The scene on Sydney Harbour was of epic proportions. Literally thousands of bobbing masts were jostling for their positions in the parading line up. And the noise of whooping and clag horns seemed almost to shake the struts of the mighty bridge. Boats of all shapes and sizes were dominated by the tall ships, replicas of those that first arrived. It was a stirring sight and a thrilling feeling to be in the middle of it all. The boats hovered and we hoovered all day and night, with food and drink in endless supply. I wondered how many would have given a thought to those poor first souls, barely alive from festering food in foul-smelling, cramped conditions, on ships barely the size of the present-day harbour ferries.

The event culminated well after sunset with a spectacular firework display framed around the famed Sydney Harbour Bridge, which was echoed with displays from bridges in the distance. It became such an overwhelming sensation to absorb that I was heard to say at one climatic moment 'Oh god, I'm coming'.

40

The Corridor Well Travelled

It was almost becoming a habit, flying back to spend Christmas with family in Adelaide, then hanging around for three months and returning in March. Before returning to the UK in 1988 I was lucky to catch an open-air production of *The Mahabharata* in the Adelaide Festival, directed by the innovative Peter Brook and staged in a quarry in the foothills. It was a profound experience watching 21 actors from 16 countries performing these epic stories of the foundations of Hindu culture. The play was in three parts, taking nine hours to perform. It went from dusk to dawn.

One can never say never, but I sense that it is unlikely there will be anyone quite like Peter Brook again. He was an originator in re-interpreting classic text. His production of *A Midsummer Night's Dream* was spellbinding. He was also responsible for a haunting film interpretation of *King Lear* with the incomparable Paul Schofield, and his memorable production of Seneca's *Oedipus* at the National Theatre. There are a number of directors taking up the classics, but from the reports I read, they end up mucking around or distorting the text so that it becomes almost unrecognisable. In my opinion, Peter Brook re-vitalised the classics, instead of reinventing them.

A very precious occasion in family life took place on 3 February 1988. My mother, at the age of 89, had her third art exhibition: a crowning day in my mother's life. My sister Eunice inherited something from our mother with her china painting. I inherited zero pictorial skills but I was good at painting pictures with words.

My sister had been keeping an eye on Mother, who lived on her own for 40 years. She was about to turn 90 years old and I was beginning to think I ought to do my bit by coming back to look after her. My career had not taken off and was probably unlikely to, so basing myself more in Adelaide became an increasingly attractive option, but not a good career move. An actor really has to live in either Sydney or Melbourne.

For the time being, back in London until the end of the year, I went through the familiar bouts of highs and lows. The trowel and shovel were picked up once again, not for masonic purposes, but to play real-life landscape gardening sketches starring Kettles and Pegge. It kept our spirits up, our bodies in shape and the pennies coming in. Throughout the rest of the year I ended up doing about 10 jobs, out of which only one was drama.

The drama role was highly suitable to the sporting actor. I was to play the part of an ex-Australian test cricketer in a new series called *Gentlemen and Players* for TVS Southampton. The stories were centred around the dynamics between village and city life. A vast number of well-heeled, privately educated gentlemen continue to work in the City of London's financial hub but live in these villages. The dynamics come from a clash of class: the villagers who worked locally versus the commuters, and the old families versus the new rich. It was a very interesting and popular series exploring these themes.

My character had been roped in to play for the gentlemen's side against the village team in the annual cricket match. There were two sequences where his skills as an ex-top player were paraded. I had to do some homework. I was fortunate to know an ex-Australian test cricketer who also came from South Australia's landed gentry. In my preparation I thought of the way he talked and walked. More difficult was appearing to play like an ex-test batman. Alf Gover's cricket school was nearby where I lived in Wandsworth. I enlisted the son John Gover to be my coach. My instructions to him were: 'You have two weeks to make me look as though I could have been an ex-test cricketer.'

John's plan was to concentrate on two shots, the pull and the off drive. Once the shape of the shot looked right, John put me in front of a bowling machine, repeating the same two shots over and over.

At my next session I arrived to find the machine being used by a very familiar face. There, at the batting crease, was Lawrence of Arabia. It was the mesmeric Peter O'Toole. We had a brief chat and I asked him if he would care for a game with the Stage Cricket Club. He said he couldn't guarantee turning up in any regular way, but that he enjoyed a net and the odd charity match. I couldn't help feeling that little flush when you have a moment with charisma.

The location for filming was a picturesque village in Hampshire. There was a short sequence in the nets, surrounded by locals watching. With some very fine, fast editing I really looked the part.

However, during the early autumnal months of 1988 various and interesting small jobs nevertheless failed to ease the growing sense of failure and disenchantment. London is a lonely city when you are not being successful. I had seen little of my friends and my relationship with Jenny was getting threadbare. I had the sense that she really wanted out but couldn't make up her mind where to go and what to do next. In addition I had to attend a funeral.

Adrian Horton had been an assuring presence and support throughout my life. The family lived next door to us in Old Windsor and I had played for his cricket team since I was 10 years old. It was as though a prop had been removed. Adrian had declared his innings in the most timely way, when hearing his side were about to win. His Gentlemen of Old Windsor Cricket Club lasted for another 25 years.

The spur to return to Australia came primarily from Susie Maizels again. This was for a part in the first mini-series about the commando raids on Singapore Harbour called *The Heroes* to be directed by Don Crombie from *Robbery Under Arms*. Even though Don was keen to use me it didn't work out this time. However, it did lead to a good part in the sequel.

What did come off was being a presenter on a pilot for a travel project promoting Australia. So it was back down the M4 to Heathrow, not to lose the war again but to put Australia on the map as an adventure-holiday destination. However, there was a slight hold up.

I arrived at the airport in good time but without my passport, only to be told the flight was delayed anyway, so had time to rush back to the flat. Jenny was still with me then, a lot of unravelling of our relationship had been going on before the travelling, which continued with another final drink. It was a drink too far as the flight had closed on return. I had missed the flight even with a second chance. After being suitably apologetic and despairing I was rewarded with an upgrade to business class the next afternoon. A brief visit from Lady Luck.

41

Pegging Out Australia

Pegging Out Australia was the title for the promotional film and the only time my name would ever appear in the top credits. The idea was to feature an urbane English travel writer thrown into all kinds of typically Australian activities in a documentary/drama style series. Dale Kelly, an ex-Olympic swimmer, was ambitious to sell Australia as a travel destination. Her only experience came out of creating a video library for farmers, for which I had fronted the promo.

With James Lingwood directing we were fortunate that the inimitable Rex Ellis was available. Rex was a top outback tour guide, mostly taking overseas guests into the interior on camels, or 'ships of the desert' as he called them. Rex is the archetypal Australian bushman: short, lean, resourceful, tough, caring, modest, deeply knowledgeable of the environment, with a wry sense of humour and a fund of stories. I spent a whole week filming with him, and he came some of the way to changing my view of the outback, blighted from touring Shakespeare to schools in the early 1960s.

A long sequence was filmed in the wine district of McLaren Vale. The opening scene was me being dumped seemingly in the middle of nowhere, sitting on a log complaining of the heat and flies, talking directly into camera. There was no set script and I found no problem being myself, muttering away. Then a lolloping camel ride through bush and vineyards, with Rex expounding the virtues of visiting Australia. Our final shot took place at Coriole, the Lloyd family winery, where we see a camel drinking from a beer can in its mushy mouth.

After editing and exhausting local avenues for funding, we decided the best option would be to pitch for part funding from the Australian Tourist Bureau. We secured $40,000. I arranged a meeting with Stuart Scowcroft, Head of

Features at the ABC, to pitch the show. I should have known something was odd when asked to wait at reception while the tape of our pilot was sent up to Scowcroft to view. The tape was returned with the familiar message of 'we'll let you know'. I didn't even get a courtesy meeting. Nothing further was heard.

A year later an ABC programme to do with adventure holidays was screened. Our worst fears materialised immediately. There, in the opening sequence, was a camel drinking a can of Coca Cola. And so that seed fed to Scowcroft a year ago was picked up and developed with absolutely no recognition of its origin. The ABC blatantly stole our idea.

We found out this was not uncommon. The ABC had a history of stealing ideas, probably part of the original covenant from its modelling on the BBC who were also known for it. The pilfered show burgeoned into multiple programmes on adventure holidays and travel destinations with celebrity presenters The lesson learnt was not to make an example of a creative idea but to get an independent company with backing to make the series. Our original idea was more in keeping with the way Michael Palin was filmed in his travel series years later – a kind of 'fish out of water' on foreign shores (pun intended).

I had a few weeks filming in the charming fishing village of Beachport, on the far south east coast of South Australia. This was a Bryan Brown/Rachel Ward film originally called *Confidence*, but released as *Sweet Talker*. It was by no means a small-budget movie, and it gave Beachport a huge economic boost. It was a very Australian film with plenty of larrikin charm and no violence. Somehow it failed to be picked up by the major distributors, who are mostly controlled from America.

The next job came out of the bread-and-butter basket with an amusing coincidence. I was cast by the memorably named Kim Tank to represent a leading obstetrician in an Adelaide hospital giving a talk on breastfeeding. Unknown to me my niece was there having her baby and exclaimed when seeing me: 'He's not a doctor! That's my uncle. He's an actor.' The teaching video may well have backfired, the tank offensive defeated!

A tradition had evolved for my mother's birthdays, and her 90th was no exception. Mother had her friends to afternoon tea in her tiny cottage. Then my friends turned up in the evening and she recited one of her monologues.

There was a moment in the afternoon when I was quite startled to hear how Mother greeted one old lady: 'Oh Daisy, how wonderful you could make it! I thought you were dead.'

But the *coup de mot* was heard later that night. It was the end of the evening and most of the guests had gone, leaving just the family and my good friend Sandy, a strapping, sporty Aussie who had a way with the ladies. He suddenly asked Mother if she would like to go dancing in a nightclub. My mother had no hesitation in saying 'What fun!' and so off we all went. There were about six of us in two cars. We got mother in without charge, showing her pension card. There she was in the middle bopping away among the groovy, club-scene girls who kept smiling and laughing with her. Mother was having the best time.

After midnight we called it a day (a lovely English anachronism). Mother was taken home in Sandy's car. We all arrived at the same time and I went in to open the front door. Turning, I found my mother in Sandy's arms being taken from the car to her bedroom. Sandy lay my mother gently down on to her bed, her arms around his neck, and said:

'There you are, Mrs Pegge. I bet you haven't had that done to you for a long time.'

To which my mother rapidly replied:

'No, and I'm not going to let you go now.'

There was little to celebrate as an actor in 1989 but being in the bosom of the family helped ease the ennui. My innate optimism was not crushed. I kept hanging on to the fading voice of Mr Micawber from *David Copperfield*: something will turn up.

42

A Long Wait

Indeed Mr Micawber had gone walkabout for six months in 1990. For the first time in Australia I had to sign on at the labour exchange. Nothing had eventuated out of the to-ing and fro-ing to Melbourne and Sydney for interviews. Getting work as an actor is not unlike the game of golf. You can hit a perfect ball off the tee and pitch to within several feet of the pin but if you can't hole the putts, you can't score. So many jobs I have gone for I have pitched well, with a good interview or screen test, but failed to score.

Salt was rubbed into the wounded ego when I found myself entertaining actor friends from England. Terry Wilton and Richard Durden were in a touring production of *Hamlet.* Terry and I had been in the Prospect Theatre Company at The Old Vic and Richard was a member of the Stage Cricket Club. I had to make out that everything was fine – happy to have returned – a few prospects in the air. All that bouncy luvvie stuff.

Eventually the drought broke, and I was cast in *Golden Fiddles* (nothing to do with violin playing or business deals). It was a feel-good television mini-series about an outback family during the Depression, battling to survive then suddenly being left a fortune.

During the filming on *Golden Fiddles* I did two screen tests. This was becoming standard practice to reduce the risk factor due to nervous producers. You were judged on what appeared on the film clip not what you had done in the past. People with no experience could be considered, some directors like using non-actors. Bob Hoskins got his first job barging in to an audition.

I have never liked or been good at doing screen tests. Often you get a small section of a script and are required to learn the lines of a short scene for the next day, without any idea of its context. Invariably your test will be recorded by an assistant to the casting director who has also been given limited information.

The next screen test was a little different. My casting director friend Susie Maizels had picked up a contract for a series of commercials to support the incumbent government of New Zealand. They would be used on behalf of the National Party in the lead-up to a general election. I learnt in plenty of time that the script for this political promotion was to be based on the Sir Humphrey character, played by Nigel Hawthorne, from the popular BBC comedy series *Yes Minister*. It was going to demand top comedy acting. To get the job I was required to get together my own screen test. I was able to lift the text from an episode my nephew happened to have just recorded, and a friend filmed it. I did the self-test well enough.

It was lucky I had a whole month before the shoot date. I received the six quasi-*Yes Minister* sketches, which required spending agonising time learning. This was occurring in the middle of the shoot on *Golden Fiddles* with three other small jobs and another screen test for a mini-series to be shot locally. The four days prior to flying to New Zealand I was filming on two separate contracts. Those old adages are true – it's either a flood or a drought.

I was met at Wellington airport by the director Nigel Hutchinson of Motion Pictures and his producer Mary Wall. During the briefing at my hotel, to my astonishment, I was told a meeting had been arranged with the Prime Minister. At the appointed hour I met the Rt. Hon. James Bolger in a parliament building called the Beehive. Now he is obviously not the Queen Bee, more the King Pin, and a charming gentleman. It may stretch credibility but he was the picture of an avuncular All Black.

I remember asking him why he would want to include in his campaign film sketches sending up government. He said *Yes Minister* was very popular and he thought a little reverse psychology might work in his favour. He was returned to power but I did hear that the series of sketches caused quite a stir in the ranks of the opposition and were prematurely taken off. Watching them now I have to say I was a convincing understudy for Sir Humphrey. The scripts sparkled with wit, which required fast, dexterous acting. I was pleased with the result. This was not my last time playing a political adviser.

My meeting was not the last contact I would have with the Prime Minister, either. He wrote a thank-you-for-your-contribution letter to me and I replied as Sir Humphrey, to which he responded in like style. Three years later I had reason to write in the same manner again, to which he responded.

The other screen test at about the same time was for *The River Kings*. This was another mini-series based on a novel by Max Fatchen, an Adelaide writer and journalist, about the paddle steamers on the Murray River in the 1920s. It was another feel-good family story about a boy who runs away from home to seek a life working on paddle steamers. They were the economic lifeline along the mighty Murray in South Australia and were a magnet for adventure. The script adaptation was by Rob George, who had become a friend.

It was necessary for me to do another screen test, as the part was a hard-working Aussie orchard farmer; the kind of part the likes of Bill Hunter or Jack Thompson would play. Fred, who throws the central character off his property for being keen on his daughter, was outside anything I had done before on screen.

Don Crombie, who knew me from NIDA and liked my work, had a feeling I might be sufficiently convincing, perhaps because within the role Fred had aspirations to be more than just a farmer. There was another level to play. I went out of my way to find out what it was like to be an orchard farmer. I spent a few days in the Waikerie area and met Noel McPherson whose family had worked his orchards for many generations. I watched the way he walked and talked. I do feel that time I spent made a difference.

It was a most enjoyable shoot, not least because in the cast were Bill Kerr and three other wonderful Aussie character actors – Willie Fennell, Lex Foxcroft and Edward Hepple. The sleepy little river town of Morgan came alive for several weeks. The local economy profited from accommodating the cast and crew (I was lucky enough to be on a houseboat) and many residents were employed. Working on location is more often than not the happiest time for an actor. You are away from home where you can more easily be in that world the film is creating. However, it is intense and in a supporting role there is invariably hours and hours of hanging around. Often nothing seems to be happening. The cause is usually to do with the light.

It seemed I was more at peace with myself having been in work during the last six months of 1990. Before heading back for what turned out to be the last throw of the dice over a long period in the UK, I lingered in Adelaide until a screen test in March took me to Sydney. As ever Susie Maizels had suggested me for another tricky role. Major Chapman, in *Heroes II: The Return*, was a dithering officer. In the story, commandos have mined ships in Singapore Harbour. Major Chapman fails to pick them up by submarine at an appointed hour, which results in their capture and executions. It was a role not unlike the one I played in *Anzacs*. Captain Young was a coward, Major Chapman a ditherer. Negativity and incompetence are always difficult to play. You have to act in a minor key with hesitation. Obviously Susie never saw me as an upfront leading-hero type. I can only deduce that these passive roles might require a strong actor, capable of subtle characterisation. I need to hope that was the case but I'm not entirely convinced.

This would be my third time being directed by Don Crombie. He had assembled a strong cast led by the up-and-coming English actor Nathaniel Parker, with John Bach and Craig McLachlan. Nathaniel was very determined to make it. We had one thing in common: we both wanted to act from early age. He was a handsome leading-man type from an upper-class background; an Old Etonian whose father was a Lord and a prominent member of parliament. He soon went to Hollywood and did appear in *The Bodyguard* with Kevin Costner and John Malkovich but that didn't seem to follow through in America. He is now a British television star in the *Inspector Lynley* detective series. The other overseas actor in the cast was Mark Lewis Jones, a Welshman who came from my UK agent's stable. He went on to establish a solid career in television, including *Game of Thrones*.

The story, researched by Peter Yeldham who wrote the script, was very closely based on historical facts. The theme was not unlike *The Guns of Navarone*. Commandos sail an old fishing vessel towards the enemy target, using submersibles to creep into Singapore harbour in order to attach limpet mines to Japanese ships. It was called 'Operation Rimau' and was a follow-up from a previously successful operation called 'Operation Jaywick', the basis for *The Heroes*, which was seen by 15 million in the UK. Both operations were among the most daring raids of the Second World War and it's surprising that it was not seen as a major film project by either Hollywood or Britain. The reason could be that 'Operation Rimau' ended in complete disaster with all the commandos captured and beheaded by the Japanese. That was caused by my character not taking firm action to keep the appointed rendezvous.

It is an apparent paradox that the medium of television seems to carry greater acceptance for the truth in story telling. Is it due to audiences being used to documentaries perhaps? In *The Great Escape* one prisoner does survive whereas in *Heroes II: The Return* none do. Anyway, it would be the third and last time I would be in a film about the loss of Singapore. Years later when performing in schools, my colleague liked telling the students: 'Edmund is a very careless actor. He has lost Singapore three times.'

43

The Last Throw of the Dice

The great dilemma of my life was wanting to be in two places at the same time. I am still agonising over this even at 75 while writing this. In the early 1990s I felt increasing pressure to curtail this migratory existence and spend more time in Australia with Mother, in her nervous 90s. So this ever-hopeful Dick Whittington was off again to London Town, hardly to seek a fortune but to make a possible final dash to resuscitate a slipping-by career. If you're out of circulation for too long you're easily forgotten.

The urge to mix it with the best has never left me. Britain's reputation for excellence in playwriting, theatre production, period drama and innovative television has never diminished. Hollywood has a stronger magnet for emerging actors from Australia. There has been a tectonic cultural shift away from the Mother Country. However, actors from all over the world still apply to get into British drama schools, where you learn the fundamentals of stage acting first. No actor can perform on stage without training the voice and body. In recent years internal acting or acting from within, required for filming, has diminished the need for a trained voice. This neglect is, in my opinion, having a profound effect not only in drama but in all aspects of vocal communication. An ultimate example of this came from the 2014 remake of *Jamaica Inn*. This BBC production received dozens of complaints from viewers who could not understand what many of the actors were saying. They had taken authenticity too far by learning the actual Cornish dialect the characters would have spoken in that period. In addition, one of the leading actors out-mumbled Marlon Brando.

It was the end of June 1991 when I returned. My first thoughts, as the plane caressed the green fields and hedgerows of England, would have drifted to the sound of ball on willow and the smell of newly mown grass. I was off the next day to play cricket on tour in the West Country. Cricket has always been an important part of my life, particularly in England. There is this myriad patchwork of clubs at every level of ability throughout the land. At most games, especially against village sides, you are served the most magnificent teas homemade by the local ladies. Mostly we play the same sides every year and get to know the oppositions. In the summer of 2015 I played my last game at Merstham for the Stage. Their umpire refused to give me out first ball as I had played against his team for 40 years. There is a comforting timelessness about the game.

As for the career, it took a long while to get going again. There was a general downturn in volume of work due to new franchising of the independent television stations. Less drama and series would be produced in-house.

Nothing came good until my agent called to ask if I would like to go to Birmingham to play a small part in an episode of *Jim'll Fix It*. It was a massively popular show whereby Jimmy Savile fulfilled a young person's wish. This young girl wanted to be Cleopatra in Egypt. The depth to which my acting career had plummeted was compounded when I stumbled uttering my one and only line announcing Cleopatra's grand entrance. I received an evil eye from Savile as we had to do another take. I think that moment was the lowest point in my career.

I was surprised to find that I was in the company of a well-known actor. This job, without doubt, would be regarded as a desperate acting gig. I was desperate but I could not see how Derek Fowlds could be. He had been a co-star in *Yes Minister*. He was a notable actor who would end up being in the country police series *Heartbeat* for many years. Of course circumstances are different for everyone.

At this point in time, although rumours abounded, Jimmy Savile was the king of popular television. Even though I could see he was being touchy-feely with this girl, we could not have imagined the extent of his systemic abuse of innocent young people.

A decent acting break came from being cast in *The Bill*. The payback for being pushed in the pool at that party, years before. Sadly, Detective Inspector Hutchinson would only appear in one episode. Although *The Bill* was not regarded as a soap opera, it demanded fast acting with minimum rehearsal.

Most of the action scenes are shot on the move with handheld cameras. Fortunately I had a sedate scene behind a desk. My scene was shot at Croydon Airport with the read-through taking place at Merton Abbey. It does beat going to the same office every day.

The mid-winter period was bleak, and made more so from building a fence on a snow-covered slope for a friend's pre-school grounds. My curses and cries of 'why am I doing this?' were extinguished by the freezing fog.

There were occasions of comfort and consolation. I attended a press launch at BAFTA in Piccadilly for *Heroes II: The Return,* which was mostly hijacked by Nathaniel Parker to launch his claim to fame. The series was televised the following week, which afforded some hope. But I came away with the feeling of being on the outside looking in.

What made the year worthwhile was attending an actor's workshop on playing Shakespeare. Patrick Tucker and his wife Christine Ozanne had recently founded a new company called the Original Shakespeare Company (OSC). Patrick was a theatre and television director and I had met him when he directed me in an episode of *Angels* for the BBC. He had gathered a band of actors who would be prepared to experiment in performing Shakespeare's plays as they were possibly done originally. He had been John Barton's assistant at the Royal Shakespeare Company and would have been steeped in text analysis.

The central tenet of his belief lay in the First Folio. Patrick believed that Shakespeare gave clues on how to play the roles within the written text of the First Folio. His research led him to formulate the working practices that were more than likely used to prepare and mount the plays in Shakespeare's time.

One key element was that actors knew nothing about the play they were going to perform other than their parts. The original actor's script only gave them a cue line for when to come on and when to speak. It was conjectured that the actors in Shakespeare's theatre companies would have thoroughly learnt their parts and been given indications as to how to speak their lines from clues embedded in the text.

Patrick believed that much has been lost from the way each generation bowdlerised the text. (Interesting that this word originated from Dr Thomas Bowdler, an American who published an expurgated edition of Shakespeare's plays in the 18th/19th centuries.) Patrick even believed that the texts used by the Royal Shakespeare Company were not exactly what he wrote in the First Folio. Over recent years it has become fashionable to modernise Shakespeare, to make his plays seem more relevant. This has gone hand-in-hand with the foolish policy that there is less cultural imperative for his plays to be taught in schools.

I can only convey a snippet example of Patrick's method from a workshop I attended. I had thoroughly prepared the powerful speech by Mark Anthony from *Julius Caesar*, beginning 'O Pardon me thou bleeding piece of Earth' following the assassination of Caesar. I had been hugely influenced by how Marlon Brando had spoken it in the movie, building to a climax on the word 'havoc', stretching the sound out and slipping down to '... and let slip the dogs of war'. I did it that way and also earlier pausing before saying 'butchers' in the line: 'That I am meek and gentle with these – butchers.'

As far as I can remember Patrick applauded the pause before 'butchers' saying that in the First Folio the word was written with a capital B which he says indicates strong emphasis, but he believed the climax was wrongly placed on 'havoc'. He said if you look at the First Folio text Shakespeare indicates pauses and emphasis through punctuation, capital lettering and line breaking. He suggested that Shakespeare intended the climax to come on 'Dogs of War' because he capitalised the words.

Of course, Shakespeare would have been the last person to be didactic about how to say his lines as he was an actor himself. He would have acted in other contemporary plays and exercised the interpretive element of an actor's craft. However, discovering the clues that lay behind how Shakespeare originally wrote his text was often a spine-tingling revelation. It was like being on an archaeological linguistic dig.

The central exciting aspect of his work lay in the resulting spontaneity in performance. Patrick would gather his cast having told them not to read the play, even though many knew it well. They received their parts well in advance but with only a three-word cue. The one day of rehearsal would be to work out entrances and exits and sort out costumes. There would be no director's notes or comments on interpretation.

I saw two full-scale performances, one of *The Comedy of Errors* at the now defunct Mermaid Theatre (run by Bernard Miles for many years), the other of *As You Like It* at the present day Globe. Both performances were electric. It was like watching a Formula One car race – waiting for something to go wrong. Amazingly, little did. And certainly what came over loud and clear was the storyline.

My good friend Greg de Polnay playing Jacques in *As You Like It* described it as terrifying. He said:

> You had to listen so hard to what actors were saying waiting for your cue, particularly for when to come on. There was no let up, even if you weren't on for a while, in case something was cut. You could almost get an electric shot from the hypertension on and off the stage.

I was asked to join but being an absolute wimp I declined. I have always struggled with learning lines and the idea of being stranded on a thrust stage makes me shudder thinking about it now.

Many well-known actors offered to participate in the OSC over the 10 years it was active. It would have been interesting to see how the likes of Ralph Fiennes, Prunella Scales, Greta Scacchi, Susannah York and Derek Fowlds handled this nervewracking method. Patrick took the OSC far and wide – Canada, USA, Australia and, of all places, Jordan. Sadly I don't believe the company exists any more. It would have required much funding. There was talk of Patrick running the Globe Theatre but it went to Mark Rylance, which I know upset Patrick. After that brief affirmation for my acting, the year ended with little to look forward to.

However, over the Christmas period of 1991 I began something that would lead to alternative work as an actor. I was staying with various friends and instead of a present to say thank you, I prepared a reading of *Memories of Christmas* by Dylan Thomas. Later in the year I was asked to put together a programme of poetry for a Harvest Festival held in the church at Beaumont Hall, a rambling 17th-century country house in Essex.

It was most reassuring for my ego to stand in the pulpit of this ancient church in the afternoon, reading aloud poems appropriate for the occasion, among amateur performers and musicians. In the evening there was a gathering around the grand piano in the oak-panelled drawing room for a bijou concert. My contribution was singing *My Darling Clementine, The Man*

Who Broke the Bank at Monte Carlo and *Mad Dogs and Englishmen* after which I received a very interesting comment. A gentleman came up and said: 'I understand you are a professional actor. We hoped you might be an inspired amateur.' It reaffirmed a comment I made when touring the outback: the further out you go from the centre of cultural activity the more sure amateurs are of being just as good as professionals.

On reflection it was probably this event that signposted the fork in the road of my career, when I took the first few steps down an allied path. It brings to mind Robert Frost's poem 'The Road Not Taken'. Its calm almost casual observation allays any mea culpa angst about making the wrong choices in life. The final lines resonate:

> *Two roads diverged in a wood, and I,*
> *I took the one less travelled by,*
> *And that has made all the difference.*

It would take a few years yet before this path would become a highway; at this junction it was a detour.

44

The London Blues

Letters written during 1992 revealed a significant mid-life crisis. I was wishing I was back in Adelaide, missing my real family and friends, finding London grim and cold, not feeling so much at home, not receiving any calls (from friends or my agent), dealing with a relationship that was falling apart again, and finding fewer and fewer parts for middle-age actors. I was obviously out of love with London and life. Samuel Johnson said that when a man is tired of London, he is tired of life. I am intrigued by Johnson's previous line, though: 'You find no man, at all intellectual, who is willing to leave London. No sir.' Perhaps my angst lay in that observation, as I'd always had feelings of intellectual inadequacy. I was in a great state of unrest and it was the nearest I ever got to experiencing something of 'the black dog': that deep feeling of alienation, of not measuring up to expectations. This was propelled, and at the same time eased, by a new affair.

Landscaping led me briefly into the arms of Jan. She was of the idealistic left-wing persuasion, a member of the agitprop fraternity who rail against the wrongs of the world. The trouble with diehard left-wing people is that they can never see the other side of an argument. There was an element of being attracted to an opposite, although I always had fundamental left-wing sympathy – care for the less fortunate and supporting measures to curtail the 'unacceptable face of capitalism'. But Jan was of the radical left, the protesting, barrier-mounting brigade. I had never met anyone quite like her. Being in this vulnerable state I suppose I was ready for some 'whips and scorns'.

She was a good talker and in an eager way attempted to thoroughly deconstruct me. It was like a short course in what I imagine Scientology to be about. She poked and prodded into my inner self, saying things like, 'You really don't believe in anything do you? Including yourself.' It was a confrontation I probably needed at that time. Nobody had challenged me in the way she did. Her forthright manner led her to be highly critical of my laissez-fare attitude to life. She made the strong point that perhaps my lack of success was due to my not having a centre, not being a definite person. She hit the nail on the head with that remark, as quite often people had said of my acting that it didn't project an inner life. Perhaps that was the innate fault observed by my drama teacher at NIDA, resulting in shallow acting. She agreed the part played in *Tenko* was an exception. This intense scrutiny made me face my shortcomings. I certainly felt cleaned out from the inside.

These 'dark night of the soul' sessions lasted over those summer months, until our relationship ended abruptly with a phone call. However, the poor girl was suffering far worse problems: she was having treatment for cancer, she was out of work, her tenant had left, her cat had died, and she had lost a grandmother's heirloom. This litany reminds me of a very funny book about a struggling New York actor called *P.S. Your Cat Is Dead*. At some point during down times, it helps if you can use a third eye, see yourself in the wider context and be able to laugh about your plight.

One lasting outcome from this relationship, however, came out of us visiting the Rembrandt exhibition at the National Gallery. We lingered over his self-portrait. That evening I wrote the following poem:

> *Hands clasped, unclasped,*
> *Feeling the sensuality of his strokes,*
> *His light illuminating our unspoken desires,*
> *His touch forever there to see*
> *Ours sealed in that instant*
> *Forever to be shared with all who have loved.*

Poetry allows you to encapsulate in few words a universal feeling that can seem to suspend that moment forever. One of the most profound and prophetic lines for me are in 'The Second Coming' by W.B. Yeats:

> *Things fall apart; the centre cannot hold;*
> *Mere anarchy is loosed upon the world*

Landscape gardening became my main source of income for five months and it was a deeply satisfying job. Despite most gardens being built in very cold weather with split hands and an aching back, to see a lasting result was compensation for the actor's fleeting legacy.

I did do the odd day's acting work here and there. I landed the main figure in a whisky commercial for Italy. It was filmed at Knebworth Hall in Herts, and I was a clan chief for two days for £2000. Suddenly in four weeks I earned £4000. It was interesting to discover that they wanted me because of my resemblance to Prince Charles.

The Royals with all their drama were a hot subject for films, especially from America. There was one film entitled *Sarah* that focused on Prince Andrew and Fergie. It was followed soon after by NBC casting for another film, this time on Prince Charles and Diana. I was able to persuade them to let me test for Prince Charles. Alas to no avail. I was pipped to the post by Roger Rees, a fine and well-known actor from the RSC. I did play Prince Charles one day, in a sketch pleading for the job of King of Australia, in a resurrected Footlights Club revue. He is fun and easy to take off.

During the down periods my father often came into my thoughts. I had inherited his cut-glass tumbler in which he would drink his evening *burra peg* (Hindi for double) whisky. I keep up his habit. It was strange how that feeling of loss when 12 years old comes back. Perhaps I was wishing I had his strength of character. I did inherit his frustration and a loud voice, which did not contribute to a harmonious domestic life, whomever I was with.

The hardest part of being a supporting actor is having so little control over your career. There are actors not deemed stars who work regularly. That was the status I failed to achieve.

With autumn well and truly closing in, my thoughts turned towards the warm and easy days at home in Adelaide. This coming period would find me more purposefully travelling down that 'road less travelled' and realising a lifelong ambition.

Part 5

From 1993

45

On the Road Again

Back in Australia and within two weeks of the new year I had an audition for a stage play. The Gordon Frost Organisation had set up a tour of Australia and New Zealand with Noël Coward's play *Fallen Angels* starring Hayley Mills and her sister Juliet. The part I was up for had been turned down by another actor, a recurring theme in my story. The role of Fred Sterroll, one of the husbands in the play, was a perfunctory one. Fred appears only in the first and last scenes but it was six months' work with an eight-week break, touring the major cities from Perth to Auckland and working with a well-known West End director, Chris Renshaw.

Hayley Mills was hugely popular, her fame reaching back to when she was a child star in Walt Disney films like *The Parent Trap* and *Whistle Down the Wind* with Alan Bates. She has latterly been seen in the UK television series *Wild at Heart.* Her elder sister Juliet had made a name for herself on American television in *Nanny and the Professor.* They were lovely people to be with and the small cast got on well. At one time in the tour the whole family was with us. We were well looked after by the management, John Frost being that rare species, a caring and generous entrepreneur. Theatre touring is not massively well paid unless you are the star. However, supporting actors get good touring allowances which meant I was able to save most of my salary.

Before rehearsals commenced in Sydney I was flown to Auckland to film a commercial for Sorbent toilet rolls, a slightly more down-to-earth credit compared to Noël's wistful words but very timely.

During rehearsals in Sydney I met up again with Tom Kenneally, author of *Schindler's Ark,* whom I had been introduced to at The Old Vic in 1978. He was interested to find out more from my association with the republican movement in the UK. My friend Dr Stephen Haseler was president of the nascent republican movement in the UK. Subsequently I became a kind of liaison person between the two movements. One of the nice surprises to come out of touring is meeting up with old friends and making new connections.

We were all flown to Perth to open at the Regal Theatre in Subiaco at the end of March. It was a gala opening with many of Perth's dignitaries. After the preview night I was told to speak louder, an issue probably caused by not working on stage for 13 years. The tenterhooks must have been too tight on the opening night, as I experienced what all actors dread – drying. I was looking at Juliet with my mouth open and nothing coming out. Juliet, of course, picked it up and completely covered for me. Nobody noticed. It is nerve-wracking because in that brief moment you are in a black hole.

The Mills sisters were rapturously received and the rest of the cast enjoyed the spilt-over effusive compliments at the traditional first night after-show party. Management were generous with presents, which was most appropriate as it was 1 April, my birthday.

Treading on the coat-tails of celebrity or basking in the shadows of stardom can be a perk or an obligation. I enjoyed the social fallout from being in their company. We dined with Alan Bond several times, went for a sail on the yacht *Aurora*, spent a day on Rottnest Island to see the quokkas and another in Margaret River, and even had a grand supper party thrown for the company by Gina Rinehart. Rinehart had arranged to have a wallaby roaming the kitchen, as Hayley had never seen one. I also caught up with some old teachers and dozens of relatives.

Touring is very full-on and sometimes you feel the performance gets in the way. We needed more time, for example, in the Margaret River district. Apart from the wonderful wines, one needed time to lie on the beach at night to behold the heavens alight. I have never seen a brighter sky; you could read a book by the light of the stars. Maybe that is why people hundreds of years ago, seeing the sky so light, could believe there was a heaven. Shakespeare often refers to heaven as being the great light in the sky and artists have painted that notion for centuries.

An unusual part of the production from the beginning was the use of real champagne. Two bottles had to be popped in every performance. It is very difficult to simulate. John Frost had cleverly got Veuve Clicquot to sponsor the tour. Hayley and Juliet took only a sip from two full glasses. Three-quarters of a bottle of French champagne could not simply be thrown down the sink.

Our next booking was in the St James Theatre, Wellington, New Zealand, where unusually the second night was bigger and more responsive than the first night. I was hoping the Prime Minister might be in the audience: I had written to him in Sir Humphrey style from the *Yes Minister* commercials I did two years ago. From his reply in like kind, which was sent by special courier to the stage door of the St James Theatre, I learnt that he was unable to attend due to an overseas commitment. I was surprised and delighted that he had the time and the style to respond.

This was a fairly comprehensive tour of both islands, taking in most major towns over a period of six weeks. On the *Male of the Species* tour in 1975 we played only Christchurch and Wellington. It seemed little had changed, even Fergus Dick (the famed name of NZ radio drama) was still working, but you could now get a decent cup of coffee. However, there was a noticeable difference in the audience. Not only did they fill the houses but they picked up the humour, reactions were quicker and applause more sustained. Even though New Zealand has always been seen as a backwater, New Zealanders tend to be more anglophile than Australians. British television dominated their content in those days. And what made us feel more at home were the many grand old theatres still standing.

Hastings in the Hawkes Bay area sported one of the last remaining theatres built by Henry Eli White. The façade of this theatre, opened in 1915, was in the Spanish Mission style with a lavish Art Nouveau interior and was like nothing we had seen before. White had also built the St James Theatre in Wellington. During the second day we visited the nearby town of Napier which had been completely rebuilt in the Art Deco style following the earthquake of 1931.

Travelling the rolling, dot-painted white-woolled pastures (New Zealand is the land of the sheep and this author is in love with Dylan Thomas) on our way to Palmerston North, we passed through Norsewood and Dannevirke, quaint villages founded by Scandinavian logging settlers in the 1870s. Little of the old forest remains. Out of the woodwork in Palmerston North came Professor Keith Thompson at the stage door. He had directed me in the opening production of the Union Hall at Adelaide University in 1958.

A cigar-like plane flew us to Hamilton where we played three shows to capacity houses in the Founder's Memorial Theatre. This was a modern 1960s-built 1200-seater with good backstage facilities. Maybe it was something to do with a wealthy rural community but all three performances were hugely appreciated, again particularly on the second night. Perhaps New Zealanders like to hedge their bets and wait to see what the first-nighters think. This would have nothing to do with Scottish settlers, of course.

With a whole week based in Hamilton and only three performances, we were able to be tourists. Spectacular formations of stalagmites and rock formations in huge cavernous areas had us awe-struck in the Waitomo Caves. They were not dissimilar from those caves I visited in Spain, but they were even more stunning because of the illumination from the resident glow-worms.

A day trip was arranged to Rotorua where we were wonderfully confronted by a haka (the Maori war dance regularly seen at rugby matches). We watched Maori carvers gently carve their artifacts; apprehensively felt the mud bubbling and the geysers blowing at the mud pools; and even witnessed Christ walking on water. St Faith's Anglican Church in Rotorua is famous for a stained-glass window depicting Christ, positioned to look as though he is walking on the real lake behind.

From Hamilton, in the middle of the North Island, we were flown to Invercargill at the very tip end of the South Island.

Invercargill is noted for an eccentric house. The outside walls are covered with embedded paua shells, which also decorated the inside walls of the living room. It was created by the appropriately named Fred and Myrtle Flutey, who were together for 64 years. Their front garden was a playground for gnomes, with a pond and shells from all over the world. The kitsch contents have now been removed to the museum in Christchurch.

We travelled the coastal road to Dunedin in a minibus mostly on dirt roads. Here is an edited account from my letter about our journey and time spent in Dunedin:

> It was a gloriously scenic route passing millions of sheep but an eerie feeling travelling for two hours through villages with no signs of human life. We stopped at Curio Bay – a fishing village with no fishermen – and stood on the point

overlooking the desolate bay in an exhilarating strong wind. I took a photo of Hayley's hair looking as though it was part of the spray from the crashing waves. There was only one tea room open but we were the only tourists.

It is a strangely familiar country with parts reminiscent of the UK, except for the extensive rainforests. The people are also familiar but strangely different. They seem to be more parochial and insular than Australians, with a dourness and a more basic sense of humour (Scots' influence perhaps). Did not see many women that appealed to me but the men were either big rugby-looking players or weedy running types. Every town was littered with joggers.

In Dunedin we played in another beautiful old theatre, the Regent, a huge 1700-seater with a great dome built in 1928 in a revived baroque style. After the first night we were invited to the Dunedin Club. Dunedin is old money. Many NZ companies began there. It turned out to be the only time the company was officially entertained and probably just as well. They didn't know what to say to us, the men making fairly boorish comments. At least I got a game of golf and tennis out of the gathering.

I do vividly recall that unique feeling stage actors experience. Both performances were packed out and we received thunderous applause from a full house. You stand looking up at the gods (the top gallery), basking in a state of euphoria. It is as though a bright light has been switched on inside you. You are glowing with pride. Of course the audience are really clapping the stars and it is reflected glory, nevertheless you are part of it. The only other character in the play that stood out other than our two stars was the maid played by Julie Godfrey. She scored many laughs and exit applauses with her taciturn manner. Paul Bertram played Willy, the other husband. They were tedious roles to play with most of the performance spent in the dressing room.

Christchurch (on the Avon) beckoned next, though its beckoning was marred by an insulting review. Sometimes a centre that has a strong amateur presence will produce a parochial response from the resident arts critic. Comments such as:

> bus-loads of eager theatre-goers crowded the Theatre Royal. They came with enthusiasm to see an imported production which was, in almost every respect, inferior to theatre presented every month in Christchurch by local groups. The Court Theatre puts on Noël Coward plays from time to time and does them with indigenous style.

The name of the critic was revealing – Imogen de la Bere. Quite what she meant by 'indigenous', I'm not sure; perhaps she had seen a Maori production of *Private Lives*. Her review was very different from another review by Melissa Chilton in the *Southern Times*:

> It was a frightfully stunning, wonderful night when two international actresses treated an Invercargill audience to a top professional performance ...

Probably every touring company will run into at least one extreme parochial resentment. However, such reviews don't seem to spoil the party. We had full houses at every performance. Some of us were obliged to see an amateur production of *Phantom of the Opera*. I wrote in my letter that 'any resemblance to Andrew Lloyd Webber's original was purely coincidental'.

There is a profound and significant difference between an amateur production and a professional one, even between a bad professional production and a good amateur one. Essentially it is about repetition. To sustain a performance over many weeks with eight performances per week requires training and technique, particularly in voice. A recent example was that of a young performer plucked by Lloyd Webber from a talent show to star in one of his productions in the West End. She lasted a week; her voice broke down.

In a good amateur show some parts will be played to a high standard but there are invariably some inconsistencies in the smaller roles. There will be noticeable differences in the pace and look of a production. Professionals have a polish, an intensity, are faster speaking and quick on cues, with a greater quality of seeming not to be acting. Comic acting is about playing for real and comic business (unspoken actions that gets a laugh) must come out of the character. An Oscar Wilde-type saying holds some truth: play comedy tragically and tragedy comically.

In addition, there will most certainly be a marked difference in production values – in stage setting, in props and in costumes. Above all are the discipline and the ethos. Few actors I know have ever missed a performance. We are very supportive of each other. In a small touring company it is like being married to 10 people for six months. At the end we exchange phone numbers and addresses, declare undying love – 'it was wonderful, darling' – and never see each other again. I have seen some worthy productions by amateurs but for that critic with the grand name, to say our production was in every respect inferior to the locals was just plainly absurd.

Our final date was in St James Theatre, Auckland, where we played to large but increasingly less responsive audiences. That, to some degree, was our fault. Despite what I have said about the difference between amateurs and professionals, we were tiring and our performances were becoming lacklustre. We needed a rest or a prod up our collective bottoms.

We said goodbye to the Long White Cloud on 12 June and flew to Brisbane. We played six performances in the Lyric Theatre, part of the relatively new cultural complex on the South Bank. Our final performance in Queensland was in a theatre in Surfers Paradise (a last-minute addition). Surfers is not my favourite place but the audience were in hysterics during the drunk scene, a scene the locals could readily identify with. It was a memorable last night followed by a great party, which included Stacey Keach, a great friend of the Mills sisters and another name to drop.

46

Living Out of a Suitcase

Actors are good at temporary nesting. I unpack everything on entering the room – putting clothes in drawers, book and clock beside the bed, photo and writing pad (now laptop) on the table. Even in the dressing room most try to make a cosy small area in front of the mirror. We respect each other's space. It is always exciting in the first few weeks but at about the eight-week mark it begins to get tiring, and you start to wish for the end.

The *Fallen Angels* tour was a little different. It had been booked in two parts with an eight-week break. I made a very brief trip back to London to find another tenant for my flat. Popping over to London was becoming a habit and it was great fun in those days with so few stringent regulations. Now air travel has become tiresome and worrying.

Rehearsals recommenced at the Comedy Theatre in Melbourne on 18 August. Our director Chris Renshaw gave us what at first seemed a strange direction for the kinds of roles Paul Bertram and I were playing. He told us to find a 'firmer truth'. Even though these kinds of English upper-class Bertie Wooster-type roles are almost one dimensional, you cannot just play bumbling fools. You have to find something to make them seem real. I found two brief notes in a diary:

Looking for Fred, beginning to find him.

Got Freddie in the first scene but lost him in the last.

To avoid 'losing' your character, you have to stay in a state of suspended animation, carrying what you came off the stage with for the entire break. This is requisite in film acting where you may have to wait for hours to capture what you have filmed from a different angle. Through training yourself you can develop a memory-block concentration, whereby you can flick a switch into what you left behind.

It was a great buzz being in Melbourne. There was some night life and a decent meal after the show at such venues as the Society Restaurant. Although I have never liked Melbourne as much as Sydney, they are two great cities of the world. There has always been great rivalry, with Melbourne being seen as the lady and Sydney the tart.

After four weeks in Melbourne we bumped into the Footbridge Theatre in Sydney. This was not a mainstream theatre. It was the old but upgraded Sydney University theatre where I had seen Germaine Greer play *Mother Courage* and many other student productions. The season extended to seven weeks owing to the limited capacity of the theatre.

This was the time when Hayley and Juliet's parents came to visit. Sir John Mills had been knighted and certainly had the air of a satisfied high achiever. He was also myopically proud of his daughters, with good reason. He and his wife, Mary Hayley Bell, were suitably gracious and complimentary. John Frost had arranged for Sir John to give a one-man performance at a theatre in Gosford, up the north coast from Sydney. We all trouped there on a Sunday night to see him give us an extraordinary lively series of music hall routines with top hat and cane. He was well into his 80s.

Sydney was where I had based myself for many years. Consequently there was much socialising. It was getting harder to keep up the energy and sharpness in performance. Our wonderfully affable company manager, Peter Adams, had to keep reminding us that every performance is the first, the one and only, for each and every audience. This is one of the most demanding disciplines in professional theatre.

Adelaide was our final destination. Performing on the wide expanse of the Festival Theatre was not ideal for an intimate play. The stalls were never more than three-quarters full, which diminished audience response. It made for a sad end to the long run. A visit backstage from Barry Humphries after the opening night lifted our spirits. I was able to tell him how untidy he used to be, as I had to clean his room at Chico Lowe's rooming house in the early days.

On the night that Mother came to the play I was able to get her on to the stage after the show with the curtain up, so she could see what it was like.

It set off her performing instinct as she began slowly and quietly to speak one of those monologues she had learnt for Lionel Logue. Gradually gaining confidence, she ended up declaiming to the gods. It was a spine-tingling moment for my sister and me.

Our producer John Frost flew over for the last night on 20 November and threw a great party, for the cast only, in the suite at the hotel Ramada. We left with presents, signed programmes and the usual intentions to stay in touch. I saw Hayley once in England but the others I never saw again. Such is the life of the 'strolling player'.

47

Taking More Control

Towards the end of 1993 after the tour, I began to feel the need to take more control over my career. It first came about through my very good friends Bill and Wendy Wauchope who had recently bought an historic house called Glen Ewin in the foothills of Adelaide, an ideal setting for any kind of open-air event.

I suggested they invite friends to bring a picnic and listen to my shortened one-man version of *Under Milk Wood*. This was readily taken up with the addition of a reading of Chaucer's 'The Miller's Tale' in the original Middle English by Tom Burton, Professor of Middle English at Adelaide University. I was sad to miss hearing the famous last lines in Neville Coghill's lively translation:

> *And Nicholas is branded on the bum,*
> *And God bring all of us to Kingdom come.*

All the same, the story came across through Burton's performing ability.

On returning to UK for a while I found little joy and little work. 'Who am I? And where do I belong?' were questions smouldering away deep inside me. Through republican friends I was seeing the irrelevance of monarchy and the inequities of the class system in the UK and realising the virtues of Australia's egalitarian society. It was an easier life in Australia, but my sensibilities kept being bruised by boorish ocker behaviour and parochial attitudes. This seemed not so prevalent in Sydney but it had become economically difficult to live there. And what I achieved at the end of 1994 in Adelaide would have been unlikely anywhere else.

Shortly after returning to Adelaide, I just missed out on a commercial for New Zealand worth $37,000 – in this case coming second is deep shit.

However, I was approached by the Independent Arts Foundation of South Australia to launch a book. It was for Blanche d'Alpuget's latest novel, *White Eye*. A friend on the committee knew of my shipboard association with her in 1965. Blanche had gained some notoriety. After completing the biography on Bob Hawke, Australia's ex Prime Minister, she married him.

After the previous year's success at Glen Ewin, and people talking of a mini open-air Glynbourne, I was invited to plan something more substantial for 1994. I came up with the simple idea of stringing together famous speeches from Shakespeare's plays, sonnets and songs on the theme of love and war. *Shakespeare's Greatest Hits* seemed an appropriate title. Judith Barr, a local celebrity, acted as Mistress of the Revels, her daughter Catriona sang the Elizabethan songs (years later she became an opera singer with seasons at Glynbourne) and my music director was an old friend from university days, Jeremy Wesley Smith (brother Martin is a widely respected modern composure).

For three months I worked alongside Jeremy, putting together the order of speeches, researching appropriate Elizabethan music and the scores for the chosen songs from the plays. Sections would be introduced and some literal comments made by the Mistress of the Revels. Songs like 'O mistress mine where are you roaming' would follow 'If music be the food of love play on' from *Twelfth Night*.

It was a hard slog learning the lines of 18 speeches, mostly soliloquies. It is much more difficult learning in a vacuum with no one to feed off. Interpretation would have to be slightly removed from the context of the plays to make clear the sense. I received valuable help locally from Professor Alan Brissenden and Frank Ford. Patrick Tucker from the Original Shakespeare Company sent me First Folio copies of the speeches.

After one dress rehearsal, the following night was my one and only performance. To give a more immediate impression of the evening here is an extract from an account I wrote to my London agent:

> Three stages were built in separate parts of the garden, by the lake, by the house and under the great wall. The musicians played from the second story balcony. At dusk with just a glimmer of purple in the sky, a spotlight glided around the audience picnicking on the lawn. As the overture from Walton's music for Olivier's

film of *Henry V* finally builds to its climax, there is a beat of silence and darkness. Then the spotlight explodes on to me standing masked on the wall 20 feet high, dressed in a flowing white Hamlet shirt and black trousers. 'All the world's a stage ...' rings out over the people and across the lake under a full moon. The spotlight was shone upon the lake so the audience could imagine Cleopatra's barge as I spoke the Enobarbus speech. 'The barge she sat in, like a burnish'd throne, Burn'd on the water ...' Then at the end of 'Once more unto the breach' I leapt off the high wall, sword in hand. Larry would have killed to have done what I did in such a magical setting. The Mistress of the Revels organised the audience to vocalise being Roman citizens throughout 'Friends, Romans, countrymen' – it got pretty lively when it came to raping and pillaging. I did manage to manipulate them at will or rather with Will and his powerful words. Then came down among the audience playing Falstaff's speech 'Honour pricks me on' in the manner of Arthur Daly from 'Minder'.

A haunting moment hung in the air after Catriona had sung the American war song 'When Johnny comes marching home' at the end of the Feast of Crispian's speech. For the finale I sang unaccompanied 'When that I was and a little tiny boy' from *Twelfth Night*, echoing the opening speech with the spotlight slowly closing on my face. Time stood still after the last note as I covered my eyes with the sad mask.

The performance, however, did not quite go to plan. My radio microphone broke down during the first speech. It couldn't be fixed so I began again with only one fixed mike on the main stage but often just relying on old-fashion voice projection. My early years of training and three months of thorough preparation rescued the evening, as I had to continually make adjustments.

Many friends could not understand that for all that work there was only one performance for which I received the princely sum of $500. The exposure hardly matched the remuneration but I had realised an ambition. I had created my own show and achieved considerable artistic success under difficult circumstances. For me that was payment enough. I have only to play the overture music from *Danses de la Renaissance* by the Clemenic Consort or the thrilling opening music from Walton's film music for *Henry V* to re-experience that lingering feeling of deep satisfaction. I had probably reached the pinnacle of my artistic ability.

Indeed, recognition of what I had achieved came from Peter Adams who had flown over especially from Sydney to help out. Peter had been our company manager on *Fallen Angels*. He was still working for John Frost and was keen to explore further possibilities for me to perform it in the eastern

States. Sadly it proved too difficult. However, the idea and structure of the show certainly interested a very famous actor who would have easily found a backer.

In the year 2000 Kenneth Branagh was filming *Rabbit-Proof Fence* in Adelaide. I told him about the show and took him to Glen Ewin. He was very keen to pick up the idea and asked if he could use my text. I still had the fanciful idea that I might do it again somewhere, even take it to England, so I declined. Of course there was no copyright on what I had devised. He could have easily devised his own but I believe he never did. His interest reaffirmed my achievement.

For the next four years a concert was staged in this open air setting for picnickers. *Duo Pianists Under the Stars* followed in 1995 with Darryl Coote and Robert Chamberlain featuring the *Grand Canyon Suite* and *Carnival of the Animals*. It was a joy to speak the witty lines of Ogden Nash resplendent in a white tuxedo. However, the moon upstaged and outshone us all. On cue for the interval, just as I was saying 'Now we reach the grand finale' the moon majestically rose over the lake, bathing the gum trees in soft golden light. There was a collective gasp and a sense of rapture. Nature won the accolades that night.

Sadly, without a professional foundation for these kinds of ventures, it couldn't last forever. Two more were staged which included *An Evening with Denis Olsen*, my old friend from NIDA days, who gave a superlative performance of Noël Coward songs. He had become Australia's leading Gilbert and Sullivan performer.

By 1998 the committee had fragmented and a more secure business was developing for storage and weddings. Cultural traditions are much harder to establish and keep going in Australia. There just isn't the population and physical culture is dominant. Whatever does keep going, like the various festivals in every city each year, requires arts funding or sponsorship.

Small events in local Australian communities seem to last for a while and then fade away like flowers in the desert. I wonder if there is any validity in the idea that humans tend to reflect the topography of their surroundings. It is certainly reflected in the Australian voice. The harsh, brittle, wide-open land required a nasal placement. Perhaps the early white settlers imitated the caw of the crow to pierce distance. The lush green fields of England and Ireland are reflected in the softer tones. The Welsh dialect goes up and down like their hills and valleys.

The dulcet sounds from concerts at Glen Ewin have long gone and raucous sounds from wedding parties have taken over but at least figs have restored the fruit-growing culture on the terraces. The legacy from Glen Ewin can be tasted in Harrods these days with their Willabrand chocolate figs.

48

Sailing Towards the End of the Century

Although there were five years to go, 'sailing' seems to be an apposite epithet to describe my journey over the last years of the 20th century – full of ups and downs with long periods of tacking. At the beginning of 1995, my old school friend Alan Cotton invited me to join *Cabaret* (the yacht we sailed in Sydney Harbour for the Bicentenary) in Port Lincoln on the West Coast of South Australia. He said it would be a gentle sail back to Adelaide, stopping over in various anchorages, with just him and his wife Bronwen. After our meal one night, with my hosts cosied in chairs in front of me at the stern, I began reading aloud *Falling for a Dolphin* by Heathcote Williams. After a very short while a chick tern alighted beside me only a few feet away. It sat there for the entire 20-minute performance and at the end it flew away. What made it come to that spot at that time and stay? Was it the small light on the book, the sound of my voice or was it an example of reincarnation? Whatever the reason, it was 'a moment on hold'.

That year turned out to be financially sustainable and encouraging for staying on. I was picking up the usual bread-and-butter work from voice-overs, training films and documentary dramas. Two of these documentaries are still being seen by international tourists in museums at Coober Pedy and Melbourne.

Then at last, in March 1995, a proper acting job came my way. It would be only my second time on stage at The State Theatre Company of South Australia, the last being in 1978 in *Cymbeline*. The offer was four roles in a satirical play called *Three Birds Alighting on a Field* by Timberlake Wertenbaker. The play had a broad canvas requiring a large cast. The subject centred on the cultural hypocrisies of the art world. The title was an apposite follow up to my one-man reading on a yacht – 'One Tern Alighting on a Stern'. Apologies for the irresistible pun.

From the day of the offer on 23 March and commencement of rehearsals on 1 May, I did a lot of research into the roles. The first was the most difficult. The play opens with an auctioneer selling a completely blank painting signed by a famous artist for $1 million to the audience. Even though I affected an auctioneer's style and method, it was fearfully difficult learning the lines. Inevitably, on one night a waggish group of my friends very volubly started bidding. I was forced to improvise.

The part of Constantin, a Romanian dissident, became a most enjoyable challenge. I was able to meet a Romanian couple and got them to speak some of my lines into a tape recorder, thereby scoring the lines in phonetics. Constantin was a loud, demanding character with a signature phrase: 'Gimme yor paintinks'.

A strange thing happened a short time after the show had closed. I met a real Constantin. He was a very loud, boisterous and very demanding Romanian athletics coach called Mario at the school where my partner's children went. Within a few minutes of meeting him I yelled 'I don't believe it, I have just finished playing you on stage'. Thereafter, whenever we met or passed each other in the street he would yell the 'gimme yor paintinks' line.

By the time rehearsals began I had done most of the preparation. Consequently, rehearsals became interminable, with endless prosaic, academic discussion about the wider and inner meanings of the text. In a multi-scened play with suggestive scenery, the choreography of each scene is of vital importance. It used to be said that great directors cast well and direct traffic.

However, what was deeply satisfying in the first quarter of 1995 was to have helped build a mini harbour on the lake at Glen Ewin. I was assisting Bill Wauchope, who employed me from time to time, fulfilling that need acquired from landscaping in the UK. Being part of a construction that had my initials carved in the steps fed my desire to leave something tangible behind. It was also great fun as Bill had a not dissimilar sense of humour to Patrick O'Grady, my landscape employer in London. They both came from a landed gentry background with an easy manner and plenty of laughs.

This three-year period was very much a transitional stage in my life, as I was looking to find ways to take more control; not just relying on other people giving me work, but creating my own.

My father had quelled riots in India with the strength of his voice, which I had inherited. I needed to use that to improve my earning capacity. I performed my own devised poetry programmes on a number of occasions, but a happenstance meeting with a fellow traveller would lead to many years of on-and-off work and almost elevate poetry to an industry. It came from connecting with Richard Potter, who once had been a disaffected school teacher.

He had been invited by the organisers of a country literary festival to devise an entertainment. It was to celebrate an anniversary of C.J. Dennis, one of Australia's best loved poets and storytellers. Poems were presented in an engaging way, some dramatised. The show was well received and the following year we performed it in the Fringe Festival. What came out of this was ongoing work. By 1997 we had become The Informing Performing Company or IPC.

Before reaching this era, which lasted for ten years, I did pick up some film work. One of them was Russell Crowe's early movie *Heaven's Burning*, and I enjoyed doing a commercial for Cottee's Jam in which I was asked to imitate David Attenborough.

The film called *Maslin's Beach* was quite another matter. The script was conceived, written and directed by Wayne Groom and was set on a nudist beach. This meant, of course, that the actors had to act in the nude. The wardrobe department missed out on this shoot. Fortunately, my part was the only one not requiring nakedness. The character was based on the famous author Henry Miller who was supposed to have had sex with his daughter. Firm concentration was needed when glancing down at the naked director, whose dangly bits were scraping the sand as he directed me in a scene with a naked actress playing my daughter. It took all those years of experience and discipline. It was damned hard work.

This self-funded film, not altogether surprisingly, became a cult movie. Five years later Wayne contacted me to pay a proper fee, having sold well overseas. Since then he has been championing these memoirs and I have reciprocated with his now completed project. *Paris or the Bush* is a two-hour documentary about a working-class rowing club called The Cods from Murray Bridge in South Australia, who almost won a gold medal at the Paris Olympics – a *Chariots of Fire* story. It has received worldwide interest. My mother would be very excited if she knew I played the Governor of South Australia.

49

What Do We Leave Behind?

My cousin Marilyn passed away around this time. While she had a brief career as an actress, her work would be scarcely remembered, so her legacy rests in her daughter. Stage actors suffer from leaving no more than their name in a programme. Their performances were witnessed and gone in an instant; only a few remain in the collected memory. Most screen actors, however, can now watch what they did 40 years ago. I have just seen for the first time a very young looking Edmund Pegge playing Meeker in *Dr Who*. It feels like watching someone else. Perhaps being an actor and not having children has prompted gestures towards immortality.

I have been prompted to ponder these things after remembering how profoundly the play *Arcadia* by Tom Stoppard affected me. In the play the young girl Thomasina, being tutored by Septimus, a friend of Byron, exclaims her horror at the burning down of the library in Alexandria. She weeps for all that knowledge lost and the great plays of the Greek theatre. He then quietly eases her fears by explaining how we can carry on:

> By counting our stock. Seven plays from Aeschylus, seven from Sophocles, nineteen from Euripides, my lady! You should no more grieve for the rest than for a buckle from your first shoe, or for your lesson book which will be lost when you are old. We shed as we pick up, like travellers who must carry everything in their arms, and what we let fall will be picked up by those behind. The procession is very long and life is very short. We die on the march. But there is nothing outside the march so nothing can be lost to it. The missing plays of Sophocles will turn up piece by piece, or be written again in another language. Ancient cures for diseases will reveal themselves once more. Mathematical discoveries glimpsed and lost to view will have their time again.

It was an assuring feeling hearing those lines: that each individual leaves behind, in some small way, something of themselves, that nothing is entirely lost; that even from the burnt-out library, something of what has been destroyed will be picked up; that along the road of discovery lost ideas like lost baggage will be picked up again, be fully restored and even embellished. These ideas lingered and deeply affected me.

These thoughts have also been connected to spending time with a high-powered chief executive. This high-profile businessman was a troubled soul and relates to a theme in these memoirs. I caught a glimpse of the real person behind the executive mask. Most of us spend the majority of our lives hiding behind a mask. Since the Greek theatre period 2000 years ago, actors have been doing that for a living. The demands made to reach the higher levels of success in our viciously capitalist society can crush the inner person. The demands of running an international company would have had some affect on his family life. There was no indication as to the extent of his inner detachment, cursed by the 'black dog'.

There was a telling moment when he visited Glen Ewin while we were building the dam. He sat there occasionally talking but keenly watching us put stone upon stone. He expressed envy at seeing us do work that would leave something tangible behind. A few years later his state of mind led him to an unexpected and untimely death. Perhaps this pushed me further to seek an outlet that would appease the hollow felt from my fleeting, look-at-me profession.

All these thoughts were reinforced with the death of my mother just before Christmas in 1998 aged 99, just missing out on her letter from the Queen. She was 95 when my sister and I felt the need to get her into care. We were very lucky to find a brand new Lutheran home which would take no more than her two-weekly pension. I did a very sneaky thing to make sure her last days were in a comfortable setting. Getting there early to move her in I found her name outside a narrow, dark room. The next room was wider and full of sunlight so I switched over the names. It was never found out and the woman next door had dementia. Mother was happy in her bright room and kept going for three more years. I have never felt any guilt.

In February 1996 I finally met the person 'without compare'. Annie Green and I have been together ever since. I espied this slim, dark-haired girl in a black and white polka-dot dress during a Test match at the Adelaide Oval.

I found myself slowly being drawn into her family life, despite making the potentially fatal error of beating the younger daughter Penny at backgammon. 'You Pommy ...' regaled my ears from this pretty, seemingly demure young 15-year-old. I could see it was going to be tricky but I eventually became accepted by her and the elder daughter Georgina. As well as my niece and nephew Linda and Grant I now have a newly found step-family, which has eased the cry of 'Who will remember me?'. It has also afforded closer experience of family life in this very different age from my upbringing. The endless drama and earnest exploration of feelings completely explains to me why soap operas are so popular. In my new-found domestic hothouse, the seed for speaking poetry burst into flower. Taking poetry performances to schools began in June 1996.

The first programme Richard and I devised was called *A Moment on Hold*. The idea was to explore Australian identity through the music of words, showing how poems resonate and expand meaning through hearing them expressively spoken. Further programmes were developed during this helter-skelter, to-and-fro period that would last more than 10 years. In addition, opportunities arose that would enable me to leave behind something material. My acting career was in no way over but it was on the wane. These new projects, however, would have me going here, there and everywhere.

50

Spreading the Word

This was going to be similar to missionary work. If we were going to hold the attention of students of all ages and backgrounds performing poetry, we were going to need a fairly muscular and entertaining programme. Teaching the rudiments and appreciation of poetry can present a daunting challenge to English teachers. Although I fervently believe you cannot apply business principles to education, we identified a need.

Richard had been an English teacher and a very good one, in the style of the Robin Williams character from the film *Dead Poets Society.* To inspire young people to value poetry, to show it wasn't boring, that you could have fun with words, were our initial aims. Over time we would expand and deepen those parameters.

The project required many hours of trawling through poetry anthologies. We had to catch in our net poems that lent themselves particularly to being spoken aloud. For example, poems such as 'The Highwayman', 'Cargoes', 'The Listeners', Roald Dahl's version of 'Little Red Riding Hood', and 'The Man from Snowy River' demanded inclusion. We also needed audience-participation poems. Another aim in the performances was to show the importance of expressive speech. We found a poem called 'Noise' by Jessie Pope in which each phrase required vocal expression the words suggested: 'The hubbub of traffic, the roar of a train'.

These kinds of poems were put into a programme called *Rollicky, Rhythm and Rhyme* developed later when we needed to entertain all levels. Keen-eyed readers will notice a misspelling. *Rollicky* was meant to be *Rollicking* but we rather liked the *ee* sound of *Rollicky* and, being a derivative of *rollick*, it has the more accurate suggestion of a frolic. This programme very soon became the most popular and widened our market.

Our baptism took place in a community centre theatre playing to pupils from state schools. Thirty-four years ago I began my professional career playing Shakespeare to students with the Young Elizabethan Players; time had come full circle. Performing to students unlikely to have heard poetry spoken before was going to be more difficult. We were surprised how well it went. It was nerve-wracking, like being on trial. I began by quoting Dylan Thomas's opening remarks from *A Few Words of a Kind*, a recording of his poetry recital from New York in 1953. Here is an extract:

> Poetry is what in a poem makes you laugh, cry, prickle, be silent, makes your toenails twinkle, makes you want to do this or that or nothing, makes you know that you are alone and not alone in the unknown world, that your bliss and suffering is forever shared and forever all your own.

Heady stuff for 15-year-old boys but we grabbed them with a wonderfully silly poem. 'Mangoes' by Richard Tipping consists of four senseless stanzas about what mangoes are, beginning with 'mangoes are not cigarettes' and ending with 'mangoes like poetry'. Demanding funny voices we settled on a brown-voiced television announcer, an over-the-top gay voice, an American cinema voice selling the next movie and a David Attenborough voice. These caricature voices made sense of the nonsense and were received with laughter and applause. With a robust rendition of 'The Man from Snowy River' and a Bruce Dawe poem on football we were able to hold them through a few lyrical ones.

The idea of performing poems written by students and picking up local poetry was a key to being accepted. Kangaroo Island, off the south coast of South Australia, was our first rural booking. We performed to all the school children and the local community over three days. Much of the success came from performing those student and local poems. Being good at sight reading was necessary.

A familiar trend and profound concern would come out of this particular programme. A key element in *A Moment on Hold* was to explore Australian identity. Familiarity of subject matter and verbal idiom was important for gaining and keeping attention. However, when asking questions after performing two poems about early Australia, we were alarmed at how little they knew about their country. Not to know when Australia was settled by

Europeans is a serious shortcoming. This became very apparent after I had delivered 'Old Botany Bay' by Dame Mary Gilmore, a poem I read on BBC TV. It was read by Jack Thompson at the opening of the 2000 Paralympics. My interpretation was very different from Jack's straight reading. I topped and tailed the six stanzas with a very strong Aussie drawl. The second was in an Irish accent, the third in London cockney, fourth in West Country and the fifth begged to be spoken with a Scottish accent. I am sure Dame Mary could hear those different accents when she was writing. By doing the poem this way it indicated that the early settlers came from all over the British Isles, sent there as convicts.

It is said that Australia was founded by the best judges of England. Very few students over the many years knew this simple fact. It seems history is not deemed important. I believe this to be a profound oversight by the educationalists, driven by capitalist demands for job training. The oft-quoted phrase 'ignore history at your peril' prevails.

In this first year we found audience response unpredictable. We went from schools in the extreme outback, including mining towns, to elite private schools in the city. On balance I think we were more appreciated in the bush. Probably something to do with the rarity of live actors performing, particularly one who had been in *Dr Who*.

A senior programme called *The World of Poetry* was taken to my old school. Included was Wilfred Owen's poem 'Dulce et Decorum Est' which I delivered at full blast pointing to our motto inscribed on the above panelling, '*Pro Deo et Patria*'. These echo the final words in the poem, '*Pro patria mori*', the message being how it was an honour to die for your country. There was a cool response to our performance befitting privileged senior students.

With juniors it was easier to get them going. In our first performance of *Rollicky, Rhythm and Rhyme* at the Junior School, it was impossible to complete performing 'Mangoes'. It came from the way I said 'mangoes' in the second stanza. Using a very elongated, sliding, high-camp voice sent the audience into convulsions. Every time I began there would be a howl of laughter which I fed by giving them a prissy, outraged look.

Years later boys would stop me in the street saying 'mangoes'. I can imagine that some educationalists might consider this an utterly inconsequential outcome. If the experience from any of our performances opened up just one young mind to poetry and the spoken word, the benefit could be quantified. It helped Churchill win the Second World War.

At one school early on we asked if any students had written a poem they would like to hear performed. Ben Hempel, a boy from a school in the outskirts of the city, was keen to hear his poem 'Swimming'. We immediately recognised it could be interpreted in two different ways, as the swimmer and as a commentator. It was a huge success and with his permission we began to include it in every performance as an example of interpretation, for which he earned royalties. Many student poems were performed along the way. Before some performances a student, having been invited to perform with us, would receive a quick performing lesson.

With all the junior programmes we would get them joining in and keep them amused by saying a poem in a Kermit the Frog voice and speaking 'Betty Botter' in world record time. My best was seven and a half seconds. These tricks meant we were able to keep their attention in more serious poems that required concentration. 'The Highwayman' was one poem needing no tricks or props. It is such a powerful, romantic story, all it needs is a dynamic vocal rendition, which is only achieved through training. It never failed.

This would be the beginning of a sea change in my professional life. It would find me engaging with young people, revealing the limitations of teacher training and identifying the perceived drop in standards of literacy and speech. In addition, I would find a writing voice, even an academic one. Before embarking more fully on this mission, I felt what I had left behind in England calling me back for a while. I was also keen to take Annie to Paris and Venice.

51

London Calling

I was back in London in June 1997, but being away for so long meant luck was needed to pick up work. I did land one interview. It was with no less a person than Lynda La Plante, the creator of *Prime Suspect*. It all went well having mentioned working with Helen Mirren in *Cause Célèbre*. I was then asked to read a section of the script. A London accent was required (à la Michael Caine) which I can do but a vowel in the line 'You can't barge in 'ere like that' betrayed me. I had given it the long, hard Australian 'a': 'You can't baarge ...' In cockney speech it is pronounced with a long soft a 'baurge'. Lynda immediately asked if I was Australian. I protested that I was not but that I had just returned from a visit. Undone by a vowel, I ended up not getting one acting job for the whole of 1997, despite many further interviews.

I was certainly not idle: I picked up landscaping work with my old colleague Kettles, prepared for Annie's visit, played many games of cricket and made many visits to the theatre.

I mentioned that Mark Rylance had been appointed director of the newly opened Globe Theatre. He is a remarkable actor and in some way took a leaf from the great Sir Laurence as an actor/manager. Of course, the top candidate for that was, and still is, Kenneth Branagh.

It was an exciting experience watching the July 1997 production of *Henry V* from the pit in front of the stage, where the groundlings would have been 500 years ago. In addition Rylance made the historical gesture to those days by casting himself in the part of Katharine. Young boy actors played the female roles then, as I did in my youth. Many years later I was astonished by his powerful performance in a modern play about gypsies called *Jerusalem*. His acting has that depth, power and panache redolent of Sir Laurence, as indeed has Branagh. Though, in my view, no one has touched, or is likely to, the sheer brilliance of Lord Olivier, as he became.

My life being a continuous working holiday, I have never felt the need to go on holiday for a rest. This was my second time being the full tourist: taking the train to Paris, a plane to Venice and a car to Scotland. Paris always lives up to its reputation, an enchanting city packed with visible history and requiring comfortable shoes.

Connections came handy in Venice. The daughter of a friend in Adelaide had married Francesco, who ran the small Hotel Dalla Mora overlooking a canal. We had breakfast underneath the washing line on the terrace above and waved at the tourists in gondolas as though we lived there. He took us around the canals in his dinghy with an outboard; not very elegant, but it gave me an excuse not to be ripped off by a gondolier. Annie never lets me forget not being gondoliered.

I caused a brief incident in one of the squares after I had handled an apple from a stall and put it back. As I was walking across the square the said apple missiled past my left ear followed by some kind of 'advice' in Italian. Renowned for its masquerades I have often wondered since what lies behind the mask of Venice.

Visiting friends around England and Scotland, where they immediately took to Annie, was an important step towards anchoring my life. Sadly Annie had to leave on 29 August, the day before a friend's wedding and on the eve of a momentous incident. On returning from the wedding in the early hours of 31 August, I happened to turn on the television and was stunned by the unfolding drama of the accident that killed Lady Di and Dodi Fayed. It had only just happened in Paris near where Annie and I had dined. The subsequent outpouring of grief was an extraordinary phenomenon. This very beautiful, privileged girl had captured the hearts of the underprivileged throughout the world. She had become a thorn in the side of the monarchy and given the republican movement a huge boost. The way she had been treated by the Queen and her court was a disgrace.

I was fast becoming anti-monarchy, influenced through my friend Dr Stephen Haseler, president of the republican movement in the UK. Many facts about the British monarchy are not readily known. Due to no written constitution, Britons are not citizens of their country; they are the Queen's subjects. There are many anomalies that have been so eloquently expressed by Geoffrey Robertson QC at various republican meetings I have attended.

At one meeting in 2001 I was invited to explain why Australia had not embraced a change, but discovered I was to speak immediately after Robertson. He oozed his thoughts across the floor without notes. I was terrified of making a fool of myself in front of mostly left-wing intellectuals. It was most unfair to follow a master of rhetoric. I explained about the clever twofold question in the referendum which asked for a choice of models instead of the simple question 'Do you want a republic?'. Friends told me I did well, though Robertson had not stayed to hear me. I still had not acquired the confidence to be myself in public. As I explained to my friends, I need a mask to hide behind.

I stayed on in London until the beginning of December exploring the possibility of touring poetry programmes to schools, but found the booking logistics overwhelming. However, two not unrelated occasions made an impression.

I was invited by a friend of the family to the Garrick Club. Founded in 1831, it encouraged members of the Establishment to mix with literary figures and actors. This was a far cry from the days when we were seen as rogues and vagabonds, though something of that still persists with insurance companies. I was like a young boy in a chocolate factory. To walk in the shadow of the great actors since David Garrick, after whom the club was named; glancing at the club's renowned collection of theatrical paintings and prints; hearing the murmur of important people; it was quietly thrilling

The next occasion would lead to a job and a return visit to the Garrick Club. Every year members of the Stage Cricket Club are invited to the Long Room at Lord's to attend the Cross Arrows dinner. Our skipper at the time was Nigel Miles Thomas. As we were preparing to leave, Nigel said to me, 'Oh by the way. Ed, been thinking. I might have something for you next year.'

Before returning to Adelaide for Christmas, I found out that he had set up London Full Circle Productions in Hong Kong to produce *Travels with My Aunt*, a play adaptation of Graham Greene's novel. It would be a tour of Southeast Asia playing in the expatriate clubs and hotels of Bangkok, Hong Kong and Singapore. Rehearsals would not be beginning until the end of March, so it was good returning to Adelaide with a firm prospect. Another example of how fortuitous an actor's life can be.

52

Acting Again!

At the end of March 1998 I flew back to London to rehearse *Travels with My Aunt*. I felt at ease early on in rehearsals, due to knowing the director. Donald Sumpter had been at Nottingham Playhouse and was someone I had admired, as was the leading actor Roger Lloyd Pack. Roger was a very fine and well-known actor who had become famous through playing Trigger in *Only Fools and Horses* and Owen Newitt in *The Vicar of Dibley* on BBC television. He was often hailed in the street even in Singapore. More importantly he was a hugely experienced stage actor and a very nice man.

Graham Greene's novel is centred on Henry Pulling, a retired bank manager, who meets his Aunt Augusta at his mother's funeral. This free-spirited, elderly aunt takes him on her travels through Paris, Turkey, Paraguay and Argentina where they meet strange people often in dangerous situations. These adventures turn his dull suburban life into an outrageous odyssey. With only four in the cast, we all had to play more than one part. Mine were Henry Pulling, Tooley (an American) and Miss Keene. Roger played mostly Aunt Augusta.

Having been working more in Australia with little theatre work, I found myself struggling to keep up the pace at which the others were working. I was mentally slower and had to work hard at finding a higher gear. More specifically I had to increase the pace of my thinking and speaking. In the early stages our director remarked on my slowness in picking up cues and my lack of sharpness in movement. Perhaps it was caused by the sun and the slower pace of life in Australia. I do find cold quickens the thinking process. It turned out to be a very intense three weeks.

The play was ideally suited for touring, and it would be staged sparingly, like those potted versions of Shakespeare to schools. The novel was skilfully adapted by Giles Havergal and first performed at Glasgow's Citizens Theatre in the early 1990s. This marvellously entertaining story is deftly told in a classically staged way: a few key pieces of furniture (rail, rostrum and stool) in front of black curtains with actors dressed in white tuxedos over white shirts with black ties. The various characters are indicated by a shawl, hat or stick but the real differentiation comes from the actor's craft, using voice, gesture and body language.

Playing a variety of roles in the same play demands a slightly different approach in preparation. The characters must have more substance than a caricature or a cut-out figure. I used Humphrey Bogart's style and vocal manner from *Casablanca* to play the American part of Tooley. It was important not to over-play femininity with Miss Keene but to focus on her actions and intent. With our director's prodding I eventually got up to speed.

After an encouraging reception from a pre-tour performance in London, we flew to Bangkok on 19 April. We were delighted to find that our accommodation and performance would be in the Shangri-La Hotel. In addition, the Singapore ambassador to Thailand would be in the audience and we were required to meet him afterwards. This caused me to neglect my next-door neighbour from Adelaide, Max Tomkins, who happened to be passing through Bangkok at that time. Southeast Asia seems to be fertile ground for chance meetings. After playing the first week in Bangkok we flew to Hong Kong where we performed and stayed in the Ritz Carlton.

In the audience were old friends from London. Andrew and Sarah Burns were residing in Hong Kong. Andrew had been appointed British Consul-General to Hong Kong and Macao. Sarah had been married to Geoff Kenion who had run the theatre company in Mallorca. It was their daughter Ella's wedding I had attended on the night of Lady Diana's accident.

These two weeks in Southeast Asia confirmed yet again the very strong impression of the sun still not having set on the British Empire. There was not a vast difference from when I was last there in 1966. Many new buildings and greater prosperity, but the Europeans were still living the 'life of Riley' in their separate clubs. We played the HK Country Club, the HK Football Club, the HK Cricket Club, the Kowloon Cricket Club, the Pacific Club, the Ladies

Recreational Club and the United Services Club. These last two were probably remnants from the Empire days.

This kind of performing echoes the ancient tradition of the strolling player. Performances were in different places with varying facilities and problems. We were never in a conventional theatre. It was great fun to perform and never tedious. We were warmly welcomed everywhere with the oft-heard comment that the play was a breath of fresh air. However, it needs to be pointed out that the well-known comic actor Derek Nimmo had been touring the area with his company for some years, playing mostly farces. I think 'the fresh air' might have implied that our play had more substance.

Sadly, Roger Lloyd Pack died early in 2014 at the age of 69. We did many things together during this short tour. My fondest memory was watching him imitating a local doing tai chi. Like his acting, he was completely absorbed with fierce concentration and would not have cared that he might have looked awkward.

The most vivid memory I have of Roger is seeing his lugubrious face in momentary shock when I dried. There was this seeming endless hiatus which was probably only three seconds. He could see I had dried through the desperation in my eyes. He soon came to the rescue and nobody noticed. It was Roger on returning to London who took me to the Garrick Club for the second time. His father was a well-known actor member.

We moved on to Singapore for the second and last week and found we were booked into the prestigious Tanglin Club where we would give our last performance. We also played the British Club, the American Club and the Dutch Club, where I was able to catch up with my old school friend Ross Clayton. Having done the two war series and a film about Singapore (*Tenko, Heroes II: The Return* and the television movie *Gordon Bennett*) I wanted to explore some of the islands that might have featured. We weren't able to go to the island where the shipwreck in *Tenko* was shot but we did find an island with gun emplacements. This position may have overlooked the submersibles coming into the harbour to blow up the ships in *Heroes II: The Return*. We were two schoolboys again, slightly older.

One evening Ross took me to an extraordinary old hotel called the Mitre (apparently still there but closed). The caretaker was a character out of a movie (Robert Newton of *Treasure Island* fame would have played him). He was looking after hundreds of suitcases and boxes filled with belongings of seamen. Singapore was one of the busiest ports in the world and seamen from every part would come to find work. I was overwhelmed gazing at so many that were never picked up. So many stories there buried in sad suitcases waiting patiently for their owners. We both felt in that cemetery of suitcases the enormous feeling of insignificance dealt to so many.

There is a passage in the play that pertains to this fleeting nature of life. It is when they are visiting Paraguay. Aunt Augusta fires a broadside at the reality of suburban marriage which Henry is about to sink into when he returns to England:

> *Aunt Augusta:* Do you know what you'll think about when you can't sleep in your double bed? You will think how every day you are getting a little closer to death. It will stand there as close as the kitchen wall. And you will become more and more afraid of the wall because nothing can prevent you coming nearer and nearer to it every night.
>
> *Henry:* … isn't it the same everywhere at our age?
>
> *Aunt Augusta:* Not here it isn't. Tomorrow you may be shot in the street by a policeman because you haven't understood Guarani … when we have our Dakota, perhaps it will crash with you over Argentina. My dear Henry, if you live with us, you won't be edging day by day across to any last wall. The wall will find you of its own accord without your help, and every day you live will seem to you like a victory.

The play certainly had substance but packaged in humour. It strikes me that this wall is coming closer to all of us today, closer than ever before, with random killings by terrorists and aircraft accidents.

Saturday 16 May 1998 turned out to be of significance. That night in Singapore at the Tanglin Club was the penultimate time I would be in a stage play. I was already on the 'road less travelled' by many actors. In no way, however, did it mean I was giving up performing as many had. This work in schools would take over and consume my time for the next ten years.

53

'Words, words, words'

By August I was touring schools again, assailing young ears with words. Our booking agent was a diamond. Her conversation sparkled with effusive plaudits of our work. She was so persuasive that we had bookings through to the end of September. She was no ordinary agent which included her name. Carole Carroll came from Wagga Wagga, went to school in Gumly Gumly and joined the Book Book tennis club. This doubling up extended to her address, which included lots of 2s in the suburb of Glenelg, which is a palindrome. These facts scored a hit at a banquet in Hong Kong in 2001 when we had brief success overseas.

Driving in the outback is tiring business requiring special care for our voices with all the dust. Carrying water was no problem; finding a decent cup of coffee was. After leaving the metropolitan area the chance of finding one becomes more and more remote. However, on the outskirts of Port Pirie, beyond the Goyder Line where rainfall is scarce, we pulled up at a delicatessen. The Italian owner did a double take when he saw me. With mouth open still gazing, he yelled to his wife and son: 'You wonta believe it. We heava Fader Murphy in de shop!'

Father Murphy was the part I played in *Home Sweet Home* for the ABC in the early 1980s. The family had been replaying a video copy the night before. After much Italian jocularity, autograph signing and a refusal to accept payment for our coffees, my mock blessing was amusingly received as we took off into the desert.

We had been invited to be artists-in-residence at the school in the remote mining town of Roxby Downs for a week. By now Richard and I had devised a creative writing workshop. With the junior and senior poetry performances, our three ninety-minute daily sessions meant our days were intense. In addition we often conducted professional development workshops with the teachers after school.

Richard's method was to gently talk students into centring themselves by closing their eyes and relaxing their bodies. Richard's vocal journey would be topped with my speaking a poem or, more often, the edited opening of *Under Milk Wood*. The students would be asked to listen to sounds around them, then to look briefly at an enlarged photo. In a very short time they were asked to write without thinking their immediate response to those stimuli.

The idea was to open the door to the subconscious. Then we would read out what they had written. They were often amazed at hearing their words spoken with expression and humour. Over the years this method produced some astonishing results, especially among underperforming students.

The rest of the year fizzled out but there was a sad ending for our family with my mother passing 'gently into that good night'. We were told the night before that she had gone into a deep sleep, and by the time we arrived in the morning she had slipped away. It took a long time to sink in that she was no longer there. I still miss her.

By the end of the 20th century speaking poetry became my primary source of income. There are few writing poets who could say the same. The speaking of poetry would lead to the writing of a manual on *how* to speak it. This in turn would lead to a CD example of how to interpret poems vocally. On the way I took up the offer of converting my diploma from NIDA to a bachelor degree. Further down this track, out of the speech manual would come a booklet on how to read a story to young children.

The speech manual came out of our visits to St Peter's College Junior School. Francesca Peel was a forthright teacher who recognised the importance of poetry in early education. It was her suggestion that I write a manual. Francesca's keenness lay in her having established an inter-school poetry speaking competition. There was very little material to guide teachers instructing vocal interpretation of poems and text. Oral presentation skills have been and still are neglected by the education authorities.

With Francesca's practical assistance and encouragement the final draft was produced at the school in February 2000. Its first title was *Speaking Poetry* and I sold it to many teachers and libraries on our travels. A final version was published in 2007. This manual was a fine example of how the baton is handed down; my text was inspired by the teachings of my mentor Musgrave Horner, who was the speech and drama lecturer at Adelaide Teacher's College in the 1950s.

Our bookings in schools became more centred around Book Week in August every year, when schools were given the budget to focus on reading and literature. In the first four years, schools as far afield as the West Coast of South Australia to the Riverlands in the East and the rich pastoral towns of the South East would invite us for whole weeks as artists-in-residence.

We visited the South East many times where we found in the towns of Naracoorte, Penola and Mount Gambier a fertile climate for writing. John Shaw Neilson and Adam Lindsay Gordon, two famous early Australian poets, had lived there for a while and seemed to have left a legacy. There was a strong literary tradition in the whole area of the Coonawarra and the Limestone Coast, noted for its myths and legends, like the Tantanoola Tiger.

We were regular visitors to St Joseph's Primary School, which was established by the world-renowned Roman Catholic saint, Mary MacKillop. But in the middle of the vast forests of the South East, we experienced a 'moment on hold' from a young student at Millicent High School. We had visited the previous year when we met and stayed with a wonderful English teacher, Diana Cook from Zimbabwe. Australia often throws up interesting people in remote areas and surprisingly talented students.

A young student, aged 13, was sitting in the front row of one of three sessions we conducted that day in 2003. Large photos of a tranquil scene with trees by a lake and a moon, followed by a winter scene in fields with a grand house in the background were presented briefly. The pupils were asked to write without thinking whatever came into their minds for two separate minutes.

This is what she wrote:

> First picture:
>
> *A sunset as beautiful*
> *as a baby sleeping with the moon as a dimple.*
> *When he smiles with a face so young and fragile*

It's amazing.
Trees as his hands
when he brushes yours away
so he isn't disturbed while he is dreaming
so peacefully.

Second picture:

A frosty day in winter with a sunrise
so beautiful with trees it's like you never want to leave again
It's so peaceful and quiet with no one there
even if there is someone there.
It's cold but you can always have fun because you are there
enjoying yourself.
as you try to picture yourself with the one you love.
There.

To our astonishment we were told that she had been deemed illiterate; that she had never written anything beyond the simplest sentences. When I was reading aloud, giving her words resonance, I glanced down to see her eyes wide open. There was a hush in the classroom. It was a 'moment on hold'. We also learnt later that being the eldest, she often had to look after her siblings.

Another memorable moment occurred at the end of our professional development workshop with the teachers. After I had spoken the above poem the principal, whom we hadn't seen all week and was a typical tick-all-the-boxes, admin-obsessive head, grabbed the poem from my hands.

'I now have something to show the school council,' he declared. In other words, he thought here at last was tangible evidence that would justify our fee.

Evidence of the value of our work came in abundance from teachers and students in their evaluation replies. There were many reports that our visit dispelled the fear of poetry and turned around under-achieving students. Teachers were awakened about their voices in workshops which, they said, should be included in their training. What came out of so many of our sessions was that everyone enjoyed them. When learning is fun it is more readily remembered.

We were hugely encouraged by the appraisal (the late) Bob Ellis gave for our work:

> There must have been a moment when a cave-dweller first understood that a mark chipped on a stone could signify a meaning, and writing was born. Or when he raised his voice in a particular way, and song was born. Edmund Pegge and Richard Potter have been seeking and igniting a similar moment in the lives of school children. It is a moment when the mightiness of the spoken word is made known to them, and the joy inherent in exploring it enraptures their young minds, leading them to change powerfully into greater creatures in learning and performances.

Our journey lifting words off the page and exciting the ears of young people took us to remote parts of South Australia and even overseas. Somehow we were invited to be part of the inaugural Hong Kong Literary Festival in May 2001.

The invitation came about through the offices of the Australian Consulate in Hong Kong. It was prompted after my contacting Sir Andrew Burns, the British Consul-General in Hong Kong, whom I had last seen in 1998 when touring in *Travels with My Aunt*. He recommended us to the British Arts Council who were mounting the festival. They approached the Australian Consulate who agreed to fund us.

Our launch was to dozens of school teachers. We performed poems and talked about our aims and method, which all went very well. We were honoured to be asked to open a new library with a series of poetry performances followed by visits to two schools. The reaction was very promising. We were able to take our agent Carole with us who did what she could to promote us. But finding someone to liaise with Carole and act as a booking agent there proved impossible. Poetry and clear speech are hard products to sell.

One incident I shall never forget. We were having a drink in a narrow, lively bar after the banquet. Our good Australian country girl of an agent, happily married, was persuaded to climb up onto a tiny dancing area on a bar, losing herself to the music and almost making a Marilyn Monroe moment. The whole enterprise was worth it for that moment.

54

Hopscotch

Pursuing this body of work touring schools among a few acting jobs caused much hopping around over the five years from 1999. In 2002 I began a long-haul project putting together a CD of poetry.

I had already got together with Rob Pippan, recording speech examples for the manual. Rob was a brilliant guitarist in a local Adelaide band and a wizard on a studio keyboard built in his home. He liked the idea of creating a backdrop of sound and music to poetry and his innovative sounds for 'Jabberwocky' enhanced the story brilliantly. I believed a CD of famous poems produced in this way would be very marketable. Rob waived his normal studio fees and we slotted in the work over a period of two years.

He was a high octane performer and amazingly fast at creating suitable music and sound effects as backing. Seventeen classic poems were recorded, among them: 'The Highwayman', 'Cargoes', 'The Listeners', 'Ozymandias' and 'The Man from Snowy River'. Sold to teachers as an aid to introducing poetry and to the public, the CD has been very well received.

I was able to slip in some work on a movie and a television series in 1999. I played a scene with Ben Cross (*Chariots of Fire*) in *The Potato Factory*, followed by a supporting role in another Rob George/Donald Crombie movie *Selkie*.

NIDA invited their alumni to a 50th year celebration in 1999. There were only a handful from the second year who were still working as actors and I found it strange that there were many attending who hadn't made it at all. It was also noticeable that of the older actors present few were high profile – probably too busy working.

Unlike in the UK and USA, there is an obsession with youth in Australia that does not reflect the community we live in. It is very definitely reflected in the casting of television drama and movies. There are token oldie parts.

Ray Meagher in *Home and Away* is one of only a few actors I know from my days. John Waters is sometimes seen and it is great that Jacki Weaver has been recognised.

There are three actors I know well from my generation in the UK who are still in regular work: Tom Georgeson (*A Fish Called Wanda*), Daniel Hill (*Judge John Deed*) and Johnathan Coy (*Rumpole of the Bailey* and *Foyle's War*). All three have achieved what I was aiming for: recognition as a regular supporting actor. I nearly made it but fell short.

My ego received a boost, however, in May 2000 when I performed Noël Coward songs in an imitation *Last Night of the Proms* concert in the Adelaide Town Hall. I had seen Jeremy Irons on television performing at the Albert Hall. I thought he was under-powered and hadn't entered into the character of the songs. It would have been foolish of me to even try imitating Coward. After auditioning for the conductor Carl Crossin, I worked hard over a period of seven weeks for a paltry fee, but it was well worth it.

Carl was the music teacher at Marryatville High School, a highly regarded music school. He was very encouraged that I proposed a more robust half-singing, half-speaking style of delivery.

Waiting backstage with musicians warming up instead of actors going *ooh aah eee* was a new experience. My part was to open the second half. My good friend from university days Tony Brooks, wit and bon vivant, was MC. Saying that my name was more than appropriate to perform Mr Coward's songs, he proceeded to regale a thousand ears with my full name – plus an extra one from my father's. Edmund Cyril Cuthbert (extra) Colbeck Pegge battled the orchestra to be heard and from all accounts won. It helped that I was required to compose my own introduction to each song. It was as well, also, that I had prepared a vigorous rendition, as Carl was not able to achieve a lightness of touch that some of the songs require.

In introducing 'Mrs Worthington' I warned people of a delicate disposition not to listen to the last verse. By all accounts the last verse had been performed very rarely by Noël Coward himself and only once in Australia. That only time was in Adelaide, to soldiers at an army camp in Woodside just after the war. There was certainly no need for lightness of touch when it came to that verse in my performance. Here it is:

Don't put your daughter on the stage Mrs Worthington
Don't put your daughter on the stage,
One look at her bandy legs should prove
She hasn't got a chance
In addition to which, the son of a bitch
Can neither sing nor dance
She's a vile girl and uglier than mortal sin
One look at her has put me in
A tearing bloody rage
That sufficed Mrs Worthington
Christ Mrs Worthington
Don't put your daughter on the stage.

Needless to say, it received rapturous applause. Having heard a rough taping of the performance, I would like to think I achieved a result that even Noël might have applauded.

In 2001 I entertained Kenneth Branagh, who was in Adelaide to shoot *Rabbit-Proof Fence*. Our first outing was dinner at the Star of Greece restaurant on the cliff tops overlooking the beach at Port Willunga. Arriving early we took a stroll. Ken began ruminating about his inability to find a partner to stay the course. I pointed out that he had been with beautiful, lively and ambitious actresses; that sparks would inevitably fly between two highly charged positive people. I simply suggested he look for someone behind the camera, which he eventually did. On hearing about his marriage I sent an email saying I was glad he had taken my advice, which he acknowledged when I caught up with him after a play he was in at the National Theatre. The play was coincidentally called *Edmund*.

Charles Dance was cast to play Roderic Chamberlain, the prosecuting lawyer, in the film *Black and White* shot in Adelaide in 2001. It was a cause célèbre case conducted in the Adelaide High Court from the 1950s, about a young Aboriginal man accused of killing a white girl. Directed by the late Craig Lahiff and produced by Helen Leak, the film was able to attract three internationally known actors, the other two being Robert Carlyle (*Macbeth*) and Kerry Fox (*The Crimson Field*). It was a strong cast which included David Ngoombujarra playing Max Stuart, the young Aborigine.

Being cast as Dawson, the offsider to Charles Dance's character, meant I would be working with him all the time. As befitted his part, Charles Dance was compelling, with an air of authority. I had arranged through a friend to watch proceedings in the criminal court with Charles, after which we had coffee and a chat. We had filmed a few scenes together before I was called to be interviewed by Phillip Satchel at the ABC.

It was an hour-long interview similar to those in Margaret Throsby's *Midday* in Australia and *Desert Island Disc* in the UK. He asked me a tricky question: 'Where do you find yourself in the league table of actors?' I said initially that I had always been a second eleven player in most things. Then I found myself slipping into the UK soccer analogy, saying the star names were in the premier league like Russell Crowe or Brad Pitt. In the next league down were very well-known actors like the actor I was working with, Charles Dance.

It didn't take me long to gather that Charles must have heard my interview. He hardly spoke to me for the rest of the shoot, presumably because he thought of himself as being in the premier league. It was confirmed as I was leaving. Driving slowly past him in a school playground area, I noticed Charles was at ease, chatting with a young female. He looked up and sardonically uttered, 'There goes Edmund Pegge, a legend in his own State'.

In a sense he was right; in Adelaide I move up a league. However, these days I feel as though I have slipped down to the fourth division in the acting league tables, like Accrington Stanley in the soccer tables – a club with a theatrical sounding name.

Just before flying back to London I had witnessed on television, to the point of saturation, the horrendous events of 9/11. It was a staggering spectacle which changed the status quo of the Western World, seemingly forever. Instead of flying with a degree of trepidation, I rationalised that it was probably the safest time for air travel with security maximised. It is mind-numbing to contemplate in any way what these terrorists think they achieve with random killing on this scale.

The London attack of 7 July 2005 happened the day after Annie (my partner), her daughter and her daughter's boyfriend arrived. I had booked to take them to see *The Lion King* in the West End, with supper afterwards at Joe Allen's around the corner. I had no hesitation in going. London streets were crawling with police. This holiday with Annie would take us back to Paris, then to Prague. The highlight was attending a performance of Mozart's *Don Giovanni* at the very theatre where the opera had its world premiere.

Over the decade from 1999 I notched up many air miles, often commuting twice a year to London. However, in 2002 I spent the whole year based in Adelaide. Our IPC work in schools reached its zenith, but I did no acting at all.

However, I did become a 'proper' actor by receiving my NIDA degree at the University of New South Wales. With no academic expectations I finally had a recognised university degree: Bachelor of Dramatic Art NIDA. It was to prove useful in the light of the educational work I was doing. Added to my diploma from Trinity College London, it certainly gave my speech manual greater authority. What pleased me most about gaining this degree was my thesis being deemed worthy of publication, albeit in a teachers' journal. My tutor and examiner Robert Brown from the University of Adelaide had rated it at the lower level of distinction. A PhD friend in the UK, whose thesis was on an English subject, rated my effort worthy of being on the way to a Master's Degree.

The year ended with a fun job. David Griggs, a fellow graduate from NIDA, handed on a request from Saatchi & Saatchi in Sydney to coach the Australian cricket team – not, of course, at cricket. Two players were required to talk in a West Indian accent for a commercial. My immediate reaction was of apprehension. Could I find an oral tape recording and do it phonetically? Connections came to my rescue, remembering a good friend's daughter was married to a West Indian. Not only was I able to transcribe the text into phonetics with his help and taped him speaking the dialogue, he was also happy to accompany me on the day.

It was during the lead-up to the 2002 Adelaide test match. Adam Gilchrist and Brett Lee were chosen. We got them to say each phrase after us. It was interesting to note that Brett Lee wanted to take the tape back to his hotel but not Adam Gilchrist. He was confident and did the commercial. You can never quite predict where the next job will take you.

The following year I did the reverse, spending seven months in the UK. Before leaving in May 2003 I had an enjoyable two days in the town of Orange in NSW. Susie Maizels cast me, without an interview, playing Judge Snedden in *Jessica*, a Bryce Courtenay television adaptation. Also in the cast were the male leads from *Lucinda Brayford*, the ABC television series filmed in 1980. Sam Neill, Barry Quin and I had a fun reunion. It doesn't happen too often that three actors from a past production end up acting together in the same scenes 23 years later.

It was necessary to spend some time working on my flat in London, which is always best in the summer months. It was a bonus landing a guest lead in one episode of an afternoon BBC series called *Doctors* starring Christopher Timothy (*All Creatures Great and Small*). Little did I know that I would be working with an actor who would soon be passing Charles Dance in the league tables. I played the part of an ex-RAF officer who has problems with his son and has a heart attack. Playing my son was Eddie Redmayne. He had just come down from Cambridge and was inexperienced in screen acting. It was almost his first job. I gave him a few elementary tips and off he went, climbing very rapidly into the top division. With his performance as Stephen Hawkins in *The Theory of Everything*, he has slipped rapidly into the premier league.

I have to admit I did not notice star quality in Eddie at that time. He had those soft, fine features that often seem to accompany upper class English boys from Eton and Harrow. He was also quiet and softly spoken, a quality that suited his character in the television series *Birdsong*, but for me he tended towards mumbling.

With winter in the November air of 2003, I was down the M4 as usual to Heathrow to be under the Southern Cross and escape the cold. I spent the whole of 2004 in Adelaide, touring schools, tidying up the manual's text for publication and recording more poems. It was another year with no acting work; my profile was inevitably fading. My agents were becoming distant. But I was so busy it didn't worry me. My ego was healthy from the applause of school children and plaudits from teachers. I was becoming a published writer, cutting a CD, and Mr Micawber was still in the wings.

55

The Last Hurrah

I arrived back to a London winter at the end of November 2004, in time to farewell my old friend Ken Hannam. He was best known in Australia for the movie *Sunday Too Far Away* and had become a high-profile television director in the UK, directing series such as *The Day of the Triffids*. There were many familiar faces from television at his funeral. I was asked by his wife Madlena Nedeva to say a few words and read an Australian poem. I read the John Shaw Neilson poem 'Song Be Delicate'. Geraldine McEwan followed me with the often-quoted lines from *The Tempest*. Ken had so wanted to return to Australia before his end but he was too ill. Madlena scattered his ashes in a park on the North Shore of Sydney.

I was entering into that era in which funerals were becoming more frequent than weddings. I have long entertained the idea that Richard Curtis should write a sequel to *Four Weddings and a Funeral*, calling it Four Funerals and a Wedding. It would provide more work for the older actors before they hop off the twig.

Having been out of the circuit since doing the *Doctors* episode in 2003 with Eddie Redmayne, I did not expect to pick up work too quickly. My agent phoned in March with an interview for a part in an episode of *Rosemary and Thyme* starring Felicity Kendall and Pam Ferris playing gardening sleuths. The episode required actors to play tennis, which appears in my résumé. I met Brian Farnham, the director, having prepared to read a scene for him. He was from the old school. His immediate response was: 'I don't need you to read. I know you can act; it shows in your résumé. I just need to see which part will fit and get a feel for you.' We had a few laughs over having a feel for me and I mentioned how different it was in Australia with mandatory screen testing.

Feeling confident I would land a part, I hoped it would be the leader of the tennis group with many scenes throughout, not the one that dies early in the story. Sure enough, I got the part of Charlie Gudgeon who is stung by a bee and jumps off a balcony within the first 20 minutes. At least he gets talked about. There was a bonus in getting a part in this episode – it would be shot in Spain.

Before the start date in April, another booking came completely out of the blue. I received a call from my agent to say I was booked to appear in a Rory Bremner sketch. Rory Bremner is a master impressionist providing political satire for Channel 4. During the period from 1999 to 2010 he and his associates, John Bird and John Fortune, wrote and filmed sketches spoofing whatever was happening in politics at the time, under the title *Bremner, Bird and Fortune*. They were absolutely brilliant, scooping many awards.

On receiving the script I found why I had been cast without sight. The filming was taking place the next day and they needed an actor to play Lynton Crosby, the Australian political adviser to the Liberal Party in Australia. He had been requisitioned by Michael Howard of the Conservative Party in the UK to run his election campaign. They would have got someone to leaf through *Spotlight* to find an actor who could play an Australian and might have a passing resemblance to Crosby. There I was aiding a politician again as in the New Zealand commercial for their PM.

A Mercedes Benz picked me up about noon, taking me to Addington Palace in Croydon. The sketch was being filmed in the London residence of the Archbishop of Canterbury. On arrival I was hastily taken to a large caravan in the car park. Rory, the director Steve Connelly and another were in manic discussion over the script. I think the other was probably a legal adviser. In no time, what I had learnt was scrapped and I was virtually asked to improvise what Crosby might say in the situation being filmed. This was way beyond my ability; I had no idea how to perform in this format without proper rehearsal. I managed to verbalise some political-sounding guff but felt out of my depth.

They seemed happy with what I did. All that was seen of me when shown, however, was my backside as I leant over a desk gesticulating to an animated Rory. For this bottom acting I received an astonishing £1000 and was driven home in the Mercedes by 5.00 pm. So much for a short journey in the fast lane.

I was doing some landscaping for a female friend in Putney soon after. We were having a drink at the end of the day when the doorbell rang. She was expecting her boyfriend who was none other than the director on the shoot, Steve Connelly. He kindly reassured me what I had done was fine. There were no further offers.

Filming in Spain at the end of April was a real treat. We were based in Mijas, a small town towards the eastern end of the Costa del Sol. The majority of the filming took place at the Lew Hoad Tennis Academy. *Rosemary and Thyme* episodes are mostly filmed on location. There were eight guest actors in the cast and all had to play good social tennis. The whole shoot turned out to be more like a paid holiday, with time for tennis, swimming and golf. It is different for leading players in most shots with lots of dialogue. Felicity and Pam were very friendly but their workload prevented them from much socialising. For us it was one of the most relaxing, fun shoots for Carnival Productions, a very actor-friendly production company led by their highly respected producer Brian Eastman of *Poirot* fame.

The opening sequence was shot in the middle of the smallest bull ring in Spain. It is the only time I have ever stood in the middle of a bull ring. I tried to imagine what it would be like to be a matador waiting for the bull to appear with the roar from the packed terraces. A small continuum from the days of Rome.

When I arrived back at Heathrow, a parting phrase from our director Brian Farnham had a prophetic outcome for me. As he was getting into a taxi I called out to him what a fun shoot it was.

'Yes,' he replied, 'but probably the last hurrah.'

Brian was referring more to restrictive budget difficulties for filming, but it would turn out to be, indeed, my last hurrah. This episode would be my last television credit in the UK. However, the whole series has been so popular I am still receiving residuals with so many repeats. The latest replay was in 2017 on Foxtel.

Soon after returning to London in 2005, I contacted Judi Dench to see if she would write a foreword to my speech manual, now titled *Expressive Speech*. She readily accepted and I was delighted to receive a glowing appraisal. This gave the prospects of finding a UK publisher a huge boost. Even so, I thought it would be very difficult. But after only a few rejections a positive response was received from a small publisher in Kent. Noel Graham of Claire Publications arranged to meet me at the Institute of Directors in Pall Mall. I felt a touch of frisson walking into this grand building, having just crossed the road with Denis Thatcher.

The manual's appearance in the UK was timely. There were rumblings about the standards of literacy and poor speaking habits. Noel Graham really believed it would sell in the education market but he only had one educational outlet in which to advertise. There were never any significant sales. However, a further response did come from another small publisher, this time in Devon.

A meeting was arranged by the resounding-sounding Drummond Johnstone. He was the owner of Southgate Publications, which specialised in supplying material to Sure Start Centres, a government network for helping the disadvantaged. He produced 'how to' information booklets.

Drummond saw something in the manual that he felt could be adapted into his genre. Specifically it was to provide practical assistance to parents and librarians for reading aloud stories to young children. On return from a hectic five weeks in Adelaide schools, I worked out a programme of basic vocal techniques required to bring a story alive, but had no idea how to put them into a booklet that would be practical. I left these limited ideas with him.

It wasn't until October of 2007 that I began work on a booklet for Drummond Johnstone. He had taken my ideas to a neighbouring colleague in Sandford. They had developed a format that would require my specific input to make the booklet practical. I was invited to stay with my co-author who had the most propitious name for writing – Alison Shakspeare, William's original spelling.

A series of children's stories had been chosen such as *We're Going on a Bear Hunt* and *Giraffes Don't Dance*. My part was to orchestrate the text with bold letters for emphasis and marks for pauses. On the side of the page were instructions on how to speak the lines. In the introduction were voice tips and then a list of animals with descriptions on how they might sound when reading aloud. Much fun was had during these sessions. I would come down to breakfast as one of these animals. The elephant was the most popular.

A very colourful booklet called *How to Enjoy Reading to Young Children* was produced. It was the beginning of a very happy period. The work that was to come out of this booklet compensated my fading career as an actor.

In this period I was beginning to gain more confidence in public speaking. I used to be reluctant to speak in front of an audience as myself. However, I had launched a book, addressed an assembly of republicans, conducted workshops and in 2006 delivered a eulogy from a pulpit. It requires some technical ability to get through speaking a eulogy; with rising emotions, clarity can suffer.

During my numerous return visits to London over these years I saw many productions: Derek Jacobi's performance in Schiller's *Don Carlos* was outstanding. Surprisingly, this classic play was in a West End theatre. It was such a treat to sit in the gods and hear every word.

Warhorse at the National Theatre in 2008 was also outstanding. It was an astonishing technical achievement telling this heart-rending story from the First World War. To see those mechanical horses come alive was so moving. Very quickly you hardly noticed the young people underneath. There were many young people in the audience and I was told every performance in those early days received standing ovations. I wonder whether the film had the same impact.

However, the crowning experience for me was staged at Sandhurst Military Academy. *The Armed Man: A Mass for Peace* by Karl Jenkins was an epic choral work. We were seated with our picnics in front of the wide main building. As the music began, lights and images were thrown on the building depicting the narrative. At climactic moments fireworks exploded in exact synchronicity with the music. The concert was sub-titled *Music on Fire*; it certainly was. I was completely uplifted by the sound and spectacle. It was the most memorable concert I have ever attended.

About this time I attended an interesting dinner party. It's purpose was to launch Boris Johnson's bid to become Lord Mayor of London. This engaging, fast-talking, ebullient figure with tousled hair was charm itself. He was amusing and stimulating. Foolish are those who think this Old Etonian is a buffoon.

Our school bookings in Australia were beginning to drop off in 2007. Our work, by its nature, really should have gone on year after year, with new students coming through all the time. We hadn't reckoned on budget cuts affecting our employment. At least during every return I was adding more poems to the *Poetry Alive* CD with Rob Pippan. I had already been selling a pilot version and was encouraged to do more. It took to the end of 2008 to complete another 15.

Earlier in 2008 my co-author Alison had come up with a great idea to make more money. She suggested I develop a speech workshop based on the booklet. It was selling well. There were Sure Start Centres and libraries in most large towns. Alison put out a flyer using my credits as bait. Mentioning that I had been in *Dr Who, The Bill, Tenko* and the recently shown *Rosemary and Thyme* did the trick. Using someone who has been on television as a selling tactic is like shining a light to attract a moth.

I conducted my first workshop on 25 June 2008. Nerves accompanied my journey by train to Southampton and then by ferry to Ryde on the Isle of Wight. I had never conducted a workshop on my own. Having prepared well, for two-and-a-half hours I hardly took breath. The key was getting them all saying things together, and then, later in the session, individually, having sussed out those who had confidence. My passion about clear and expressive speech carried me through. It is fundamental in any form of oral presentation – passion articulates what we have to say because according to my mantra, it's not just what you say, it's the way you say it.

This first workshop seemed out of place among the yachting fraternity. The Isle of Wight is known for having been the summer residence of Queen Victoria. My next booking took me to the other end of the social spectrum. It was a long journey by train to the outer reaches of the East End of London. Thurrock is way down the Thames Estuary, beyond where I left for Australia from Tilbury Docks. Grays Central Library was in the middle of a wasteland of old factories, slowly being rejuvenated. The librarians, teachers and parents (mostly women) who attended more than made up for the bleak surroundings. It was an uproarious session. East Enders have a keen ear for a joke, are not afraid to have a go and have that famous strong sense of community. I returned to London in great relief, seeing the surroundings in a warmer light.

Returning to Adelaide between early July and September 2008 to pick up the usual school bookings, I approached the head of library services. The idea of selling the reading aloud booklet and conducting workshops for librarians was cautiously received; a very Australian reaction. Just one workshop was managed, which did go well, before returning to London. In the meantime, Alison Shakspeare had put on her agent's hat and booked a wide-ranging tour of the UK.

The second tour began with a small group of international people in the old Marylebone Library near Edgware Road. Sheffield and Reading followed, and then I was flown to Belfast where I was picked up and taken to Ballymena.

The town is known for manufacturing buses. Even Boris Johnson has a route-master bus named after him by the Wrightbus Company. A week later I was in Powys in Wales, then another flight to Aberdeen in the north of Scotland. A booking in Bexley brought me nearer home. My final workshops were in the towns of Street in Somerset and Blandford in Dorset.

I had very little time to explore these towns but did manage a visit to the Ballymena museum. Reading a sweeping history of Northern Ireland, I came to understand something of how the accent came about. The soft tones of the Southern Irish accent were gradually hardened and nasalised from the influx of Scottish people from South West Scotland. To prove my untried theory I need to ask a Glaswegian to imitate a southern Irish brogue.

Grey stones and grey skies belied the warm welcome in Aberdeen. I found myself slipping into their accent, which is slightly different from the very polite Edinburgh accent. But what surprised me was the only just understandable written dialect called *Doric*. A copy of a Roald Dahl story written in *Doric* was given to me. I have always been fascinated how accents and dialects develop. During my time at Nottingham Playhouse in the 1960s I was told that, not so long ago, you only had to walk over a bridge on the river Trent to hear the difference between the Nottinghamshire and Derbyshire accents.

From 2009, the cutting budget imperatives were beginning to be exercised in both countries. I became increasingly dismayed that my recognised contribution to lifting standards of speech and literacy was to be short lived. My last booking was in the small town of Knowles outside Liverpool on 18 October 2011, where I had been before. Some librarians like Geraldine Williams could see the ongoing value of what I was doing, but she said the government did not. It seems that anything not showing an immediate outcome or which cannot easily be evaluated gets the chop. Sure Start Centres were closing and library budgets were slashed.

Despite a few attempts to persuade education ministers at the top level in the UK and Australia that what I was doing was fundamental to achieving higher standards in literacy, it has been to no avail. I was even invited to the Houses of Parliament. The UK Volunteer Reading Charity was invited to attend a nibbles-and-drinks thank-you from the Minister of Education. The organisers had been told of my work and included me. This is an organisation of retired people who give their spare time reading to children. Governments like charity; it lessens their obligation and saves money. Any form of speech training seems to be totally ignored by teaching authorities. Later, in the work force, many find they have to get up in front of a gathering and make an oral presentation. Realising they have had no training, they rush off to find a presentation coach. There is an increasing number of these – usually ex-actors.

At times of extreme frustration with politicians, I can understand the attempt by Guy Fawkes in the Gunpowder Plot to blow up the whole bloody lot. But it was a thrill to enter the premises. To gaze across the Thames from the ornate dining room, feeling the history around me among the babble of posh accents. It was a special moment. It wasn't quite the last hurrah for everything but with only a few school bookings and one workshop, 2009 was the beginning of the end for work on the adjacent path.

In February 2009 I attended the Founder's Day Celebration of NIDA in Sydney. I felt awfully old. Four girls from the second year and I tried to brush away the years. Five of us did a *Singing in the Rain* arrival down the red carpet. Inevitably, those from the earliest years numbered the fewest but there was a sense that those who hadn't really made it weren't important or remembered. Later, in the UK, a cricket match, some royalties and a little financial security eased a creeping feeling of not quite making it.

Playing cricket in England is a great joy. You can keep playing into the fading years as long as you can see the ball or even turn your arm over. There are clubs that play at all levels of cricket. This is not so in Australia which is probably why Australians are so good; the game is taken very seriously throughout all levels. In the Stage Cricket Club our president Brian Jackson was still bowling at 80 years of age.

The pinnacle of my cricketing life came at the age of 70. The Stage were

STAGE	C.C v/s	NPL & LENSBURY C.C	VENUE NPL		DATE 5/7/07	WEATHER FINE/Muggy
INNINGS OF NPL	TOSS WON BY STAGE		TYPE OF MATCH 40 OVERS · START		FINISH	OF INNINGS

	BATSMAN		HOW OUT	BOWLER	TOTAL
1	J. VITTS	4 4 4 1 4 1 3 4 · 1 · 4 1 · 6 · 1 1 1 4	BOWLED	PEGGE	82
2	C. CHURCHMAN	1 4 4 4 4 4 1 1 1 4 1 1 4 1	STUMPED DAVIS	SADLER	44
3	M KELLY	1 ·	CT VORA	PEGGE	27
4	FRANK		CT G·SMITH	PEGGE	6
5	D. INDIKA		LBW	PEGGE	16
6	T. PITTS		NOT OUT		9
7	D. MERCHANT (snr)		CT CLINTON	PEGGE	0
8	K. NAYLOR		BOWLED	PEGGE	2
9	B. SCOTT		NOT OUT		0
10	D. MERCHANT (jnr)				
11	CHRIS				

* CAPTAIN
· WICKET KEEPER

		TOTAL BALLS RECEIVED			TOTAL BOUNDARIES SCORED			
FALL OF WICKET	1	2	3	4	5	6	7	8	9	10
SCORE	149									
OUTGOING BAT & SCORE	2 / 34									
N.O. BAT & SCORE	1 / 45									
PARTNERSHIP	100									
TIME/OVER NO	16									

BYES 4·1
LEG BYES
WIDES 1·1·3·2·5·5
NO BALLS 1·1
PENALTY PREV INN
PENALTY THIS INN

SUB TOTAL
EXTRAS
TOTAL

BOWLER	BOWLING ANALYSIS [ALL NO BALLS AND WIDES NOW ATTRIBUTED AGAINST BOWLER]																				TOTALS	O	M	R	W	
	1	2	3	4	5	6	7	8	9	10	11	12	13	14	15	16	17	18	19	20	WD NB					
1 CHURCHSMITH																						8	–	48	–	
2 CLINTON							13	11														6	1	51	–	
3 SADLER							2	3														8	–	28	1	
4 T. WHYTE	M		M		1	2	3	4	1													8	2	28	–	
5 Y. VORA	3	10	2	6	1	8																6	–	30	–	
6 E. PEGGE				W																		4	1	14	6	
7																										

playing against NPL Lensbury in Teddington. In 2007 I had very good bowling figures against them – 5 wickets for 40 runs in 9 overs. In the 2009 match I was thrown the ball when they were about 120 for 1 after we had scored a huge total. It was a placid pitch. To everyone's astonishment, not least mine, in 4 overs I had taken 6 wickets for 14 runs. The opposition was captained by Indika, a professional Sri Lankan cricketer, whose wicket I took. For an actor in downtime such a performance gives a tremendous boost to the ego, which is why I mention it here.

The royalty payments from the reading aloud booklet sounded wonderful but it would never be 'a nice little earner' at five pence a copy. It was a good feeling to be able to say we had sold 30,000 copies. At last, however, through the sale of my cottage in Adelaide, I had some capital for the first time in my life. Enough to complete the modernisation of my flat in London.

My only disappointment from the last 10 years is that I am no longer working on a regular basis. Our work in schools was highly acclaimed, as were my workshops in libraries. The responses were unanimously positive. So many asked the question why there was no voice element in training. In the UK the librarians were most generous in their praise. Many reported that what I had taught them worked. In Australia the absolute vindication of our poetry and creative writing sessions came from the students themselves when asked to evaluate our visits. We had opened their eyes and made a difference.

In both countries there have been massive cutbacks in funding for – what might well be termed by those in authority – extra-curricular activities, suggesting it is not essential. Clear and expressive speech is not only mandatory for oral communication (critical if you are an air traffic controller) but also underpins quality of life. I haven't given up on this crusade but it has been like swimming upstream against a very strong current.

56

P.S. My Cat is Not Dead

There is a very funny novel written by James Kirkwood called *P.S. Your Cat is Dead*, in which everything seems to go wrong in the life of a hopeless New York actor. My story opened with the yellow eyes of a cat calling back my memories, so it is an apposite title to end my last chapter and to say overall, things went okay for me.

Gauging success is very difficult among people on the lower rungs of the ladder. Particularly in a profession obsessed with creating stars in a population craving to worship something tangible. In my own small way I have experienced something of this phenomenon, even though my standing has dropped into a lower league now. I have received fan mail over many years and recently seem to have acquired a small, loyal circle.

The question is whether one has maximised one's potential. That requires honest, down-to-earth self-evaluation. Looking back over the last 55 years as a professional actor, I suspect I did. I was certainly no manqué actor and I was more than just a jobbing actor. If I had stayed in London my career might have gone further, as indeed it might have in Australia living in Sydney. But along the way I changed direction and began travelling down an adjacent path, in which I became very successful. Its continuum, however, depended on outside factors mainly involving funding. By no means have I come to the end of my working ride, even though I was given a strong, somewhat amusing, reminder of my mortality later in 2010.

Residing more in Adelaide, I had picked up with old university friends, particularly those who were in the Footlights Club. I was persuaded to join the cast of a current revue early in the year, resuscitated in the old format. My old friend Tony Brooks had written a brilliant script for me to play Prince Charles looking for a job to be King of Australia. I couldn't resist.

It can, however, be awkward for a professional actor to perform with non-professionals. You have to be at your best to allay silent murmurings. In a small town, as I described when touring New Zealand, some locals can't see the difference. It was not the case in the revue. It did me enormous good to walk out on to a stage and work an audience. It was something I had not done for many years and it was another full circle: Shakespeare in the outback with touring poetry to schools and now the university revues.

More than a nudge concerning my mortality happened one afternoon in England on a weekend jolly with old friends in August 2010. Soon after arriving to stay with friends in Kent, blood appeared in my urine. I yelled out, 'Anyone for a glass of red on tap?'. That night I was very sick, but in the morning I was fine. On returning to London, I saw my GP, whose name would turn out to be appropriate in this context – Dr Staples, a lovely Sri Lankan lady. She advised an immediate scan on my return to Australia.

Before leaving I was privileged to catch Judi Dench on the run with a spot of lunch. She was on her way back home after a costume fitting at Bermans for the movie to be shot in India called *The Best Exotic Marigold Hotel*. I said a spot of lunch because the spot became a tremendous downpour. We were on a roof garden restaurant and laughed so much we hardly ate anything, mainly because our meals were floating. Judi Dench is the most intoxicating person I have ever met and so kind and generous. Furthermore, we greeted each other with the same famous phrase from Dicken's novel *Great Expectations* – 'What larks, Pip!'. We must have both been thinking of those happy, fun days at Nottingham Playhouse.

Shortly after returning I had an MRI scan and was subsequently diagnosed with cancer in one of my kidneys. I was fortunate to be referred to a wonderful surgeon. Dr Stapleton took out the damaged kidney and told me I was lucky the cancer was contained and not spread. There was a long period of recovery but eventually 32 staples were taken out of my side by my stepdaughter, Penny (a nurse). While attending to this bloated whale, as she described me, I said to her, 'What with Dr Staples in London, Dr Stapleton here and all these staples you're taking out, I've been properly stitched up.' I think it healthy to make a joke about something that could have been fatal.

It was fatal for one of my very good friends. Oliver Horsbrugh, whom I knew at St Paul's School, was diagnosed with exactly the same condition a few years ago. It had not been picked up in time. His cancer had spread. Within two months he was dead. I was extremely lucky to have that early sign.

In fact I have been very blessed with good health throughout my life and fortunate not to have had any serious accidents. It is all a bit of a lottery, but I do believe a positive outlook helps to keep chance or good fortune on your side. In 2013 I did have to pay a series of visits to the Oscopy family. I was sorted out by the father, Dr Willy Kneebum!

These circles in my life were reinforced in 2012 when I made my last stage appearance. I once described the maverick commentator/writer/ filmmaker Bob Ellis as 'Sydney's bumbling intellectual Falstaff, lording it over lesser mortals'. Before his too-early demise, Bob had teamed up with Denny Lawrence to write a play about the missing years of Shakespeare's life from 1581 to 1583. The play was called *Shakespeare in Italy*. It was a persuasive proposition that he had remained a secret Catholic but was sent as a spy to Rome on behalf of the Anglican Queen Elizabeth. Privately funded by the author, it was staged in the small Holden Street Theatre on the outskirts of Adelaide's CBD. It was an interesting but over-written play and sadly did not do well. We had to cancel one performance when nobody turned up.

For me it was like a re-visit to those early days in repertory theatre combined with my first professional job – playing Shakespeare in the outback. I enjoyed playing the English Ambassador to Rome in a costume approximating Elizabethan. I was challenged by a strong performance from Lucy Slattery playing my wife, a much neglected young local actress. Unfortunately, the most memorable part of this production happened on the way home after the last night. I was arrested by the police and thrown into jail.

It was after midnight on a Saturday. I had only had a couple of drinks, but on an empty stomach. I began heading for home in my VW Polo but decided to change direction and go through the city. Suddenly I heard the sirens of a police car behind me. Thinking it couldn't be me as I had done nothing wrong, I kept going. I found myself having to stop due to a sort of road block with a taxi across the road. As soon as I had pulled up my car door was yanked open and I was ordered to get out.

'What for? I've done nothing wrong,' I protested.

The aggressive policeman grabbed my arm, hauled me out, slammed me against the car and handcuffed me. I was put into another car, my head pressed down as they do in the movies, and driven to the central lockup, to which my car had been driven by another policeman. I was invited to occupy a cell and told to remove my shoelaces and belt, presumably in case I decided to commit suicide.

This fearful turn of events had me 'dashed, diddled and dumbfounded' as my mother used to say. I was actually in a complete state of shock. I was breathalysed, photographed and finger printed. There I was, a criminal in a real-life situation. After I had been two hours in a cell, they realised it was an arrest too far and let me drive my car home. I was only charged with 'failure to obey a police instruction'.

At my court hearing I began my brilliantly written speech pleading for clemency, but in no time I was interrupted by the magistrate. 'Thank you Mr Pegge, two hours in a cell has been sufficient punishment. Just pay the court costs.' The brief glimpse of being in a cell was all good experience for an actor, but for me there is probably little opportunity now to put it into practice.

The merry-go-round is still turning: I lost the First World War recently, playing General Joffre, or rather singing him. It was a bizarre filmed operatic account of the first month called *August Watershed*. I had some fun playing a dementia patient in a training film; I told the director I was a method actor and would be fine learning the lines but once in character they would be forgotten (she believed me for a minute). Mother would have been disappointed with the part I played in *Changed Forever*, yet another series about Gallipoli, where I was demoted to playing a butler. Latterly and yet again, I was brutally smash up and killed in the television series of *Wolf Creek*, but it took 15 takes to put me down.

I am looking forward to the next stage of my life. Who knows, new doors may open and old ones even wider. I am ready to pick up anything left behind, even be killed again. In the final analysis regarding success though, I believe the eyes have it. They were too close together.

Index

Wakefield Press is an independent publishing and
distribution company based in Adelaide, South Australia.
We love good stories and publish beautiful books.
To see our full range of books, please visit our website at
www.wakefieldpress.com.au
where all titles are available for purchase.

Find us!

Twitter: www.twitter.com/wakefieldpress
Facebook: www.facebook.com/wakefield.press
Instagram: instagram.com/wakefieldpress

Printed in Australia
AUOW01n1823241117
291918AU00003B/3

9 781743 054987